Teenagers Learn What They Live

*Parenting to Inspire
Integrity & Independence*

BY DOROTHY LAW NOLTE, Ph.D.
and RACHEL HARRIS, Ph.D.

WORKMAN PUBLISHING • NEW YORK

Library of Congress Cataloging-in-Publication Data

Nolte, Dorothy.
  Teenagers learn what they live : parenting to inspire integrity
  & independence / by Dorothy Law Nolte and Rachel Harris.
  p. cm.
  ISBN 0-7611-2138-2 (alk. paper)
  1. Parenting, 2. Parent and teenager. 3. Adolescent psychology.
  4. Values in adolescence. 5. Autonomy in adolescence.
  I. Harris, Rachel. II. Title.
HQ755.8 .N625 2002
649'.1—dc21

                                                    2002028830

Workman books are available at special discount when
purchased in bulk for premiums and sales promotions
as well as for fund-raising or educational use. Special editions
or book excerpts also can be created to specification.
For details, contact the Special Sales Director at the
address below.

Workman Publishing Company, Inc.
708 Broadway
New York, NY 10003-9555
www.workman.com

Manufactured in the United States of America

First printing December 2002
10   9   8   7   6   5   4   3   2   1

To all teenagers:
May light and inspiration surround you.
—Dorothy Law Nolte

To my own teenager, Ashley, and all her friends
for teaching me so much.
—Rachel Harris

◆◆◆

ACKNOWLEDGMENTS

Our deepest appreciation to our editor, Margot Herrera,
for her careful thinking, common sense, and calm demeanor.
We are also grateful to Janet Hulstrand for her editorial
contributions and our agent, Bob Silverstein.

CONTENTS

Teenagers Learn What They Live

by Dorothy Law Nolte
and Rachel Harris

If teenagers live with pressure, they learn
to be stressed.

If teenagers live with failure, they learn to give up.

If teenagers live with rejection, they learn to feel lost.

If teenagers live with too many rules,
they learn to get around them.

If teenagers live with too few rules, they learn to ignore
the needs of others.

If teenagers live with broken promises, they learn
to be disappointed.

If teenagers live with respect, they learn
to honor others.

※

If teenagers live with trust, they learn to tell
the truth.

※

If teenagers live with openness, they learn
to discover themselves.

※

If teenagers live with natural consequences,
they learn to be accountable.

※

If teenagers live with responsibility, they learn
to be self-reliant.

※

If teenagers live with healthy habits, they learn
to be kind to their bodies.

※

If teenagers live with support, they learn
to feel good about themselves.

※

If teenagers live with creativity, they learn
to share who they are.

※

If teenagers live with caring attention,
they learn how to love.

※

If teenagers live with positive expectations,
they learn to help build a better world.

Introduction

*T*eenagers Learn What They Live is an extension of the parenting philosophy expressed in *Children Learn What They Live,* both the poem and the book by the same title. Our message is that children and teenagers learn from our example—from what we do, not what we say. The way we live our lives, the choices we make, how we spend our time, and especially the quality of our relationships are the most powerful legacy we pass on to the next generation.

Our teenagers are learning from us even while they're rebelling against us. They're especially sensitive and critical of any contradictions between what we say and what we do, and they seem almost to take pleasure in noticing any inconsistency. Also, they can be practically allergic to our most informative lectures, regardless of how well intentioned we might be. Therefore, we can't transmit our values by words alone; we have to inspire them through our behavior. We, ourselves, are the model we present to our teenagers.

No matter how resistant or even mature our teenagers appear, the reality is that they still need us. Our kids need our time and attention, our energy and concern, and yes, even our guidance, whether or not they are willing to admit it. We need to give our teens the message that we are there for them in seemingly insignificant everyday interactions as well as moments of crisis throughout all the years of adolescence. They are never too old for this caring reassurance. It's the basis of the parenting relationship.

We hope that *Teenagers Learn What They Live* will inspire you to "become the parent you have always wanted to be," as Jack Canfield said in his forward to *Children Learn What They Live*. That said, we must admit that it's likely there'll be times when you'll try your utmost to be the best parent you can be, yet things will still not work out the way you want. Parents of teens can legitimately feel helpless and powerless no matter how conscientiously they've raised their kids.

Many parents endure some challenging times during their children's adolescence—a crisis, a year from hell, or at best, seemingly endless worry about real risks and dangers. Most teens come through these difficult periods having grown older and wiser from their experience. But some will not. Parents need to make their own decisions about when to seek professional help, since every situation is both complex and unique. We can assure you, though, that sooner is better than later. If you are concerned about your teenager's health and well-being, don't hesitate to seek professional advice, psychotherapy, or family counseling. This book is not intended to replace such help.

Teenagers Learn What They Live focuses on the relationships between parents and teens, not the problems. We need a warm, caring, and open relationship with our kids so that they'll be honest with us about their day-to-day lives. Our greatest opportunity to influence our teenagers during these critical years is through our relationship with them. The better our connection, the more they'll be willing to listen to us and consider our perspective and guidance. And we need to make sure we're well connected to our kids before they enter puberty with all its accompanying hormonal changes. We want to start the journey of adolescence with our teens feeling that they are of primary importance to us, that they are the priority in our lives. These years are our last chance to help them prepare for their future and young adulthood.

Adolescence is a time of transformation for both parents and teenagers, as well as for their relationship. We have to let go of our teens while we stay connected to them, judiciously balancing these opposing energies according to our teenagers' needs. Inevitably we'll both hold on too tightly at times and let go too soon at other times.

Our teens need to become more independent and to strengthen their sense of identity. Yet they also need to learn about interdependence and the human reality that we all need and depend on each other in families, schools, communities, and the emerging global village.

Our relationship with our teenagers evolves into our relationship with our adult children. The more we can respect our teens' right to be self-determining through the process of becoming independent, the more respect they'll have for us in our future adult-adult relationship.

We know the roller coaster ride of adolescence challenges the essence of who we are as people, not just as parents. It's how we respond to these inevitable ups and downs in our day-to-day family life that shows our teenagers who we are. *We* are the best example we can give our teens as they become their own person.

It's our hope that this book will inspire and guide your relationship with your child through the journey of adolescence. We know we speak to the heart of parenting when we say *teenagers learn what they live.*

If teenagers live with pressure, they learn to be stressed

S tress may be an inevitable part of life. The world we live in is packed full of professional, social, and personal obligations that seem to keep us running from one task to another, no matter what.

Life can be just as busy for our teenagers with homework, sports, extracurricular activities, lessons, household chores, and sometimes jobs. Our teens may feel pressured from all directions—to achieve, to fit in, to behave, to take risks, to compete, and finally, to understand themselves and learn about others.

Our teenagers learn how to handle the pressure in their lives by watching how we handle it in ours. And even during adolescence, when it might seem we don't "count" so much anymore, we continue to be our children's first and most important teachers. Our capacity to gracefully juggle the multifaceted demands of our own lives is the model we give our teens.

Thirteen-year-old Rebecca is fretting about an art project that is due at school. She's been trying to get her mom's attention so she can talk about her concern, but with the demands of deadlines at work, the requirements of running a household, errands, family responsibilities, trying to squeeze in trips to the health club, not to mention a sick cat, it's been hard to get Mom's attention. All Rebecca's been able to get out of her mother, in fact, is a somewhat impatient admonition not to be "so stressed out" before she flies off to the next thing.

Like most teens, Rebecca will not miss the contradiction between her mother's advice and her own behavior. One day, as she and Rebecca are driving around together doing errands, Mom asks, or more precisely, nags Rebecca about a never-ending list of things to be done: "When is that history report due? Did you send a thank-you note to your Aunt Mariah? Have you called back Mrs. Walsh about baby-sitting this weekend?" And of course she repeats the frequent refrain, "Would you please clean up your room tonight?"

Rebecca stares blankly out the window, feeling overwhelmed. By now she has a highly developed skill for tuning her mother out even when they are physically close within the confines of the car. Her body may be present, but her mind is free—to rehearse rap lyrics, plan what she'll wear to school tomorrow, or imagine what she'll say to that cute guy in the hall. Unfortunately, Mom has lost her.

As parents we don't usually think of ourselves as modeling stress-filled lives. Nor do we realize the ways in which we may be contributing to the pressure our teens feel. Instead, we like to think we are doing everything we can to give them all they need. From our point of view, our reminders to them about their responsibilities are meant to help them take charge of their lives. But we need to be mindful that the way in which we do this can make all the difference in whether they feel supported and understood as they seek to meet these demands, or whether they feel overwhelmed.

It would be better for Rebecca's mom to admit to herself that she's the one who's stressed and then to acknowledge Rebecca's needs. "I can't talk to you about that right now, Honey," she could say to her daughter. "How about if we discuss it after dinner?" Then, of course, Mom needs to set aside some quiet time that evening to focus on Rebecca and listen to her concerns. Similarly, if Mom has a number of things she wants her daughter to do, it's more effective to write them down so Rebecca can refer to the list, checking them off as she does them.

It's important for us to remember, especially when we feel we're being tuned out, that we are still a major influence in the lives of our teenagers. It's very easy to lose this perspective when they seem to ignore us or openly rebel against us. But we are leaving an imprint on our teenagers that will emerge when they're out on their own as young adults, making decisions about how to live their lives. In the meantime, we must remember that our influence is conveyed much more strongly by how we actually live our lives than by how we tell our kids to live theirs.

Teens Are Busy, Too

Our teenagers can be every bit as overscheduled as we are. We start our children on a treadmill of activities when they're still toddlers and keep them busy throughout grade school. By the time they're teenagers, they may think this is the only way to live.

We enter into this whirlwind of activity because we want our kids to have the opportunity to experience all the options available and to get a "leg up" on the competition. As one father put it, "If my son doesn't go to football camp the first year it's offered, when he gets to middle school he'll be behind all the other kids." It may seem to us that if our teens are not on the treadmill, they're falling behind. Although early exposure to activities can give kids the chance to excel at things they might not otherwise, it's also important to maintain a healthy balance of activity and time to rest.

Fourteen-year-old Natasha's schedule is packed full of worthwhile activities: "I go to dance classes twice a week and gymnastics every Wednesday. I have piano Fridays and choir rehearsal after that. I'm on the swim team at school, and we put in about twelve hours of pool time a week. Oh, and I almost forgot, I see my math tutor one evening a week. I think that's it, but I may have forgotten something."

Her mom nods approvingly. "You forgot that you've been babysitting for the neighbor's two-year-old twins for about a year now."

Natasha is very organized and competent, but she seems like a miniature grown-up with her electronic daily planner and cell phone. She has an air of efficiency about her that seems too businesslike for an adolescent. Where is this all leading? Will she burn out at an early age as a result of this hectic pace, or will she just continue to compulsively add more and more activities with each passing year? Has she had time to think about where she's going and what she wants to do with her life?

Parents in one suburban town in Connecticut got together and decided that overscheduling kids was becoming a community-wide problem. They ran a public service campaign encouraging everyone to "Just Stay Home" for one designated Family Night each month. They worked together with the schools, asking teachers not to assign homework for that night. They encouraged parents and teens to turn off their televisions and computers and simply spend a quiet evening at home together.

Through this experiment, families rediscovered the old-fashioned pleasure of sitting around the kitchen table playing cards or board games, talking with one another as they played. It was a healthy reminder of how being together as a family and sharing simple fun at home is an important activity, too, and worth making time for. If we simply "go with the flow," we are likely to get caught up in the rush that seems to be the norm in our society. We have to make a conscious decision that we are going to plan our lives in such a way that there's space between the activities—time for quiet, for "downtime," for family time together. If we never take time to step off the treadmill, we're in danger of forgetting what it's like *not* to be stressed.

Planning for College

Some of the pressure that leads to overscheduling our kids comes from our desire to help them build a résumé that will get them into their first-choice college. The idea of teenagers even having résumés is a relatively new development, a result of the growing competitiveness of the college application process.

Parents may begin planning college application strategies for their kids before they even enter high school: What activities should he participate in to show how "well-rounded" he is? What can she do that's extraordinary, so her application will stand out? This kind of planning soon evolves into a year-round approach in which summer is not vacation time anymore, but a time for working on activities, programs, and achievements that will look good on the college application.

It's difficult to convey the amount of intense pressure this puts on teenagers. Their adolescent years can become entirely dominated by the specter of the college application competition, a process that can be both mysterious and unfair. It's not always clear why certain teens are accepted by the elite schools and others aren't. So for some kids, years of stressful effort, planning, and dreaming can end in major disappointment. Then we have seventeen-year-olds, bright kids on the brink of their adult lives, who feel as if they've already failed their parents, teachers, coaches, and themselves. What's wrong with this picture?

Gael, a senior in high school, is anxiously watching the mail, waiting for a thick envelope to arrive, announcing her acceptance into the college of her choice. It doesn't happen: she is rejected by her first-choice school. She is distraught, and so are her parents.

"I can't believe this!" she says, finally able to talk about her disappointment after a whole day spent alternating between anguished tears and silence.

"I can't either," her mom agrees, leaning against the wall in the family room with her arms crossed over her chest. She sighs, and looks defeated.

Gael gets a dazed look in her eyes and mumbles, "I'm sorry."

Where can the conversation go from here? Mom is so overinvested in her daughter's getting into one particular school that she is as distraught as Gael is. She's not able to offer Gael a more mature viewpoint, or help her find a way to accept this setback and pick another dream for the future. Gael has to deal not only with her own disappointment but with knowing that she's also disappointed her mother. This is an extra, unnecessary burden on her in an already difficult time.

Both parents and kids may get so caught up in the competition for college admission that they lose sight of the overall goal and the fact that many paths can lead to the same desired outcome: a good education and preparation for the future.

Parents need to let their teens live their own lives. There's already enough pressure inherent in the college application process. Our kids don't need us making it more intense with our overinvolvement. We can encourage and guide them, provide resources, take them to visit colleges, listen to them talk about their ambitions and anxieties, read their essays, and hope for the best. But we shouldn't *need* them to get into any one college to fulfill our own dreams.

We want to be there to support our teens if they are disappointed in this process. If Mom had been less emotionally invested in a particular outcome herself, she might have responded quite differently to her daughter. How would that look? Let's play it again:

"I can't believe this!" Gael says, finally able to talk about her disappointment after a day alternating between anguished tears and silence.

"I'm so sorry, Honey," Mom replies, sitting down next to her daughter and putting her arm around her. "I know how much you wanted this."

Gael now has the opening she needs to talk about how she feels and to express her disappointment. She has her mother's sympathetic ear and warm, supportive embrace. Mom understands that Gael has to work her way through all her feelings of disappointment before she's ready to think about her remaining options. She doesn't pressure her daughter now by asking about her second-choice college but gives Gael as much time as she needs—in a number of conversations, over a period of time—to come to terms with her disappointment.

We want our teens' high school years to be filled with opportunities for them to explore their interests and dreams, to discover what they have a passion for and what gives them a sense of purpose in their lives. We don't want them to be so pressured by the college application process that they begin to define themselves not by their own dreams and passions but by what college they get into. In order to guide them in this direction, we need to make sure that we don't lose our own perspective.

Our Teenagers Are Our Priority

The best antidote to the challenges of daily stress is maintaining a balanced schedule, based on our priorities. We all know how difficult that is to achieve. Perhaps the best we can realistically do is constantly to remind ourselves to keep our teens at the top of our list, to the extent this is possible. Often, this means we must be willing to interrupt what we're doing to respond to our kids. For instance, if our normal pattern is to be always "multitasking"—driving the car while talking on the cell phone, or preparing dinner and watching the news—we leave very little opportunity for our teenagers to engage us in conversation. And when they are asked, teenagers say, over and over again, that what they want most from their parents is more relaxed time together, and their full attention.

Maintaining clarity about our own priorities is necessary so that we are able to respond to our teens when they ask us for attention. Often their requests come at inconvenient times, over matters that may seem relatively insignificant to us. But if we don't respond to our teens' requests for attention over "the little things," we can hardly fault them for not turning to us when more difficult issues arise.

Mom is working at the computer when sixteen-year-old Sumona comes home unexpectedly early from the mall, where she has been shopping with friends. She is filled with excitement over a dress she'd seen and wanted months before that is now marked down to a price she can afford. Oblivious to the fact that her mother is busy, Sumona launches into a detailed description of her "great find."

"It'd be great for the prom," she practically sings, "and it fits me perfectly!"

Mom puts aside what she's doing and joins her daughter at the kitchen table, where she is wolfing down a quick lunch before running off to meet her friends again. This mother-daughter interlude takes only about ten minutes, but in that short time, Mom learns a lot about Sumona. She learns that her daughter is a careful shopper and a good planner (the prom is still five months away); most important, she realizes that Sumona still wants and needs her mother's approval before making an important purchase.

Mom is able to keep her priorities straight, and see that these few moments spent together are an ideal opportunity for an important kind of sharing. Through her response, she gives Sumona an important, unspoken message: "I'm never too busy to give you the attention you need when you need it." Sumona's mom understands that it's normal for teenagers to be bursting with enthusiasm over their own concerns, and sometimes be slightly insensitive to the needs of others. So, rather than respond to the interruption with irritation, or lecture her daughter about the need to respect her work, she joins in Sumona's excitement and makes a plan to go to the mall with her to help her make the final decision.

Through this incident, Sumona has learned that she can get her mother's full attention when something's important to her, and that her mother will respond to her needs. When Sumona comes home from a party one day upset about the peer pressure to drink, or when she is grappling with a difficult situation at school, she is more likely to be willing to talk to her mom. She knows that her mother will be there for her.

Freedom to Hang Out

Even though our lives may be overscheduled and stressful, we need to remember that our teenagers need plenty of downtime. We have to be very careful not to overload them by always imposing a goal-directed schedule. After all, the main job of adolescents is to discover who they are. This is their time to explore friendships and love, their talents and dreams, poetry and football. No other goal is as important or will have as great an impact on the rest of their lives. We need to make sure that our teens have the unstructured time they need to just "hang out" and do "nothing" while they discover who they really are—and who they want to become.

Thirteen-year-old Grant was playing on two different soccer teams, volunteering at the local food bank, and continuing his study of the cello. Working out a schedule for the family was a challenge, especially since Grant had two younger brothers who were equally involved in sports and other activities. But Mom had been a corporate vice president before she had children and was exceptionally well organized, so she was able somehow to make it all happen. However, there were problems: Dad sometimes complained about having too many games to watch, or having to miss one of the boys' games due to scheduling conflicts. Both he and his wife wanted to be able to support all of their children in their various activities, but it was becoming impossible to do so.

One evening after dinner, Dad raised the question of where the family should take their vacation this year. Grant immediately asked, "Could we just stay home and not go anywhere?" Mom and Dad were shocked—they had expected the usual debate over mountains versus beach, but not this.

"I really would just like a chance to do nothing," Grant continued. "Maybe go to the movies or something, but basically just hang out."

At that moment, Grant's parents realized how overloaded their son's life had become. Here they had been stressing themselves to keep up with his schedule, and it turned out that what he really needed was some downtime. It's as if the family had gotten on a fast-moving treadmill and didn't know how to get off. Grant's honest plea shocked them into the realization that they didn't have to live their lives on such a hectic schedule.

Mom and Dad realized they had to make some important decisions about their everyday lifestyle, not just vacation. Together they began to set firm priorities and limits. They encouraged Grant to choose the soccer team that was more important to him and to drop the other one. Grant also decided that he could do his volunteer work on alternating weeks, opening up a little time for relaxation in his schedule. Even though he was the first to admit he needed more time to himself, it was still difficult for him to carry through his decision to quit one of the teams; however, once he had, his relief was clear.

As parents, we need to respect the time our teenagers need for their own self-discovery. What looks to us like "hanging out" and doing "nothing" may be extremely important time for them to reflect, relax, and figure out where they're going. This is an important part of growing up, and it prepares teens for the inevitable stresses of their young adulthood. In a few short years they will be making decisions about college, careers, and love relationships that will shape the rest of their lives. The more they learn about themselves now, the wiser they will be when it comes to making those decisions.

When Kids Work

Some teens work to make extra spending money, but many have to work to support themselves or contribute to their family income, even though it may affect their grades and limit their ability to participate in extracurricular activities. These kids don't have the luxury of having time to hang out and do nothing; they have entered the world of adult responsibility and financial pressure at an early age.

Other teenagers contribute to the family by taking over parental responsibilities at home while their parents work. At fifteen, Leah is the oldest of four children. Her mom is a working single parent struggling to provide a decent home for her kids and keep them out of trouble. Leah comes straight home from school every day to make sure her younger brothers and sister get home safely and help them get started on their homework. By the time Mom arrives at 6:30, Leah has straightened up the house and made dinner. She is usually able to start her homework by 8:00, but by then she's pretty tired and it's a struggle.

Mom understands the sacrifice her oldest child is making, and tries to lighten the burden on her as much as possible, but the basic schedule of the workweek can't be altered. The fact is that there are some situations in which teenagers have to grow up early, and they lose out on some of their childhood to take on the pressures and responsibilities of the adult world. When this is our situation, we need to remember that despite the adult responsibilities they're shouldering, these teens are still our children. Whenever possible, we should look for small ways we can appreciate and continue to nurture them.

The night before Leah's sixteenth birthday, Mom brings home a birthday cake for her. The younger children are all in on the surprise, and have prepared small gifts to give Leah. Leah is clearly pleased with being pampered and having her family do something special for her. No matter how grown-up some teenagers seem, they all still want to be fussed over on their birthdays.

Mom is also concerned that Leah not get "stuck" in the role of caretaker. As Leah turns sixteen, her brother Sam is turning thirteen. Mom thinks he's now old enough to begin sharing in the care of the two elementary school–age children, thus relieving Leah of some of her responsibility. Sam takes over two days a week so Leah can stay after school to pursue her interest in taking photographs for the school yearbook. This is good for everyone—Leah gets a break, and Sam is proud to take on additional responsibilities, seeing it as an acknowledgment of his increasing maturity.

Coping with Peer Pressure

Because their relationships with their peers are of such paramount importance to our teenagers, they are vulnerable to a host of problems having to do with various kinds of peer pressure. Although they may be extremely defensive in discussing the various dilemmas they face with their parents, this is one area in which they really need our help and an adult perspective to help guide them.

Clyde, a high school sophomore, maintains honor grades in all his advanced placement courses and still finds time to be a student manager on the basketball team. It happens that Clyde is also one of the first kids in his grade to turn sixteen, get his driver's license, and own his own car. He immediately discovers that he has more "friends" than he'd ever imagined. Kids he knows only casually are calling him up to go to parties and, oh yes, by the way, to drive them there. His closest buddies also want him to drive them here, there, and everywhere. Clyde is totally unprepared for this sudden on-slaught of popularity and the peer pressure that goes with it. Though it doesn't involve pressure to do anything wrong, Clyde just doesn't know how to handle his new social position.

He feels pressure from his parents to continue to study hard and pressure from his peers to be more social. This is a common dilemma for teens—their parents want them to be careful and work hard, while their friends want them to take risks and "party hardy."

Dad understands the pressure Clyde is feeling from his buddies. One day, out for a ride with his son at the wheel, Dad begins reminiscing, "I remember how excited I was when I first got my driver's license." Then he pauses. "It opened up a whole new world for me, but I also had to grow up fast."

The last remark catches Clyde's attention. "What do you mean?" he asks.

"Well," Dad continues, "one of my friends wanted me to drive him and his girlfriend somewhere, and I just didn't feel comfortable getting involved."

"Where'd they want you to take them?" Clyde asks, becoming more and more interested.

Dad hesitates, then takes a deep breath. "Well, um, to a motel," he answers, trying to maintain a calm voice.

"Oh," Clyde mumbles, "I know what you mean. My friends are always asking me to do stuff with them, drive them places I don't really want to go."

At this point in the conversation, Dad's choices are clear. He can begin asking pointed questions, like a detective, to find out what Clyde's friends are up to, or he can give Clyde some high-handed advice on how to "just say no." Instead Dad quietly asks, "How do you handle that?"

This question gives Clyde room to talk about what's going on in his life, without feeling that he is being cross-examined or pressured in one direction or another. For his part, Dad really wants to learn more about his son, so he just listens, while Clyde drives and talks openly about some of the pressures he's been under.

These are the kinds of talks our teens are most likely to remember. These are the moments we need to recognize as opportunities to draw closer to our teens, to let them get to know us in a different way—more as equals—and to give them an uninterrupted chance to talk. Once our kids know they will really be heard, it may surprise us how much they're willing to open up. We just have to remember to control our impulse to give them what we see as guidance and what they often see as just more pressure.

Stress Is Contagious

When our teens do come to us with a problem, it's important not to overreact to the overly dramatic way they may present it. Teenagers can be extremely emotional, and they have a way of talking about normal adolescent challenges as if they're the end of the world. When they do, we need to control our own anxiety so that we don't respond in a way that makes things worse.

By the third week of ninth grade, Cathy is totally stressed out about the amount of homework she's getting in high school. "It's twice as much as last year," she tells her mom as they're getting dinner ready. "There's no way I can keep up."

Mom listens quietly while she works, but she can feel her own tension building as Cathy elaborates on her worst fears. "I'll never get all the reading done. The other kids are so much smarter than me. I didn't understand a thing in math today, and I was too scared to ask."

Cathy is building to a crescendo when her mother can't contain herself and interrupts her. "How can you say you're not as smart as the other kids? That's the dumbest thing I've ever heard! You're just overreacting. You'll adjust to high school. Everyone does."

Cathy pauses, but only for a second. "You don't understand. You never do!" she cries, and runs out of the kitchen in tears, locking herself in her bedroom upstairs.

Mom stands alone in the kitchen, her face flushed and her pulse racing. She realizes immediately that she has said the wrong thing—again—but it's too late. She has added to Cathy's pressure by allowing herself to "catch" her daughter's anxiety and stress.

As parents, it's very difficult for us to remain calm when our teens are upset, especially if their stress is about something that was painful for us during our own adolescence. It turns out that when she was younger, Cathy's mom had felt insecure academically and had had an especially hard time with math. Stress is most contagious when it hits close to home in some way.

Cathy's mother wishes she had been able to recognize the pressure rising within her as she listened to her daughter. Then she could have calmed herself first, by taking a few deep breaths and reminding herself that this is just a momentary thing. She needed to reassure herself before she could reassure Cathy and help her begin to solve her problem.

We need to understand and accept that our teenagers are on an emotional roller coaster. Just as toddlers regularly fall down and we encourage them to get back up again, so will our teenagers fall into the depths of despair and need to be encouraged to pull themselves together and keep going. We need to find a way to help them make the shift from being caught up in their emotional dramas to figuring out what they're going to do about them. If Mom could have continued to listen patiently to Cathy for just a few minutes, nodding or murmuring an understanding "uh-huh" here and there, Cathy might have eventually said something like, "They give us so much homework, I don't even know where to start."

"Well, there's a good question," Mom might say. "How *do* you decide what to do first?"

Now focusing on developing a strategy, Cathy might decide to attack the biology assignment first. "That's easiest for me, but it's not due till the end of the week."

"What's due tomorrow?" Mom could then prompt, helping Cathy to focus on a more effective approach.

Then they would be in a problem-solving mode, and the emotional crisis would be over, at least for the time being. Together they could explore various options, from dropping a class to hiring a tutor.

Stress During a Crisis

Dealing with stress during a true crisis is qualitatively different than dealing with day-to-day pressures. It's far more intense, and this sometimes makes it difficult to function in everyday life.

Teenagers often receive *less* support from their parents during a family crisis, just when they need it the most, because their parents are dealing with their own reactions to the situation. It takes careful consideration to communicate with our teens during a crisis without overwhelming them with adult fears and responsibilities. Our teenagers need to be both informed and protected during these times. It's a difficult balancing act, but it can be done.

Fourteen-year-old Sonya's mother comes home from work one day with the bad news that she has to undergo extensive testing for cancer. She knows Sonya will take this news hard, as they've been very close since Sonya's dad moved away many years ago. Sonya doesn't show much of an outward reaction to the news, but inside it feels as though her world is crumbling. She immediately imagines the worst possible outcome and wonders how she could possibly live without her mother and all the little things her mom does for her.

But she doesn't talk about any of this. Instead, she retreats to her room where she listens to her music, talks on the phone with her friends, and watches her favorite TV show. But the next morning she has trouble getting out of bed, and she can barely get herself to school on time. Mom understands that this is not normal behavior for Sonya, and is gentle and supportive, even offering to give her a ride to school. She understands that this is her daughter's reaction to her own life-threatening illness.

In the following weeks, Mom keeps Sonya apprised of all the medical testing and results, always relaying the news in a calm, factual manner. She listens to Sonya's questions and answers them honestly, to the best of her ability.

"I'm scared, Mommy," Sonya says after one of their talks. She hasn't called her mother "Mommy" in years.

"I know, Sweetie. I am, too," her mom responds. "But I feel like everything will work out okay."

For her own emotional support, Mom turns to her older sister and her close friends about her fears, and asks them for the help she needs to get through this crisis. She knows she can't protect Sonya from the realistic threat of her devastating illness, but she can protect her from her own reaction to the stress, and from worrying about grown-up problems. She knows she needs to be strong for Sonya, and to gather the strength she needs from others, not from her daughter.

The Stress of Divorce

When parents separate or divorce, everyone in the family is highly stressed. Often there is parental conflict before, during, and after the divorce, and teenagers feel torn between their loyalties to both parents, as their world is quite literally being split apart. Because the parents are also upset, their ability to parent effectively during a divorce can be compromised. The parents may be unable to remember what their child told them just last night. They may lose patience more easily, or even explode over small, insignificant things. Sadly, just when the teenager needs his or her parents the most, they are the least available.

Sixteen-year-old Frank's parents were in the middle of a divorce, living apart, angry, and fighting through their attorneys over the financial settlement. Frank seemed aloof and uninvolved in the whole process, as if the divorce had no impact on him. However, one night Frank, usually a safe driver, had a minor car accident. It was only a "fender bender," but Frank was completely distraught. Moreover, his parents were in no condition to talk with him about this crisis—when he told them, his mother burst into tears and his father blasted him.

There are times when an entire family is too stressed to handle one more crisis, even one as ultimately insignificant as a minor car accident. This is when we need the help and support of extended family, close friends, or some other support network. As parents, we need to recognize when we are beyond our limits, and be wise enough to ask for help when we need it.

In this case, Mom called her sister-in-law, Elaine. Although she had been close to her husband's sister, they hadn't spoken much since the separation. But Elaine and her husband had always taken a special interest in Frank, and they understood immediately that the car accident was most likely a sign of his distress over his parents' divorce.

Elaine advised her brother and sister-in-law to try to calm down, and she and her husband offered to take Frank for the weekend. Frank was happy to get away from both of his parents. He didn't talk much to his aunt and uncle over the weekend, but before he went home, he thanked them and admitted that he hadn't realized how upset he was. His uncle hugged him and said the worst time he'd had when he was growing up was when his parents were going through a divorce. Frank looked at him in surprise, and then asked if he could come back soon.

Both Mom and Dad had mixed feelings of failure and guilt over the way they had responded to Frank and his car accident. However, they were grateful and relieved that Elaine and her husband had been able to step in and help their family through this stressful time. Teenagers need many adults who are intimately involved in their lives. When we as parents are too stressed to parent the way we want to, the best thing we can do is to ask for help.

Learning How to Relax

Different people exhibit stress in different ways: the signs can range from sleeping a lot to not enough, from overeating to skipping meals, from being compulsively organized to wildly disorganized. Every teen has his own unique style of responding to stress. As parents, we need to be tuned in to our kids' patterns and willing to ask what's bothering them when it seems something is wrong. The more we know about what's going on in their lives, the better our chance of understanding what may be upsetting them.

In addition, since no one can avoid stress altogether, our teenagers need to learn how to deal with it as part of their preparation for life. They need to recognize their own stress signals early, and to learn how to calm themselves down so they are better able to respond to stress constructively instead of with anxiety.

Again, the most important way we teach our teenagers how to handle stress is through our own example. Our teenagers know when we're stressed out and they're experts at reading our moods. If we become irritable and short-tempered when we're stressed, this is the example we give them.

Mom had an important deadline to meet at the office, which was going to require her working long hours for a couple of weeks, both evenings and weekends. In advance, she put the whole family on notice that they would have to pick up some of the slack and help out around the house more than usual. Dad offered to bring home dinner a few of the nights, and the kids agreed that they would help with the after-dinner duties Mom usually took care of. Mom let the family know exactly what she would need from them while she was under extra pressure at work, and they were prepared to rise to the occasion.

When her project was over, she was once again more available to the family. One night Joyce, her fourteen-year-old daughter, asked her to come into her room at bedtime. Pleased to share this quiet time with her daughter, Mom said, teasingly, "I haven't tucked you into bed in a long time."

"I know, Mom," Joyce said, as her mother sat down on the edge of the bed and fussed with the covers. After a pause Joyce mentioned, "I'm worried about school. Tennis tryouts are coming up, and I have to write a term paper at the same time. I don't know how I'm going to get through it."

"Oh," Mom said, rearranging the covers. "That's a lot of pressure."

"I have trouble concentrating in class because I'm thinking about the tennis match after school," Joyce continued. "Then I can't concentrate on the court because I'm worried about all the research I should be doing for that paper. It's driving me nuts!"

"I know what you mean," Mom responded. "I just went through that kind of thing myself, with my project at work. And you know what? The more I worried, the less I was able to concentrate."

"Yeah, that's the problem," Joyce exclaimed, relieved to be understood.

"Well, do you want to know my secret?" Mom asked. Joyce waited expectantly.

"You remember how I would sit in my reading chair every evening before turning on the computer? I was doing a breathing exercise before I started, so I could calm down my worries and focus on what I needed to accomplish that night. You want me to teach it to you?"

Joyce nodded and snuggled under the covers.

"This is easy to do," she said, "and you can do it anywhere, in any position, even standing up. But since you're in bed, let's try it lying down." Then Joyce's mother proceeded to guide her through the steps. "Breathe in for four counts, and then pause for two counts at the top of your inhale. Breathe out for four counts, and again pause for two counts at the bottom of your exhale." Then she told her daughter how, as you exhale, you can imagine that you are letting go of whatever worries you need to let go of for this moment.

For a few minutes, mother and daughter rested quietly in the stillness together, each of them breathing and counting silently to herself. Then Joyce opened her eyes and saw that her mom's eyes were still closed. She saw a serenity in her mother's face. When she gently touched her mother's hand, Mom opened her eyes and smiled.

"Thanks," Joyce said. "I think that might really help."

"Good night," Mom answered as she bent over to kiss her daughter's forehead.

Both by her example and by direct teaching, Mom is helping Joyce learn how to manage stress effectively. By learning how to handle the very earliest signs of stress, Joyce will be able to direct her energy in a more constructive way—regaining concentration and clearly setting her priorities.

Mom has also modeled for Joyce how she herself is able to temporarily put some of her family responsibilities on hold, asking others to step in and fill the gap so she can meet her deadline at work.

This is a clear lesson in how to manage the fact that we can't have it all, all the time. Joyce is lucky to have a mom who recognizes her own limitations and plans constructively around them. Later in her own life, Joyce will be able to draw on this example of balancing the demands of work and family.

Younger teenagers are likely to be more receptive to parental guidance of this kind than older ones are. Older teens might be enthusiastic about learning the benefits of breathing techniques, but not if it comes from their parents. This is another reason why it's so important to have many adults involved in a teenager's life and available to them. They might be very willing to take advice from a favorite teacher, aunt, or coach and then come home eager to tell their own parents about what they've learned. When they do, wise parents will listen, be impressed and not even mention that "they already knew that."

Teenagers Still Need Our Approval

As our children move through adolescence, their capacity to handle stress grows. If we encourage them, they can come up with creative solutions that we would never have considered. It's important for us to remember that they are preparing for a future which is theirs, not ours. It's our job as parents to acknowledge their developing ability to manage the pressures in their lives, and to respect the way they do that.

We can look for opportunities to compliment them on the way they handle themselves and relate to others in stressful situations. And we should never forget that our teenagers need our approval as much as they did when they were youngsters, even though they may not always show that they do.

Phil, a senior in high school, has been the stage manager of the school plays since his sophomore year. Gradually he has taken on more and more responsibility until he is truly functioning at a near professional level. This year the school musical is an over-the-top extravaganza with a bigger budget, larger cast, and more complicated scenery and costume changes than ever before. Phil oversees the whole thing, and he does a great job at it. Even when the faculty director loses his patience, Phil is there to calm things down. He makes phone calls to remind the cast of rehearsal schedules and to make sure everyone is doing okay. Using his computer, he creates a program that includes a brief paragraph about each of the actors in the production. Phil is everywhere at once, and he still manages to maintain his grades and his position on the honors council.

His parents have frankly never been thrilled that their son has become so involved in theater. They have always dreamed he'd become a doctor, though they can see things may be heading in a different direction. However, they do appreciate their son's level of competence in dealing with not only his own stress but helping others manage theirs as well.

After the show is over, Phil's mom and dad each write him a letter describing how proud they are of his managerial skills, and recognizing specific examples of how Phil has been able to manage his own stress as well as that of the entire theater company.

Reading the notes helps Phil understand that his parents are trying to appreciate him for who he is and what he does, even when it comes into conflict with their own hopes and dreams for his career.

As parents, we should not look to have our dreams fulfilled by our children. We would be much wiser to focus on what they're doing that will serve them well in the future rather than on what we want them to do to please us. We shouldn't expect them to fulfill our dreams, but to find and fulfill their own.

One way or another, our teenagers do take us with them when they leave home and strike out into the world at large. Our words and behavior are imprinted in their hearts and minds for better or worse, forever. The way we deal with stressful situations will be remembered by them in detail. Furthermore, the advice we have offered them about how to deal with stress and the amount of confidence we have in their ability to deal with stress will affect how they respond to their own personal challenges in life. And no matter how much they may resist our input as teenagers, our kids do in fact continue to learn from us throughout adolescence and beyond.

If teenagers live with failure, they learn to give up

The teenage years are a time for exploration and experimentation. Our teenagers will be trying out different roles and taking on a variety of activities. In the process, they will inevitably experience both success and failure. When our teens experience failure, for whatever reason, we don't want them to give up on themselves. We want them to come through the experience with hope for their future intact and a realistic optimism about who they can become and what they can do with their lives.

If teenagers consistently fail at too many things, they may become demoralized and lose faith in themselves. They may think they don't have what it takes to succeed. Teenagers who feel this way are in danger of growing up feeling inherently flawed, as if they lack some essential quality, and that no matter what they do, they're doomed to failure.

Once the expectation of failure sets in, teenagers may lose

confidence and stop trying. They may give up on themselves; it might seem too painful to keep on trying and failing. Though teens certainly wouldn't express it in those terms, they have come to the conclusion that the only way to protect themselves from failure is to stop trying.

It's our job as parents to recognize this kind of negative, self-fulfilling prophecy when it begins to occur, and to help our teens find an alternative approach to life. We want to help them face their feelings of disappointment and encourage them to persist, or find a new and better direction, when they feel like giving up.

To do this, we need to be quite involved with the daily ups and downs of their lives. That's the only way we'll know when the normal adolescent disappointments and losses are mounting and our kids are beginning to feel an overwhelming sense of failure. Different kids have different levels of tolerance for frustration, so it's important to know when your child needs help or encouragement, and to be there to offer it.

Staying Connected with Our Kids

Eighth-graders Xavier and Carlos were the two most experienced members of their school's debate team. This was their last year of middle school, and they were hoping to win the state championship, but things were not going well. Although the scores were close at each meet, they were losing one debate after another, and the whole team was becoming discouraged.

Feeling that there was no hope for the team, Xavier began to withdraw emotionally and to question whether he would even join the high school debate team next year. Carlos had the opposite response—he was energized by the challenge and determined to overcome it. He found some college-level debate videos at the library and took them home to study.

These two boys had very different responses to the same situation. Xavier needed extra support and the encouragement of adults to sustain him during the string of losses his team was experiencing. Many teens do need the advice and support of the adults in their lives when they face discouragement, even though they may rebuff the initial efforts of their parents or others to give it.

Xavier's father was a lawyer, and he had been following the progress of the debate team closely. He saw that his son's spirits were beginning to decline and realized he was close to giving up. Quitting an activity in adolescence is different from losing interest in a hobby during the elementary school years. Adolescence is the prime time for exploring a variety of adult roles and professions. It's a time to explore possibilities and new directions. Dad knew that the experience of feeling defeated and giving up on an area of interest can be prematurely limiting for teens, and he didn't want his son to fall into this trap. He decided he would offer his assistance to his son, knowing that he risked being pushed away.

On the way home after yet another loss, Xavier's dad remarked on what a close debate it had been.

Xavier grunted, "Yeah."

"Just a few points could have made the difference," Dad continued.

No response.

"I think I've got an idea for a strategy that might make that difference," Dad said.

Again, there was no response from Xavier. Dad let the subject drop, and they rode the rest of the way home in silence.

But a few days later, after dinner, Xavier sauntered over to where his dad was reading the newspaper. "Okay, let's hear it," Xavier said, as if he were continuing the same conversation. It took a minute for Dad to realize this was the opening he had hoped for the other day, but he quickly put his paper down and picked up the conversation where they'd left off, without missing a beat.

As it turned out, Dad's ideas weren't the answer to the team's problem, and they continued their losing streak. However, with his dad's support, Xavier decided he didn't give want to give up on debate. He went on to argue successfully on the high school team. In the process he learned an important lesson about persistence and determination in the face of discouragement.

Carlos's parents were supportive of his participation in the debate team, too, but for Carlos their encouragement was not crucial. He had the resiliency needed to sustain himself in spite of the bad season.

As every parent of more than one child knows, even kids from the same family can have very different capacities for resilience. When a teenager is discouraged, the active involvement of a parent can make a crucial difference. It's important to be able to see when a teen is reaching the limits of his ability to deal with failure, recognize that he needs extra support, and be willing to step in and help. Staying in close touch with what's happening in our teens' lives is the key to timing that offer of support. When the timing is right, a little help is received well and can go a long way. If Xavier's father had pushed too hard when his son wasn't ready to talk, his words would have fallen on deaf ears. And if he hadn't noticed what was happening until his son had dropped out of debate the following year, it might well have been too late for encouragement.

Helping Teens Develop Realistic Expectations

Sometimes parents are surprised to realize that teenagers don't seem to understand the connection between hard work and success. Certainly the images of success as depicted in the media rarely show the years of struggle and practice that musicians, actors, or athletes engage in before their "instant" successes. Impressionable teens may well see the glossy final product and imagine that success really can happen "overnight." Often they don't know the long story of struggle and persistence behind success—that Michael Jordan was cut from his high school basketball team in tenth grade, or that Julia Stiles was not called back after many of her early auditions. Small doses of this kind of information can help awaken teenagers to the fact that perseverance in the face of failure is an essential ingredient in anyone's success.

Thirteen-year-old Allie learned how to play chess one summer at sleep-away camp. She fell in love with the game, but lost most of her matches. When her parents picked her up at the end of camp, the chess tournament was both her biggest news and her biggest disappointment.

"But, Allie," Dad said, "winning at chess takes a lot of practice."

"No it doesn't," Allie answered, frustrated that her dad just didn't understand. "My mind just doesn't work that way."

"Dad's right," Mom chimed in. "You get better by playing and learning from each game you play. That's how I learned."

Allie was surprised to learn that her mother had some inside knowledge. "You play chess?" she asked.

Her parents both laughed. "We used to," Dad said. "We haven't played much in a while. Your mother always used to beat me," he added. Allie was amazed.

"Oh yeah, I did," Mom admitted. "Grandpa taught me when I was a kid, and we used to play chess whenever it rained."

All that year Allie played chess with her parents. She lost matches for many months and began to feel discouraged. But her parents did not believe in "letting" her win. Instead, they encouraged her to persevere and do it on her own, and discussed winning strategies with her after their matches. When Allie finally beat her father for the first time, her parents gave her a computer chess program as a gift. It took Allie a lot longer to beat her mother, but she advanced much further in the camp chess tournament the following summer and was able to see how far she had come in a year.

Sometimes we forget that our teens don't see things the way we do simply because they haven't had enough life experience. Most teenagers haven't yet learned how small, almost imperceptible improvements can eventually lead to dramatic transformations. They haven't yet developed a sense of patience and the long-range perspective needed to realize for themselves the crucial link between hard work and success.

Modeling Persistence for Our Teens

The way we persist in the face of discouragement is a powerful model for our teenagers. No matter what we say about the value of perseverance, the example of how we deal with our own challenges will have a much more profound impact on our teens. This is an especially difficult realization to make if we ourselves didn't grow up with the support we needed to overcome our own feelings of failure and discouragement. When this is the case, somehow we have to find within ourselves the resolve we need to show our teens how they can develop it in their own lives.

Sixteen-year-old Charlotte's mother has decided to redo the guest bedroom. Her plan is to remove the old wallpaper and paint the room in time for her mother's annual visit. Charlotte is busy with her own life, and has no interest in "manual labor." Also, she is not too excited about her grandmother's visit, because her grandmother is a very critical person who often makes everyone around her unhappy.

"I don't see why you're going to all this trouble for Grandma," Charlotte tells her mom. "She's not going to appreciate it."

"I know that," Mom says. "She's always been that way. I'm fixing this room up for myself. I want to move my desk out of the TV room and in here so I can have my own space."

"Well, Grandma's already complained to me that you'll never have it done in time and she'll have to be breathing in all the paint fumes while she sleeps," Charlotte tells her mom.

In fact, Mom doesn't finish the room in time for her mother's visit. The wallpaper is difficult to remove and the process takes much longer than she had ever imagined it would. Grandma arrives and complains about the mess throughout her visit. Finally, Charlotte's mom completes the project, a full six weeks later.

Charlotte is impressed. "I think I would have given up," Charlotte says, as she admires the new room. "I can't believe you finally finished it."

"There were plenty of times I felt like giving up," Mom admits. "But I just kept focused on the small signs of progress week by week. The hardest time was when Grandma was here."

Mom doesn't have to lecture Charlotte about the value of hard work and perseverance. Her behavior has said it all, more powerfully than any lecture ever could. Being able to complete the project in spite of her own mother's negativity and discouraging remarks is perhaps the even bigger success story. Grandma's expectations of her ultimate failure didn't faze Charlotte's mom. This is precisely the kind of example we want to set for our teenagers.

Seeing Failure as an Opportunity for Success

Just as we don't always succeed in meeting our own goals, our teens won't always be able to live up to their own, let alone our, expectations of them. Disappointment and feelings of failure are a natural part of life. The question is what attitude we assume when we face these situations, and what actions we take in response to them. Sometimes the experience of failing at something important gives our teens a valuable opportunity to answer these questions for themselves. It's learning the "hard way," but it's learning!

Perhaps there's no better way to explore feelings of success or failure than through the adolescent ritual of the college board exams. For some teens this process begins as early as the PSATs in seventh grade. Even though the instructions state that you can't "fail" the college boards, every teen knows that you will feel like a failure if your scores are disappointing. To make matters worse, those harsh, cold numerical scores have a way of traveling swiftly through the grapevine, so that by the end of the day pretty much everyone knows who did well and who didn't.

"How'd you do?" Dad asks sixteen-year-old Dean the minute he arrives home from work on the big day. Dean hands over his SAT scores.

Clearly Dean is disappointed in his scores, as well as nervous about his father's reaction to them. Dad's first impulse is either to say nothing at all—the "silent treatment"—or to yell at Dean. Instead he takes a deep breath and says, "Okay, give me a minute to change my clothes, then we can talk about this."

Dean waits for him in the next room, anxious.

"I know you can do better than this," Dad begins when they sit down to talk.

Dean immediately begins to offer a series of flimsy explanations and excuses for his very low scores.

"I really don't want to hear it," Dad says. "The bottom line is you didn't prepare. Did you even use that computer program we bought for you?"

Dean doesn't have much to say in his defense. He knows his dad is right, and that he blew it.

"The question is, what are you going to do now?" Dad asks, looking his son in the eyes.

Dad is right to hold Dean responsible for his disappointing college board scores. There's no question that Dean could have done much better with even a minimum of effort. However, Dad doesn't dwell on this point. Having established it, he quickly moves on, asking what Dean's plan is for the next time he will take the exams.

A few days later, when both Dad and Dean have calmed down, they talk about it again. "Well, now that we know your *bottom* scores," Dad says, his sense of humor returning, "I wonder what your *top scores* would look like."

"Me, too," Dean answers. "Well, at least I get another chance to try."

"Right," Dad agrees, adding, "That won't always be the case, you know."

"I know," Dean says soberly.

A humbling experience of failure can spur some teens into positive action. These kids seem to need to see what they can get away with before they buckle down to work. When this happens, the key is to hold the teen responsible for his failure, while continuing to have confidence and faith in his ability to do better next time.

When All Else Fails . . .

Not everyone has the necessary determination to succeed. Some teens may already have surpassed their tolerance for failure and given up. They no longer try, proclaim they don't care, and may even be hardened to adults' offers of help. When kids lose hope they become emotionally vulnerable, even though they don't show it, and they are more likely to get into trouble. These teens are difficult to reach and may already be beyond their parents' influence. When things have come to this point, the best strategy for parents may be to try to identify another adult who may be able to get through to the teen—a coach, minister, therapist, relative, teacher, neighbor, or even the parent of one of his friends. Finding just one person who can get through to a teen who is shutting himself off from the world is extremely important. It only takes one adult to make a difference in the rest of that kid's life.

This is one of the reasons it's important to maintain a strong extended family and friendship network and to draw on community resources for help with raising our children. Sometimes teenagers just need more than their parents can give them. At those times, we don't want them to fall through the cracks. Unfortunately, there are not enough mentors available to meet the needs of all the teenagers at risk in our world. Also, as teens grow older, they may be less open to accepting help than younger teens are. Sadly, some may remain unreachable no matter what.

Sometimes the best we can do as parents is to create the opportunity for mentoring relationships, preferably before trouble begins. We can arrange for after-school or evening programs for our young teenagers, so that they are kept busy with constructive activities and under the influence of caring, responsible adults. The greater the number of adults involved with our teens throughout these treacherous years, the more likely our teens will succeed.

Thirteen-year-old Tyrone was well liked by both kids and teachers at school, but he wasn't much of a student. He had difficulty reading, so he never wanted to do his homework; furthermore, he claimed that he just didn't care. His mother worked six days a week, and his father was largely absent. So Tyrone, an only child, was on his own a lot. The only time he and his mom did anything together was on Sunday morning, when they went to church.

The choir director, knowing that Tyrone was having problems with school, had his eye on him. He convinced Tyrone to join the church choir and, to everyone's surprise, that's where he began to shine. When Tyrone's voice changed, he developed a beautiful, warm baritone, and eventually went on to lead that section of the choir.

As Tyrone moved through his adolescent years, he was still not very motivated in school, and he did just enough to get by. He often did his homework during breaks in choir practice, which had expanded to three nights a week. Under the choir director's attentive eye, Tyrone began conducting the junior chorus and singing in an a cappella men's group.

From his success in the choir, Tyrone learned that dedication and diligence paid off. He developed an interest in pursuing a career in music education, and realized he would have to work harder in school so he could go to college. With this goal in mind, Tyrone studied more and his grades did in fact improve.

Before the choir director's intervention, Tyrone was definitely a teen with a high-risk profile. The director's sensitivity to both Tyrone's talents and his needs meant all the difference between Tyrone's finding success and fulfillment in his life and falling by the wayside.

Whose Life Is It, Anyway?

It's very important that when we set our teens up to succeed we do it in a way that suits their individual needs and talents. If we are constantly comparing our kids to their siblings, the neighbors, or some nonexistent adolescent ideal, we will miss what is most unique about our own teenagers, and what they have to give. Satisfaction in life depends upon pursuing one's own personal passions and talents, so we especially want our teens to have the chance to explore whatever truly interests them, free of unreasonable expectations from others.

Pete's family sent him to a rigorous private school in hopes of preparing him for an Ivy League education. It was a great school, but it wasn't right for Pete. From early on, Pete was the class clown, the last one in his seat in the morning, and the first one out when the bell rang at the end of the day. He was good-natured and fun, and the other kids accepted him exactly as he was. Gradually the teachers and Pete's parents came to accept what the kids knew all along—Pete was a bright but extremely active "hands-on" kind of kid who was not well suited for a rigorous academic curriculum.

By ninth grade, as the academic pressure began to intensify,

Pete was really struggling. Because he couldn't compete with the others academically, Pete began to feel that he didn't "fit in," that he was "stupid," and that it was all his fault.

Fortunately, during his freshman year, Pete found his way to the basement of the school and into the woodworking shop. There he began taking industrial arts as an elective course. With each ensuing year, Pete's projects grew in size, complexity, and beauty. His handcrafted furniture was soon on display in the school's art shows and began to fill his parents' home.

By his senior year, many of Pete's friends were headed for the Ivy League colleges his parents had originally wanted for him. Pete was the only one in the whole graduating class who was going to a technical school. But by this time, Pete and his parents had come a long way and were accepting of both his talents and his limitations. Because of this change, Pete was able to see himself as being successful in work that he loved, rather than as a failure in work he hated. At the graduation ceremonies, when the industrial arts teacher came on stage to announce the art award, everyone rose to their feet. Pete's friends, teachers, and family give him the only standing ovation of the day.

Knowing When to Change Direction

There are times when it makes sense to give up on an inappropriate goal and replace it with a more realistic or more appropriate one. Some teens throw their hearts into their dreams, and end up knocking their heads against an immovable wall. We have to be alert to this possibility, so that if it occurs, we can help redirect our teens' energies and save them from needless experiences of failure.

Thirteen-year-old Carly had been in ballet classes since third grade. Unfortunately she was not built for ballet, and no matter how hard she tried, she would never excel at it. But she loved to dance and so she continued the classes. However, as a young teenager, her frustration with ballet was beginning to have a negative effect on her self-image.

"I'm the fattest one in the class," she told her mom one afternoon after ballet, "*and* the slowest."

Mom, preoccupied with her own thoughts, absentmindedly responded, "I'm sure that's not true, dear."

Carly didn't say another word.

It's very easy to miss what's really going on in our teenagers' lives. Carly's mom was not uncaring or negligent. She was just distracted, thinking about her own schedule for the evening, so she missed the significance of her daughter's statement. Carly was attending ballet class two or three times a week, and for her to be feeling so badly about herself so often was just too frustrating and painful. Teenagers feel emotionally vulnerable enough as it is, so having to deal with constant criticism about something over which they have no control can be harmful to their developing sense of self.

A few weeks later, after class, Carly announced she was quitting ballet. Her mother was shocked.

"What! After all those years of study?" her mom said. "And you've gotten so good!"

"You just don't get it!" Carly exploded. Her mother had had a tough day herself and was all ready to shout back, but instead she paused for a moment. Carly remained silent, and Mom took a breath to compose herself.

"I'm just no good at it," Carly said, switching from anger to tears. "I've studied longer than the others, but I'll never be really good."

Mom realized that Carly was right, and that a superficial expression of support or encouragement was not what she needed. How frustrating it must be, trying so hard for so many years only to see others pass her by!

"I'm sorry," Mom said, simply and quietly, reaching out to give her daughter a hug.

Carly nodded, and her body relaxed with the relief of being understood.

"Ballet isn't right for you, but do you really want to give up dance altogether?" Mom asked.

"No, not really," Carly admitted.

"Maybe you could try modern dance or jazz," Mom suggested.

"Yeah, maybe," Carly agreed.

Once Mom understood what was going on for Carly, she could see that Carly's decision to quit ballet was the right one for her. Ballet classes had been a good thing for her for many years, but now that had changed, and Carly needed to make a change, too.

Teenagers can easily be overwhelmed by their own emotions, especially when they feel as though they're failing at something important to them. They aren't always able to see what other options may be available. We can help them in these times by remaining calm and objective, by asking questions so that we can understand what they're going through, by providing empathy, and by helping them move on to find alternative solutions. If Mom had gotten caught up in the emotions of the moment and snapped back at Carly, the real issues at hand would have been lost in an escalating battle between mother and daughter. Instead, Mom was able to help Carly see that when persistent effort isn't paying off, it may be better to change direction than to give up entirely.

It's Not About Winning

Our teenagers are very sensitive to our judgments about them, even though they're experts at appearing not to notice or care about what we think. They are extremely tuned in to our feelings and know when we're disappointed, no matter how much we may try to hide our true reactions.

Seventeen-year-old Olivia had been nominated for a statewide history award. The nomination in itself was a big honor, whether or not she went on to win the state competition. Unfortunately, Olivia's parents were overinvested in her winning. They wanted to be able to brag about her to their friends, and they also wanted her to achieve at a level higher than they had been able to achieve in their lives. Parents sometimes confuse their own unfulfilled hopes and dreams with what's best for their children.

Olivia's parents had told her how proud they were of her, but they made such a big deal about the banquet where the winner was to be announced that she almost didn't want to go. As the awards ceremony approached, Olivia felt the pressure building. It was interfering with her ability to enjoy the honor of having been nominated.

When Olivia didn't win the award, despite their protestations to the contrary, she knew her parents were terribly disappointed, and she ended up feeling like a failure. What's sad about this story is that what should have been a success, Olivia experienced as a failure. The same thing happens when a kid comes home with a B-plus on a test and the parent says, "If you'd only done such and such, you'd have gotten an A." The parent's disappointment takes away from the teen's legitimate accomplishment. If this is a pattern, the adolescent may give up on trying to succeed, or wanting to please the parent, or both.

It's not fair for us to expect our teens to win, to be the best, or to succeed at everything. Often the outcome is beyond their ability or control. We *can* expect them to do their personal best, but our expectations need to be clear and appropriate to our teens' interests or abilities, and based on what they want for themselves.

The way we communicate these expectations to them can make all the difference. If Dad tells fifteen-year-old Angelina before an important ice hockey game, "Get in there and score big tonight. You can do it!" it may sound like encouragement, but it's really a form of pressure. Angelina's team could win but, if she didn't personally score, she could end up feeling like a failure. Alternately she could play her very best game but, if the other team had a better defense and her team lost, she might still end up feeling like a failure.

If he simply said, "Play your best," Dad would express confidence in Angelina's ability and give her the freedom to play the game the best way she knows how.

Our kids are extremely sensitive to our expectations, the quality of our attention, and our words. As they grow older, we need to respect their right to decide what's important to them and support them to do their best in whatever arena they've chosen. We want to give our teens strong, clear messages that we believe in them and are there to support them. We want them to hear messages that encourage them—that invite them to succeed in their lives.

If teenagers live with rejection, they learn to feel lost

Because teenagers quite naturally feel insecure even under the best of circumstances, they can be exquisitely sensitive to rejection. Of course, rejection can be painful for us too, but at least we have an adult perspective gained from experience that enables us to view the rejection as a temporary disappointment. To our teenagers, rejection may seem like the end of the world. It doesn't matter whether the rejection comes from parents, peers, or is just in the teenager's own imagination. Teenagers' fear that they're not cool enough, not cute enough, not whatever-enough can be practically unbearable.

Since our teens are still developing their sense of self, even the hint of rejection, or an imagined slight, sometimes leads to acute feelings of alienation. If our teenagers feel so isolated that they don't know who to turn to, they can end up feeling lost. As they seek relief from this emotional pain, teens can be very vulnerable to peer pressure, even to the point of risking danger in order to "fit in." This is one of the reasons why teens need their homes to be places of "safe haven," where they can count on being unconditionally accepted for who they are. We want them to be able to come home to relax and know that they can be themselves, without undue pressure. Our teens need this kind of accepting atmosphere in order to build the strength and resilience they need to handle the ups and downs of their lives without feeling lost.

Fourteen-year-old Sophie is a quiet but intensely emotional teenager who likes to read and write poetry. She has one close girlfriend with whom she goes to the movies, and that constitutes her whole social life. No one else ever calls. In contrast, her mother is quite extroverted, active in the school PTA, and knows everyone.

"Why don't you call Lila to go out?" Mom suggests one day. She is always trying to encourage Sophie to be more social. "I'm sure she's a nice girl—her mother's very nice."

"I don't think so," Sophie answers.

"You don't think she's nice or you don't think you'll call her?" Mom asks, her exasperation clear.

"It doesn't matter," Sophie responds. "I'm just not calling her."

"I wish you could be a bit friendlier, Sophie," Mom says, shifting to a pleading tone. "You'd have more fun."

"I have enough fun," Sophie retorts. "And besides, I'm not like you!" She ends the conversation by angrily leaving the room.

That stops Mom in her tracks. She is just trying to help her daughter, and she doesn't understand why Sophie has gotten so upset. Mom "knows" she is right—Sophie *would* have more fun if she could only be friendlier.

But Sophie just can't do that. It isn't her way, and she really isn't all that interested in having a more social life. She's involved with her own preferred activities, and she doesn't want to be pressured into being different from who she is. What her mother sees as well-intentioned encouragement feels like criticism and rejection to Sophie.

The more we can accept and value our teens' basic personality traits, the more comfortable they'll be with us and the more willing to spend time at home. If the suggestions we offer our teenagers require them to change their basic personality style, naturally they'll feel as though we're criticizing them. And because their developing sense of self is still quite fragile, they may be particularly sensitive to any hint of parental rejection.

If Sophie's mom is concerned about her social life, it is better to ask Sophie about it than to assume something is wrong. "How're you doing with kids at school?" she might ask. "Do you feel like you have enough friends?" This will give Sophie the chance to answer, honestly, that she is getting along just fine.

"Wouldn't you like to go out more?" Mom might press.

"I'm okay, Mom, really," Sophie could say, with a reassuring smile.

Mom needs to accept Sophie's personal preference for spending most of her time alone engaged in quiet intellectual pursuits rather than pursuing a social life. She could ask her daughter what she's reading as a way of acknowledging and respecting what's important to Sophie.

We want to stay connected with our teenagers. By not accepting them as they are, we risk losing them to their peer group or to lonely isolation. Generally, we'll do much better with our teens if we're truly interested in what they're doing and if we don't try to pressure them to be someone other than who they are.

Dealing with Rejection

No one survives adolescence, or life for that matter, without experiencing some rejection along the way. The acceptance we give our teenagers at home will help them to be more resilient when they encounter rejection outside the home. During their younger teenage years, we can offset upsetting experiences with extra support and understanding, assuring them that we accept them for who they are. As they grow older, and their sense of self matures and becomes stronger, they will be better able to handle such rejections themselves, and even learn from them. Certainly the college application process and job hunting will include inevitable rejections. By then we hope our teens will have learned to absorb disappointment without losing momentum or confidence in themselves. Of course, even then they will still need our support.

When thirteen-year-old Scott's application was not accepted to be a peer counselor at school he was distraught. His best friend was chosen but he wasn't, and he didn't know why. It was driving him crazy. Nothing his mother said made him feel any better. Finally his dad took a different approach.

"How many times have you not gotten what you wanted?" he asked his son.

Scott had to think. "Not very often," he replied.

"Do you feel rejected in any other parts of your life—at home, at school, with your friends, with your soccer team, at camp?" Dad persisted.

"No," Scott had to admit, again and again.

"Does the fact that you've been turned down this time make any difference in what you'll be doing with all these other activities?" Dad went on.

"Okay, Dad, I get it, I get it," Scott said, even cracking a little smile. And he really did get his father's point. He realized that he had to take a different perspective regarding this one rejection. He was still disappointed, but he didn't feel badly about *himself* anymore. He knew this was just one small setback in a life full of good things.

Dad felt great about being able to help his son recover from a disappointment and learn how to shift his perspective in order to take a broader view. The conversation was a brief one, but the impact was profound for both father and son. Scott knew his dad was really involved in his life, that he cared about what was happening to him, and was willing to help him deal with it. For his part, Dad saw that he could be instrumental in helping his son develop a more mature attitude. This seemingly small interaction was actually an important basis for a positive connection between the two of them as they headed toward more complicated issues of adolescence.

Get Ready, Get Set . . .

Fostering positive connections with our teens is extremely important as puberty begins. We want to start down the challenging road of adolescence with our kids feeling that we are well-connected to them and that they are a priority in our lives. We can't afford to let them enter or move through their teenage years feeling lost or alone. The stakes are just too high.

The battles begin early these days. Twelve-year-old Molly and her mom are beginning to argue over what clothes Molly can wear to school and how often she has to practice her violin. Molly is beginning to exhibit flat-out rebellion over some of the rules of the house—at times she can look right through her mother and disregard any request she makes. Mom is beginning to feel as if she has no control, which makes her frustrated and angry. This describes a negative cycle that can only get worse as Molly enters full-blown adolescence.

One evening, after a few very frustrating days culminating in a major screaming match, Mom reaches her limit. She sinks into a chair in front of the TV and tries not to imagine what the next six years of life with Molly are going to be like. She is so overwhelmed, she completely tunes Molly out and simply stops responding to her. Molly runs upstairs to her room in tears. A few minutes later, Dad comes down from his study, where he's been working on the computer and hands Mom a note.

Molly has sent her dad a fax from her bedroom computer, asking for his help. The fax says, "Please tell Mom to talk to me."

No matter how badly our teens are behaving, they still desperately want to stay connected with us. Unfortunately, sometimes parents and teens become locked in a vicious circle of anger, criticism, rejection, and acting out from which there appears to be no exit. "My dad is such a jerk," the teenager says. Dad defends the harshness of his position by saying, "I have to let him know what he's doing wrong so he'll learn." And so the endless cycle continues. In these situations, both the parents and the teenager lose, and, sadly, what they lose is each other.

Our teenagers are in a volatile time of their lives, surrounded by other volatile kids, in a social atmosphere that is full of insecurity, fear, and a multitude of ways to go wrong. If we don't want them to be swept away by the hormonal changes that are rocking them from within and the teen culture that is constantly challenging them from without, we have to make every effort we possibly can to nurture our relationship with them. One of the cruelest things we can do to our kids is to ignore them.

No matter how bad the behavior gets, above all we want to stay connected to our teenagers. It's only by maintaining our relationship with our teens that we have any opportunity at all for guiding them. There is nothing to be gained by withholding our time, attention, or affection from them. Certainly teens' needs change as they mature; but they need our love, support, and guidance every bit as much as they did when they were babies. We have to be flexible so that our relationship with our teens can evolve in keeping with their changing needs through adolescence into young adulthood.

When Kids Are Gay . . .

A certain percentage of teenagers are in the process of discovering that they are gay; some of them have known this for years, and others still don't know what they are or who they will become. Human sexual orientation exists along a flexible continuum, and our sexual identities are not defined by a single experience or even a single major "crush." It's important for us to know, as our teens navigate this extremely delicate and sensitive part of growing up, that sexual orientation is not a lifestyle "choice"—it's a part of who we are. We want to create an environment in which the least of our teenagers' concerns is whether or not we will *accept* them for who they are. After all, *knowing* who you are is hard enough.

Teens who aren't clearly heterosexual are very vulnerable to rejection and harassment by their peers. They can even be at physical risk. They need all the support they can get—and they most certainly don't need to be rejected by their own families. Unfortunately some gay and lesbian teens are so afraid of such rejection that they choose to live secret lives, hiding their true feelings and identities from their families well into adulthood.

Parents have very different reactions upon realizing that their child is gay. Some are immediately accepting; others need time to work through their own feelings. Most parents need some education about what the future might look like for their teens. If they're willing to learn about their gay teen's world, they'll discover that gay teens have all the same hopes and dreams as straight teens—they want to find true love, meaningful work, success, a long-term relationship, and perhaps children.

Parents who cannot accept an openly gay teen are at risk of losing their child. And if teens are so concerned about their parents' reactions to finding out "who I am" that they cannot accept their own sexual identity, they will lose a central part of themselves. This is not the kind of burden we want to place on our children.

Madeline knew she had always somehow been "different." Ever since elementary school she'd had trouble fitting in and developing close friendships. She was cute, athletic, and very bright, but she was often alone. Her parents had no clue what the problem was, nor how they could help her

When Madeline was fifteen, she went to a wilderness summer program that trained teens in survival skills. There she blossomed socially and, for the first time, fell in love . . . with another girl. Madeline was just beginning to understand who she was and it helped immensely that the summer camp community accepted both Madeline and her new girlfriend totally. She returned home radiant. She tried to talk to her parents about her experiences but they seemed not to want to hear about them, so her sexuality remained unspoken.

As Madeline progressed through adolescence, she quietly developed friendships with lesbians from nearby high schools. This allowed her to explore her relationships more discreetly than she could in her own hometown, and she avoided having to deal with her parents' disapproval. During her senior year, however, Madeline took an art class and for her final project painted a large, abstract oil painting which was full of emotional expression. To make sure that she was completely understood, she wrote a collection of poems to accompany her painting. These were a very honest description of her personal journey and they were, in essence, her "coming out."

The art teacher selected Madeline's mixed media project for the honors art show. Horrified, her parents pressured and threatened Madeline until she agreed not to include the poems. They were adamant, despite Madeline's anguish and the support of her art teacher. They didn't see that by censoring Madeline's artistic expression and "coming out," they were rejecting a central aspect of their daughter's identity.

As parents, we would be wise to keep a long-range perspective on our relationship with our teenagers. Our kids will soon move out of our homes and become independent adults. The seeds of our lifelong relationship with our grown children are sown during childhood and adolescence. We want this relationship to be based on a history of encouragement and acceptance, not control and rejection.

Clothing: The Teenager's Declaration of Independence

It's important to remember that when we reject our teens' appearance they may experience it as a rejection of who they are. To many teens, the image they project can be a central part of their developing identity. Our whole culture feeds on and encourages this misguided belief that "you are what you wear." As adults, we're really only slightly less susceptible to the influence of the powerful fashion industry than our teens. And since our teens are not quite sure yet of who they really are *inside,* it's easy for them to develop a more clear-cut identity by what they look like on the outside.

Cliques in high schools are easily recognized by their styles of dress. This lends clique members a sense of belonging. Simple reassurances like "You look great today" from parents won't help very much as our kids enter their teens. After all, it's not the parents' reaction the teen is interested in—it's that of the other kids. With the right approach, this aspect of teen culture can actually be used to good effect.

Thirteen-year-old Jared was slightly mentally disabled and he was "mainstreamed" into a high-achieving high school. His facial expressions, way of speaking, and slight limp gave him an odd appearance. Although Jared was in the best educational program for him, his parents were concerned about how the other kids would treat him.

The psychiatrist they consulted was direct. "Dress him in the latest clothes from the Gap," he said. Jared's parents were surprised by this advice, which they at first thought was shallow. But the doctor explained, "This will help the other kids overlook what's unusual about Jared and be more accepting of him."

Jared's parents followed the psychiatrist's advice, and it was exactly the right thing to do. With all the "right clothes," it was much easier for Jared to fit in with the other kids, and this made his life easier than it might have been otherwise. His parents said it was the best professional advice they had ever received, and the best money they ever spent on their son.

The Fashion Wars

As a part of discovering who they are, teens experiment with their appearance, and much of the time their parents are offended by the results. In fact, the very fashion statements teens adore and parents abhor no doubt defines the battleground, whether it's about hair, clothes, make-up, body piercings, or tattoos. The more vehemently the parents reject and try to prohibit certain fashion statements, the more important they become to the teen. This is why sometimes the best strategy is to keep our opinions to ourselves and try to remember what we looked like as teenagers, and how we felt when our parents criticized us for what we were wearing.

We need to keep in mind that fashion is not a life-threatening issue. Sometimes in the heat of battle, we forget that. We would be wise to save our strongest parental stands for the larger and much more important issues of alcohol, drugs, driving, and sex. If we keep this in mind, it may be easier to tolerate our teens' clothing fads, no matter how distasteful they may seem to us.

With years of shopping experience between them, Mom and her sixteen-year-old daughter, Ashley, had a well-established code. Whenever Ashley tried on something her mother didn't like, Mom would say, evenly, "That does nothing for you." When Ashley was younger, she would automatically put the offending item back on the rack. However, by age sixteen, Ashley had a mind of her own.

"I like it," she asserted, admiring herself in the mirror, bedecked in a bright orange, tightly fitted top with a garish design. Mom, horrified, tried her usual hint, but it didn't work this time. Ashley just laughed, undeterred, and said, "I'm buying it!"

Mom could scarcely conceal her dismay, but she said not another word. She knew that taking away Ashley's right to decide would take away from her daughter's growing sense of herself. Teenagers need the chance to explore and experiment with their appearance as a way of discovering who they are.

What Not to Say

"You look like a prostitute," Mom says to her sixteen-year-old daughter, who is an honor student and a leader in her highly competitive school.

"Boy, you look like a loser," Dad, a high-achieving executive, tells his disheveled fourteen-year-old son.

"I'm ashamed to be seen with you." "That looks awful." "I'll disown you if you get a tattoo," or "Anybody who wants to have her nose pierced must be sick." Believe it or not, these are actual quotes from real people. We even know of one parent who tore the metal ring out of his seventeen-year-old daughter's eyebrow.

Until our teens grow up and are safely through adolescence, when they can begin to develop more confidence in their inner sense of self, they will rely on using their appearance to broadcast to the world and to themselves who they are or who they hope to be. When we reject their fashion statements, we are rejecting them. When we do that, where will they turn?

There is no fashion ugly enough to be the cause of a rupture in our relationship with our teens. While we can ask our teens to dress appropriately for the situation, and hope that they will do so at least some of the time, we should also keep in mind that we are not alone. All of the other parents are having the same struggles with their teenagers—and the ones who choose to focus on what's *most* important are the ones who will be more likely to maintain a close relationship with their children into their adulthood.

My Body, My Self

Teenagers are even more self-conscious about their bodies than they are about their clothes. For both males and females, body image is an important part of their developing sense of self. It's how they see themselves, and this image influences how they feel about themselves. Though we may all be concerned with our body image, the matter is far more intense for teenagers.

Our media-rich culture has emphasized an extreme standard of beauty, something only a tiny percentage of people can achieve. This makes real life more difficult for everyone, especially teens. The cultural pressure only adds to the amount of self-criticism and self-rejection teenagers regularly heap on themselves: "My thighs are too big." "I'm puny." "My stomach should be flatter." "My breasts are too small [or too big]." "Why am I so short?" The list is endless, but the theme is consistent. No matter what, we're not good enough.

With all this self-rejection going on, we, as parents, have to be especially careful what we say around our kids. For instance, if we have our own concerns and struggles with our body image, we want to be careful not to make our weight issues a frequent topic of conversation. Dwelling on our own personal list of shortcomings does not give our teens a good model of how to relate in a healthy way to their bodies. Whether or not we're happy with our body image, we can at least keep our negative comments to ourselves. Our children need the most positive model we can give them to counteract the negative messages they are bombarded with by the culture that surrounds us.

Teenagers have enough anxiety about their bodies as it is. Their bodies are changing drastically, and they're experiencing more intense sexual feelings and awareness. This can lead to a significant amount of confusion and anxiety. They don't need the extra burden of Mom or Dad worrying, "Will she grow up to be fat like me?"

Drawing attention to a teen's body is fraught with risk. We need to be careful not to say anything that might be construed negatively, even jokingly. Even one comment, especially from a father to an adolescent daughter, can be the trigger for a serious eating disorder. After all, Daddy will always be the first man in his daughter's life and his opinion has special meaning.

Eighteen-year-old Amber is on her way out with friends when her father asks if he can speak with her privately for a minute.

"Sure, Dad, what's up?" she asks.

In a misguided attempt to be helpful, Dad says, "I'm concerned about your weight. It looks to me like you've put on a few pounds at college." Dad has a tendency to be overweight, and he is especially anxious that his daughter not gain weight.

Amber is furious. Weight is an issue for her, as it is for most freshman girls, and she is already well aware of the extra pounds she's put on. She doesn't need her dad's comment, especially right before going out with her friends.

Fortunately, Amber is smart enough to know that this is her father's problem, not hers. She knows he is very unhappy with his weight, and she also knows that that has nothing to do with her need to lose a few pounds. If Amber were not so clear about the dynamic here, she might find herself repeating her father's words to herself in a personally destructive way.

It's much more constructive for fathers to praise their daughters about their looks. This gives daughters a positive model to use as a standard for choosing a boyfriend and, eventually, a mate.

The Friends They Choose

Just as our teens will adorn their bodies in ways that run counter to our taste, they will also hang out with friends we don't like. The conventional wisdom is correct in this situation—the more we reject their friends, the more attached our teens will be to them. After all, teens have to separate from their parents as part of the important process of establishing their own identity. What better way to do so than to choose friends who represent the opposite of what their parents stand for?

When Rita was thirteen she finally gained admittance to what she thought was the most exciting group in her middle school. Unfortunately this group of kids also happened to include some of the lowest achievers, the ones who were always getting in trouble, the ones most likely to get pregnant and drop out of school. Rita's whole social life began to consist of going to the movies and hanging out on the street. Sometimes the group would get together at the Dairy Queen. Rita was thrilled that she was a part of this exciting life. Her parents were not.

Rita wanted to invite her friends over for a sleepover, but she wasn't sure her parents would let her. Surprisingly, they were very gracious, buying special food for the kids, renting a stack of videos, and doing more than their share of driving the kids home afterward. Rita's mom was happy to chat with any of the other parents about logistics, even though only one parent called. All the kids had such a good time they wanted to come back to Rita's house more often, and her parents welcomed them back.

Rita's parents were still not happy about her friends, but through their hospitality they got to know all of the kids by name and even met a few of their parents. They'd also established their house as a fun, welcoming place to hang out. Moreover, they could now talk to Rita about her friends as individuals, rather than just rejecting the group en masse. By acknowledging the things Rita liked about her new friends, her parents could now also express their concerns in a way that their daughter could hear. For example, Mom said, "I really like Mary but I'm worried that she's not doing too well in school." Feeling secure that her mom truly accepted her friends, Rita could be open to her concerns.

After a while, the members of the group begin to go their separate ways; some of them remain friends with Rita, and some of them do not. The main point is that Rita is able to allow these friendships to run their natural course, all under the concerned and watchful eye of her parents. She was not forced to choose her friends over her parents, and she was not pushed into spending more and more time away from home in order to be with them.

Respecting Romance

For our teens, the only thing worse than rejecting their friends is rejecting their boyfriends or girlfriends. Teens can form unusually tight bonds in their romantic relationships and tend to overidentify with each other, so they take comments about their "significant other" very personally. Any criticism of their love interest will be seen as a rejection of them, too, and is likely to push them in exactly the opposite direction of what we want.

Our teens may be more intimately involved in their relationships than we realize or can bear to admit. We may see their current relationship as just a passing fancy, or a mild flirtation, but the truth is, we have no way of knowing for sure. Almost three-quarters of American teenagers are sexually active by the time they graduate from high school. These teen years are an incredible soup of hormones, romance, budding independence, music, passion, curiosity, loneliness, and late-night talks.

As parents, we are often the last to know what our teenagers are up to. So we need to be thoughtful about the way we react to the kids they've chosen to become close to. It's very easy to criticize our teens' romantic relationships without realizing the full impact and meaning our words may have.

"He couldn't even carry on a decent conversation. He just mumbled and wouldn't make eye contact," Dad complains about Cody, the boyfriend his beautiful, brilliant, sixteen-year-old daughter has introduced him to at the high school during parents' night.

"He's just shy, Dad," Laura explains, "Lay off, will ya?"

"Lay off? Are you kidding? Who is this kid? And what kind of a name is Cody anyhow?" Dad immediately escalates the criticism, in reaction to his daughter's challenge.

Dad has no idea how important Cody is to his daughter. He thinks Cody is just one of the many kids she hangs out with at the mall. In fact, they've been seeing each other exclusively for a few months and are very infatuated with each other. Dad is shocked at how intensely Laura defends Cody, who he now surmises is a boyfriend.

Laura is annoyed by her dad's remarks and hurt by his cluelessness about her life and how important Cody is to her. When our teens feel we don't understand them, they can begin to lose an important point of connection to family and home. We don't want them to separate from us out of frustration and alienation.

Dad could have kept his negative first impressions to himself and simply told his daughter, "I was glad to meet the guy you've been hanging out with. How's that going?"

Laura may or may not have opened up at that point, but at least she would have recognized the fact that her dad is interested in her friends. We want to know what's going on with our teens in a very practical way—whom they hang out with, what their romantic relationships are, how they're feeling about themselves. If we can stay connected to our kids in this way through adolescence, we can give our teens the protection and guidance they need to mature.

Broken Hearts

One of the possible precipitating factors for teenage suicide is the breakup of a romance. Although not every broken heart leads to such a crisis, we should always take our teenagers' threats or expressions of emotional suffering seriously. If we don't, they may feel lost and abandoned. This is a time when they desperately need us to be there for them with support and understanding.

No matter how we feel about this particular breakup, we must respect and acknowledge the intensity of what our teen is experiencing, and be supportive and understanding as he works his way through the grief. After all, your child's first broken heart may be the most traumatic experience he has gone through in his whole life. If we downplay the suffering he is feeling, we are adding parental rejection to romantic rejection.

Fifteen-year-old Anthony is truly heartbroken. Though he and Victoria barely kissed and were together for only four months, she was the love of his life. "We were soul mates," he says mournfully. He is inconsolable.

Consumed with sorrow, self-pity, and longing, Anthony's grades begin to plummet. That's when his parents realize they have a child who is on the verge of clinical depression. Before this they thought his problem was just "puppy love" and actually thought that it was all kind of cute—something he'd get over quickly. When they realize the depth of his feelings, neither Mom nor Dad knows what to say to Anthony to make things better. However, Dad is elected to go up to Anthony's bedroom and talk to him.

He begins as honestly as he can: "Son, I don't know what I can say that will help, but Mom and I want you to know we are worried about you."

"I know, Dad. I'm okay," Anthony responds glumly.

"We didn't realize how very important Victoria was to you," Dad continues. "Can't you just be friends now?"

Anthony looks up at his father to see whether he could possibly be serious. "Just friends? Oh wow, thanks a lot for your help," Anthony spits out in total disgust.

Realizing his mistake, Dad tries again. "I'm sorry, Anthony," he says. He sits there for a couple of moments, trying to think what to say next. Finally, he offers, "I remember my first break-up. I was a little older than you, but it was awful. I felt like my whole world caved in on me."

"It's pretty bad," Anthony admits.

This is a decision point for Dad in the conversation. He can continue talking about memories of his own first love while his son drifts away, or he can keep the focus on Anthony.

"What can we do to help?" Dad asks, resisting the urge to reminisce, and concentrating on his son.

"I don't know," Anthony says honestly. Then he adds, "Just don't yell at me about this report card. I know it's going to be lousy."

Dad thinks for a minute about that. Grades are important to him, but Anthony is even more important. "Okay," Dad agrees. "As long as we can help you find a way to get back on track."

After this conversation Anthony no longer feels quite so alone. Maybe his dad does understand some of what he's going through after all, and at least his parents aren't harassing him about his grades. Anthony feels as though he couldn't take much more at the moment.

Matters of the heart need to be treated delicately at all ages. Parents need to tread lightly and slowly, accepting both the depth and the seriousness of their teens' feelings. We don't want our teens to feel all alone with their suffering, whatever the cause of their pain. Since emotions are experienced more intensely during adolescence, our teens can become overwhelmed and imagine that they're going to feel this way forever. We need to keep close tabs on their day-to-day life so we know what's going on with them. Even if we can't make it all better, as we often could when they were young, we can at least let them know they're not alone.

Notice that Dad didn't let Anthony off the hook indefinitely when it came to his grades. He set the standard by letting Anthony know that although he understands the special circumstance and will help him through it, he wants him "back on track" academically. Being sensitive to our teens' feelings of rejection does not mean we accept all their behavior, no matter what. We always accept who our teenagers are and what they're feeling, but we have the right to reject unacceptable behavior.

The standards we set have to be realistic. Parental expectations that are too high result in the teenagers never feeling good enough and eventually not caring. That's when we lose them.

Ignoring Is Rejecting

Just as a pattern of criticism, put-downs, and insults can make our teens feel rejected, so can a pattern of being ignored. Perhaps a general lack of acknowledgment is the greatest rejection of all. Teenagers can easily feel as if they don't matter or don't even exist when they receive hardly any attention from their parents. In this situation, some teens may even look for negative ways to draw attention to themselves.

"My old man doesn't even know I'm alive unless he has to pick me up at the police station," Tom says, half-bragging and half-complaining. "And even then, all he ever says is, 'Next time I'm leaving you there.'"

Tom would never admit to feelings of being rejected by his dad or to feeling that nobody cares. At fifteen, he's already too "tough" for that. But ask him how he would want to raise his own son someday, and he has a lot of ideas.

"I'd want to do things with him," Tom says, not realizing how transparent his own unfulfilled wishes are. "I'd take him to baseball games. And maybe on a camping trip or something."

No matter how tough some teenagers may seem, it's helpful to remember that in many ways, underneath all their bravado, they are still emotionally vulnerable children. Every teenager, no matter how outrageous his or her appearance or behavior has become, needs as much warm acceptance and loving attention as we can give.

We also have to remember to be concerned about the teens who appear to be "too good." They may be polite, well-groomed, and high-achieving, but unless we spend regular time with them we have no idea what's going on beneath the surface. We can't assume everything's fine just because they appear to be doing okay and don't seem to need any "special attention." These teens may live with internal pressures that they need to be able to discuss with someone once in a while, in order to relieve the tension. We need to ask our children how they're doing, and be prepared to listen when they answer.

Sometimes this is not easy to do—we may be working long hours to earn extra money for their college tuition, or we may be stressed at work. But important as this is, we have to carve out time to be with our teens. Scholarships and loans can make up for a shortfall in cash, but nothing can take the place of precious time spent with our kids during these years.

The adolescent years mark the end of our living together as a family and give us one of our last chances to make a significant impact on our teenagers' lives. As parents we need to be willing to invest time and energy into our relationships with our teens—as much as they're willing to tolerate. It's our job to remain available to them, and their job to grow in independence. Without our help and concern, our teenagers can lose their way.

Stay Connected

We want our teenagers to be able to achieve their independence while maintaining a real connection to the family. That connection will, at times, need to be extremely elastic in order to accommodate all the tensions and tugging that are a normal part of adolescence. This is not easy to do, especially when we're upset.

Many parents vacillate between being worried about their teenagers to being extremely irritated with them.

When we get caught in a pattern of emotional reactivity, we can lose the very flexibility that is needed to respond appropriately to our teenagers through these changing years of adolescence. If teens do not feel connected to us, they can feel lost and alone. This can add inordinately to the normal amount of teenage suffering.

As parents, we need to remember at all times that the whole purpose of adolescence is for teenagers to find themselves—to discover who they are inside, to develop a strong sense of self so they can enter the world and all their future relationships on their own terms.

It's not easy to be either an adolescent or the parent of one. This can be a very challenging decade for everyone, and emotions can get out of hand. The most important thing to remember is that it is absolutely essential to stay connected as a family.

Emma and her mom have a private joke that they both use when things get rough between them and emotions are running high. To break the tension, one of them will ask the other, "Do you hate me?" For both mother and daughter, this question represents their worst nightmare, and quickly reminds them that however angry they are at the moment, they still love each other. They know that as long as they can reassure each other of their love, they will remain connected and things will be okay.

If we can maintain the relationship with our teens through these turbulent years, we are less likely to lose them. And if they are able to stay connected to us, they are less likely to lose themselves.

If teenagers live with too many rules, they learn to get around them

We may think we can control our teenagers for "their own good" with a long list of rules, but it just doesn't work. With each passing year, they become more sophisticated and more adept at getting around our rules without our even realizing it. This is part of their growing up. We have to accept our waning power as our children move toward greater autonomy and independence. If we resist this process by trying to maintain control, we only doom ourselves and them to endless battles and invite deception.

We can, however, continue to be the strongest influence on our teens all the way through adolescence and into young adulthood. Our influence stems from our relationship with them, including our ability to understand and discuss things openly. It's a two-way street: the more we listen respectfully to our teenagers, the more likely they'll listen respectfully to us.

Our relationship has to evolve gradually through these years, responding to our teenagers' developing sense of independence. It may be difficult for us as parents to let go graciously, but this is what is required of us during the adolescent years. Naturally, we don't like to give up control, especially when we think we're protecting our teens. Sometimes it's hard for us to believe that our children, who only "yesterday" learned how to ride a bike, can now take care of themselves out in the real world.

The passage of time between their childhood and adolescence is life-changing for them, but not for us. If anything, we may be in denial that our "babies" are growing up, for that means admitting that we're getting older, too. But whether or not we're aware of it, or accepting of it, our teens are rushing ahead into their lives as young adults—learning how to drive, earning their own money, and gaining their freedom. Their future is calling them, while we may be stuck in the past, still trying to catch up with putting their baby pictures into photo albums.

The art of parenting a teenager is a subtle dance between our need to hold on and control and their need to be free and independent. If we resort to constricting them with too many rules, we only create a battleground for rebellion. The challenge is to gracefully balance their increasing freedom with greater responsibility and to move forward together gradually, step by step, with their increasing maturity.

Fifteen-year-old Anton wanted to go to a rock concert with his friends, one of whom was old enough to drive. His parents knew there would be drugs and alcohol at the concert and categorically refused to let him go. Anton begged and pleaded, but his parents were steadfast in their decision and deaf to his pleas.

A few months later Anton made arrangements to sleep over at

a friend's house. His parents didn't think twice about it—it was a weekend and the boy was a friend they knew and liked. That night, the kids went to a rock concert. They had a great time, and Anton's parents never found out.

Teenagers are exceptionally resourceful when it comes to getting around parental rules. We cannot possibly know where they are at all times, who they're with, and what they're doing. If we try to control them with inflexible rules and leave no room for discussion, we lose the opportunity to communicate with them about really important issues.

In this instance, both Anton and his parents lost out. It would have been far better for them to find a compromise that they could all live with than to tempt Anton to engage in deception by their inflexibility. We may have to remind ourselves from time to time that maintaining open communication with our teenagers is more important than asserting control over them.

Perhaps Anton's parents could have offered to drive the kids to and from the concert, or Anton could have promised to keep in close contact with his parents by cell phone. This would at least have kept the possibility open for Anton to share with his parents his experience of the concert, including his own observations and decisions about drug and alcohol use. But because he ended up deceiving them, he is left to struggle with whatever difficult issues may arise on his own, without their help and guidance.

The Purpose of Rules

Some of us may have difficulty accepting how little control we have over our teenage children. If we react to this by making the rules stricter, becoming detectives and snooping through their rooms, and punishing them when we "catch" them in wrongdoing, what does this do to our relationship with our teens? And does it really protect them?

Rules should be designed to guide our teenagers toward making good decisions, especially in situations that are potentially dangerous. And since we are not usually present to protect our teenagers at the critical moments, their fate depends on their ability to make good decisions on their own. We hope they will be strong and independent enough to evaluate the pros and cons of a situation; weigh the risks and benefits, the immediate result versus the long-term consequences; and make good choices. Imposing an autocratic set of rules will not help them develop this level of maturity. We can only influence our teenagers if we maintain open communication with them. It is through their relationship with us—through our careful listening and gentle guidance—that teens gradually learn how to make good decisions for themselves.

Sixteen-year-old Karen finally passed her behind-the-wheel test, after failing at parallel parking in her first two attempts. All her friends wanted to celebrate by going out for a ride, but her parents' rule was that she couldn't drive with other kids in the car for at least three months.

Karen and her parents had talked about the reason for this rule—that having friends in the car can be extremely distracting, a dangerous situation for an inexperienced driver. She understood her parents' point of view, but she didn't want to disappoint her friends and thought she could handle the situation. Her parents suggested that they go out for a test-drive together first, to see how well she could handle distractions. As they drove to the mall, her dad turned up the radio and made wisecracks and remarks about people in other cars. Her mom asked her questions about what she was going to wear to an upcoming school dance and her parents whispered and laughed together. After almost going through a stop sign, Karen pulled over to the side of the road, shaken. "Okay," she said turning to her parents, not knowing whether to be upset with them or with herself. "You win."

"It's not about winning, but about being safe," Mom said. "No new driver can handle this much distraction, and we know your friends will be even more distracting than we were."

"And there isn't much traffic now," Dad added nervously. "Can you imagine what it would be like in rush hour with a car full of kids?"

The next time her friends told her they wanted to go for a ride, Karen said, "No," and this time she felt as though it was her decision, not her parents'. However, they provided her with an easy out. She felt more comfortable telling her friends, "My parents won't let me," than admitting, "I'm just not ready to drive with other kids in the car yet." In this case, her parents' rule gave Karen the extra protection she needed to be safe and the time she needed to become a more experienced driver.

Leaving Room for Negotiation

The more our teens are able to participate in the process of making the rules, the more likely they are to follow them even when we're not there to enforce them. The best rules emerge out of open communication between parent and teen, and are agreements that everyone can live with. Understanding each other's point of view and making deeply held values explicit will lead both parent and teen to having clear expectations of each other.

This process of communication includes an element of negotiation between parent and teen—a genuine sharing of power that acknowledges the teenager's perspective while maintaining a strong parental role. Parent and teen must both know that the rules are flexible and open for revision, depending on the situation and evolving over time, and that they will reflect and respect the teen's growing independence and maturity. When the rules are agreed upon by both parties, they really can work as a safety net, protecting the teen from unnecessary danger and the parent from needless worry.

Fourteen-year-old Michael wants to stay out until midnight, but his curfew is 11:00 P.M. Thinking his chances for leniency are better with his dad, Michael presents his case to him on the way home from a basketball practice one night. "Sometimes the movie is extra long and doesn't let out till 10:30, and everybody goes to get something to eat, but I can't because I have to go right home," he objects.

Dad listens attentively, receptive to the point Michael is making. "I know you don't want to miss going out to eat with the kids and it's a drag to leave in the middle of an evening. Tell me, how often does the movie run that late?" he asks, knowing full well that it's usually over by 9:30.

"Well, only every once in a while," Michael acknowledges.

"How about if you check the time of the movie before going out, and when it's going to run late, we can extend your curfew to midnight?" Dad suggests. He is giving Michael increased responsibility—assigning *him* the duty of keeping track of the movie schedule—and at the same time offering him extended freedom.

"Well, I guess I could do that. But you know, all the other kids stay out later than me," Michael says, pushing for more.

"I know they do," Dad replies. "I see them hanging out on the street outside the restaurant. I don't want you hanging around late at night in a group of kids with nothing to do. That's how kids get in trouble."

Michael knows he's gotten all he's going to get from his dad on this round, but he also knows he can reopen this discussion at a later time. He knows his dad is firm about certain things, like hanging out late at night; he also knows that his dad is the one who is always willing to come pick him up, and drive his friends home, too. He decides to let the matter go for now, figuring maybe he'll be able to stay out later when he's a little older.

In this conversation, Dad has acknowledged what is important to Michael, has respected his son's growing ability to plan responsibly, and has revised a rule, giving it some flexibility, while maintaining clear and sensible limits. As long as Michael feels he can influence his father, he'll keep coming back for these discussions. It's when teens feel they are totally powerless regarding the decision-making process that they begin to search for ways to get around the rules.

Picking Battles

Thirteen-year-old Diana was supposed to pick up her room before she went out on weekends. Mom had explained this rule to her daughter more than once. "I don't bug you about your room on school days, when you're too busy to clean it up. But by the time the weekend comes, I can't stand it any longer. I think it's a fair compromise that you clean up your room on Friday afternoon."

Unfortunately, this was a unilateral rule—Mom's. Diana had never agreed to it. So inevitably, every Friday after school, Diana found something better to do. She went to a girlfriend's house, stayed at school for a football game, or went to the mall. The rule wasn't working, and Mom was getting more frustrated with every passing week.

Diana understood that cleaning up her room was important to her mother, but it wasn't important to her, and she thought she should be able to have her room the way she wanted it—messy.

"This is my house," her mother said for the umpteenth time when Diana expressed her opinion. "And as long as you live under my roof, you'll abide by my standards."

So every Thursday evening, Diana would shove whatever mess was spread around her floor under her bed and into her closet. Mom would peek in and compliment her on the condition of her room. Eventually, of course, as it became harder and harder for Diana to find clean clothes and other things she needed, it also became clear that this rule was not working for either of them.

In order for rules to be effective, they need to be based on a shared understanding, mutual agreement, and a real willingness to abide by them. Without these elements, all the punishments in the world won't get your teenager to cooperate. Our teens will not consistently follow a rule just because "we say so." They will procrastinate, make lame excuses, "forget," find a way to do things behind our back, or just plain defy us.

When a rule isn't working, we may need to examine it, and possibly replace it with a new one. In discussing the situation with our teenager, it may help to ask the following questions: What needs to happen? How would we like this to turn out? How can we make it work?

Things will go a lot better if, during most of this conversation, the parents are listening rather than talking. There's no point pretending to be communicating when we are, in fact, reprimanding, lecturing, or otherwise trying to control our teens' behavior. We all know our kids are supersensitive to these attempts to control them and will only respond with greater defensiveness and rebellion.

One day Mom decided to take a slightly different approach. She asked Diana, "So, when do *you* want to clean up your room?"

"What would really work for me is about once a month," Diana answered. "And I would rather do it when I want to, like on a rainy Sunday afternoon."

"Uh-huh," Mom responded. She suddenly realized that she would be wise to let Diana set her own standards for her room, and took a deep breath.

"You have the rest of the house your way. I want *my* little corner of the house *my* way," Diana continued.

Mom nodded. "You've got a point," she acknowledged. "Okay. I'll respect your right to keep your room the way you want if you'll respect my right to have the rest of the house look nice, by keeping it free of your junk."

"You mean my precious belongings?" Diana teased.

"Yes, your precious belongings," Mom laughed.

"Agreed," Diana said with a smile.

Over the next few months, the rest of the house became neater, and Diana's room became messier and messier. With great effort, Mom managed to ignore the situation in her daughter's room, often biting her tongue when the temptation to make a critical remark was nearly irresistible. Finally Diana decided on her own that she didn't like living in such a mess, and she decided to redecorate. She threw out a lot of her old stuff and reorganized her closet. Then she put up new posters and hung strands of small Christmas lights, intertwined with silk flowers, all around the windows and door. The room was clearly her masterpiece. Mom was not thrilled about the thumb-tacks in the walls, but she knew that was a small price to pay. She was proud of Diana's efforts to design her own personal space, even though she still tended to let it get too messy at times by her own standards.

The condition of a teenager's room is a great place for parents to demonstrate their flexibility and respect for their kid's right to be self-determining. After all, the state of a room is insignificant when compared to the major issues of adolescence—drugs, alcohol, driving, and sex. We would be wise to let go of our urge to control our teens over these smaller issues and keep our focus on the larger ones.

In general, we need to control any urge we may have to micro-manage our teens. When we're too involved in the details of our teens' lives, and don't trust them to handle things on their own, we are micromanaging. We cross the line when we're too controlling about what they say, how they look, or what they wear. Sometimes our expectations of our teens function like unspoken rules, and that places our kids in a bind, because it's hard to engage in open communication over unspoken rules. It's like fighting an invisible enemy.

Our kids have their way of letting us know when we're getting too controlling. "Get a life," "Back off," or "Give me a break" are some of the phrases that can tip us off that we're coming down too hard on them. When we hear these words, unless we're dealing with a life-threatening issue, we might be wise to step back and reconsider whether this matter is really worth fighting over.

No Nagging!

Nagging is one of the most frequent symptoms of micromanagement and a common parental habit, even though we all know it doesn't work. There are times we need to find subtle ways to remind our teens of important responsibilities, but nagging isn't the way.

Sixteen-year-old Bill was applying to a special summer program in computer science. Aware that the deadline was fast approaching, Mom casually asked him if he needed a parental signature on his application. Bill grunted something unintelligible and Mom let it go at that, despite the temptation to persist in a line of questioning. "Have you . . . ? Did you . . . ? So when will you . . . ?" However, mom doesn't want her son to make a mistake he'll regret, so she tries another approach a couple of days later. "You know, I'd really hate to see you miss out on the opportunity to take part in that course this summer," she said. "I know you're looking forward to learning more about programming." This gives Bill the chance to act responsibly before it's too late—or to let his Mom know that he's actually not all that interested in taking the course.

With matters of less importance, it may be better just to laugh it off. When fifteen-year-old Greg came home from a sleepover with newly dyed, flame-red hair, at first Mom was horrified and could not think of anything decent to say. When she finally opened her mouth, she managed to say, calmly, "Well, I guess I can get used to this, though I have to say I like your natural color the best."

She got no response from Greg, but Mom was too wise to push a confrontation. She reminded herself that hair color is not really all that big a deal and that in a few short years, Greg will figure out what suits him best. She knows that respecting Greg's right to choose his own style may make him more likely to respect her decision when she weighs in on the truly important issues. By letting go of the "small stuff," we recognize our teens' right to experiment and discover their own choices. This is part of the process of growing up, and a major task of adolescence.

Helping Our Teens Make Good Decisions

Ultimately, the purpose of making external rules should be to help our teenagers develop their own internal rules, so that the decisions they make come from within them, not from outside pressure. The process of learning to be inner-directed, capable of making good decisions, independent of parental rules, and, even more important, independent of peer pressure, is a gradual one. Our kids need us to be there, present but in the background as much as possible, while they learn to make good decisions for themselves.

Roger's parents didn't smoke and they were very clear that they didn't want Roger to start such an unhealthy habit. Their influence over their son was powerful enough for Roger to resist all the peer pressure and availability of cigarettes until about age fifteen. Then, as the peer pressure grew stronger, Roger began to want to try a cigarette just once, since so many of his friends were already smoking regularly.

Roger's parents didn't know he had begun to experiment with cigarettes, but they had noticed that other kids from his grade were smoking. So they talked about it with Roger.

"I saw Ned and Curt in town the other day," Dad stated matter-of-factly. "They were both smoking."

"I know," Roger said. "What did they do when you caught them?"

"Well, it's not my job to 'catch them,'" Dad said. "But they sort of hid their cigarettes behind them as they waved to me."

"I'm sorry to hear they've started smoking," Mom chimed in. "It's so hard to quit once you've started."

Roger was silent, no doubt hoping for a change in conversation.

Then Dad took a calculated risk. "Did you know I used to smoke?" he asked Roger.

"No!" Roger exclaimed, surprised and relieved to have the spotlight shift.

"Yeah, one summer I started smoking, and by the time basketball season came around, I knew I was in trouble. I couldn't get into shape. So I quit, cold turkey. That was no fun."

After this conversation, Roger began to pay attention to who smoked and who didn't. He noticed that most of the athletes didn't smoke, and that none of the best athletes did. Roger decided he didn't want to start smoking, either.

The really important decisions, the ones that will alter the course of our teenagers' lives, will come from within them. We can provide the groundwork—giving them our support, sharing our values, making rules to help guide them, and communicating with them about what's important—but ultimately they will make up their own minds about what they're going to do. They will make many of these decisions when they're out with friends, beyond our control. We want them to be confident enough to be able to resist peer pressure and assert their right to decide for themselves. Our teens' ability to be inner-directed, to think things through and come to their own conclusions, independent of what their friends are doing, is what will make the difference in their lives.

Rules that Grow with the Teen

As our teenagers grow in maturity and responsibility, our rules need to loosen up to reflect their developing independence. We need to remind ourselves to be flexible, though, because often we are the last ones to realize that our teens are well on their way to growing up. This is partly because our image of our own kids tends to get stuck in certain ways, and partly because our kids tend to save their worst behaviors for their parents.

When Sally was fifteen she lost her parents' credit card and was too afraid to tell them. Of course, her parents found out when the bill arrived with a list of mysterious charges and they had to deal with the police and the bank. Since then, her parents have insisted that Sally pay for things only by check or cash. Now seventeen, Sally is beginning to travel on her own to visit college campuses and is far more responsible.

"You know," she begins casually over the dinner table one night, "I think I need my own credit card."

Her parents look at each other, remembering the lost card disaster.

Unfazed, Sally continues, "I know what you're thinking, but I've learned to be more responsible in the past two years. I'll be leaving for college soon, and I'll need my own card then anyway."

"It's still ten months, away, Sally, it's not that soon," Mom answers quickly.

"That's not the point," Sally says. "I'm a different person now than when I lost your card. I understand that I have to report that kind of thing right away. And you can put a limit on the card."

Mom and Dad don't know what to say. Sally is a different person now, but they are not. Two years ago seems like an eternity to Sally, but to Mom and Dad it's just yesterday. They have to catch up with their daughter, and learn to see her differently.

Finally Dad breaks the silence. "Give us an evening to get used to the idea, and we'll discuss it further tomorrow," he says.

Sally smiles. She knows she's ready for more independence, and she trusts that her parents will see it, too.

Our teens tend to grow in developmental leaps, not unlike when they were toddlers and went, seemingly overnight, from babbling to talking in complete sentences. One month our teenagers are upset, moaning, "I'll never be able to pass this test," and the next month they're training to be volunteer emergency medics, learning how to deliver babies or treat heart attack victims. We are not changing at the same dramatic rate, and can often miss their developmental breakthroughs. We need to be aware of and sensitive to our teens' spurts of growth toward maturity in order to remain current with their increasing ability to handle greater responsibility. And our rules need to be flexible enough that we can adjust them to these new circumstances. Often our teenagers are the ones to remind us that they are ready to take on greater responsibility. We need to listen to them respectfully when they do and consider the possibility that we may not be keeping up with their rapid pace of growth.

Helping Our Teens Learn How to Handle Freedom

Teenagers are naturally rebellious. They are always testing the limits, finding ways to get around the rules. It's part of the challenge of adolescence. And if we're honest with ourselves, aren't some of our own fondest teenage memories about how *we* got away with things? Rolling up our skirts before we went into the school? Slipping off oversized shirts to reveal something skimpy underneath? Sneaking in and out of our homes without waking up our parents? Or just doing something wild and crazy for its own sake?

But there are some situations, usually having to do with health and safety, that are more serious. When a teen consistently breaks these kinds of rules, often it's a cry for help. These are the kids who skip school repeatedly, get in trouble with the police, and put themselves or others in danger. In these situations, parents need professional help to understand what's going on and to find ways to help their teens.

Unfortunately, it's not always clear what will help a teen in trouble. Professionals don't necessarily have the right answer for every situation, and this can be very confusing and frustrating to parents. Sometimes there are no guidelines for families, and parents don't know whether to keep trying with a teen, or turn to "tough love" and cut off support. Even professionals may give conflicting advice. The frightening reality is that sometimes nothing works and tragedy results. In more fortunate cases, the teen finally grows up a little and begins to come around before the consequences are too grave. We don't always know what makes the difference. Still, the percentage of teens who get into really deep trouble is quite small compared to the majority who grow through adolescence into productive adulthood.

At the other extreme are the teens who seem to be "too good." Always compliant and cooperative, they spend most of their time alone or with the family. This type of teen may be missing out on a lot of the social learning that goes on during adolescence. They might have trouble later, when they leave home, becoming either too isolated or too wild.

Mary was a shy, studious teen all through high school. Her family was very close and her parents were very strict. When Mary got to college, where suddenly there were no rules or adult supervision, she changed completely. She began going to parties for the first time in her life, but she had no experience in handling peer pressure or alcohol. She was out of control by Thanksgiving, and by winter break she was on academic probation.

Fortunately for Mary, her parents were more concerned than angry. They listened to her as she spilled out the whole story of those first few months at college, on her own for the first time. Together they came up with a plan to have her live at home the next semester and attend a nearby college. They agreed that she could continue to have the same freedom she'd had in the dorm, but helped her devise some limits of her own so that she could keep up with her academic work. Spending that semester in her parents' home gave Mary the chance to learn how to balance her life. Her parents didn't restrict her in any major way, but their presence and daily communication helped her stay focused and learn how to manage her new independence.

Sharing Our Values

Teenagers do not learn values from rules. They learn values because we talk to them about our deeply held beliefs, and they see us living our lives according to these beliefs. Having a "No Drinking" rule is not enough by itself: our teens are watching us to see how *we* handle alcohol and drugs.

We need to have many talks about alcohol over the years, gradually moving the conversation into more serious territory as our child matures. We want to begin talking about drinking and driving years before our teens begin to drive. We want to begin talking about binge drinking and sex long before our kids even consider going to teenage parties. We want our teens to know clearly how we feel about drinking in general, and about their drinking specifically. We want them to be able to talk to us about how they see other kids and adults handling alcohol. Most of all, we want them to come to us with their questions as they think through their own decisions about handling alcohol, drugs, and driving. Saying "No" to alcohol or drugs is just one step at one point in time over a whole process, which extends over many years and depends on our ability to listen to them. We influence our teenagers through our relationship and through open communication.

Seventeen-year-old Sarah is rushing to get ready for a party. Dad gives her a quick hug as she heads for the door, "You know, I'll always be happy to come and pick you up," he reminds her as she's going out. "Don't get into a car if the driver's been drinking."

"I know, Daddy," Sarah says, hugging him back, taking care not to smudge her makeup.

"And I'll drive all your friends home, too," he adds. "Don't worry about the cars. They can be dealt with later."

She pauses and smiles at him, "Remember that time you came out late at night to pick me and Annie up at Roger's house?"

"I sure do," Dad replies, "and it was a good thing I did, too."

"Thanks, Dad," Sarah says. "I'll call if I need you."

It's not enough to tell our teens not to drink and drive. We have to provide them with an easy and clear alternative for risky situations. Often this means being willing to go out of our way for them. Our teens learn from our behavior, not from our lectures. It's our ability and willingness to support them, especially when it involves being inconvenienced late at night, that lets them know we really care. It's consistently giving our interest, energy, and time in support of mutually agreed-upon rules. Our teens learn their values from watching what we do, and from the example we give them.

Romeo and Juliet Forever!

There's a reason this love story has been retold for centuries. It's a classic tale of parents interfering in their teenagers' romantic passions, setting the scene for disaster. We know this, yet we also feel we can't sit idly by and watch our teens run with the wrong crowd or fall in love with someone who is not a good influence.

We all know that insisting on too many rules in these situations only strengthens our teens' resistance, and adds romance and drama to their sense of "It's us against them." We still want to look out for and protect our teenagers, but we can no longer control their lives, and we need to respect their right to make their own choices. This is the standard parental dilemma during adolescence.

What's the solution to this conflict? Unfortunately there is no single, simple answer. Different things work in different families; and sometimes, unfortunately, nothing works. Then all we can do is hope that time and our kids' slowly developing maturity will solve the problem.

Sixteen-year-old Lorrayne was in love. The boy was three years older; he had already flunked out of college and was living at home hopping from one odd job to another. Lorrayne's parents, both physicians, were not pleased. They hoped the infatuation would pass quickly, and that their daughter would not become pregnant or run off with this boy in the meantime. They were worried that if the relationship lasted into the fall, it would interfere with Lorrayne's studying. Already they could see that Lorrayne was spending too much time and energy catering to the boyfriend, trying to shore up his faltering sense of himself. They didn't want Lorrayne to fall into the trap of sacrificing herself and her own ambitions to take care of a lost soul.

Perhaps what was most worrisome to Lorrayne's parents was that their daughter was hanging out at the boyfriend's house with his family most of the summer. The kids instinctively knew which set of parents accepted their relationship, and they felt more welcome there than with Lorrayne's family. Lorrayne started coming home mentioning how "hip" his mom was dressed, or what a brilliant remark his father had made. She even said she was more comfortable with the boyfriend's parents, since they were more casual and relaxed than her parents, who were more formal and "uptight." Lorrayne's parents felt as if they were losing their daughter.

Even Lorrayne's friends were not happy about the boyfriend she had chosen, or with the amount of time she was spending with him. They too were reluctant to say anything, because they didn't want her to get angry with them. However, in a moment of desperation or a fit of honesty, one of her friends finally said to Lorrayne what her parents could not have said in a million years: "Why are you hanging around with him so much? He's such a loser!"

Lorrayne told her parents what her friend said only because she had already decided to break up with the boy, and because they had kept their mouths shut. Lorrayne had certainly known that they didn't like him very much, but they hadn't made an issue of it, forcing her to defend him. They wisely underplayed their relief at this news, but did congratulate their daughter on exercising good judgment.

This is one of the most classic and most difficult situations for parents of adolescents. It's when we truly realize how little control we have over our teens, and how we could actually lose them. And what's so difficult about this is that sometimes our best strategy is to do nothing—especially when what we want most is to do something, anything, to bring our child back into the family fold. The truth is, rules have no meaning at this point. We are relatively powerless to compete against the power and passion of adolescent romance. We don't even want to think about the sexual aspect, even though we may have already had all the conversations about being sexually responsible and safe. When a star-crossed love relationship gets started, the only thing we have going for us is time. We can hope that Romeo and Juliet will get on each other's nerves within a few months and decide to return to their respective homes. Then we can be there to welcome them back with open arms, knowing that they're now older and wiser.

Admitting When We're Wrong

If we're really honest with ourselves, we know that we break rules all the time. We exceed the speed limit, make personal phone calls at work, don't report tips as income, and return merchandise that has been used, claiming it is new. We also break the more subtle "rules" of considerate treatment in our relationships—we miss anniversaries, forget to phone home when we're late, make hurtful assumptions about the ones we love, and lose our temper.

We are not perfect role models for our teenagers, nor do we need to be. However, we do need to admit our mistakes and apologize when we're wrong. Think about the last time a police officer pulled you over and asked politely, "Do you know why I stopped you?"

When a police officer points out that we're wrong, we graciously admit it. We should do the same when our teens "catch us in the act."

Dad came home late for dinner one night, and as he walked through the garage, he noticed a smashed fender on the family car. His blood pressure and his temper rose with every step as he approached the dining room. Immediately upon entering the room, without asking any questions, he began to blast his sixteen-year-old son, Nick, who was sitting at the dinner table, happily consuming a large mound of mashed potatoes. Nick and his mother looked up in surprise. It was unusual for Dad to lose his temper this way.

"I did it," Mom said simply, interrupting Dad midstream.

Dad looked from one to the other. "Did what?"

"I smashed the fender," Mom repeated. Nick smiled.

Now Dad didn't know what to do. So Mom continued, explaining what had happened, how the accident wasn't her fault, and telling him that the other driver's insurance would cover the repairs. Dad gradually calmed down.

"So, ah, Dad . . . ?" Nick began.

"I'm sorry. I plead temporary insanity and jumping to conclusions," Dad admitted with an embarrassed grin.

Nick was gracious about the incident, and was even a bit pleased knowing he would be able to tease his father about this for a very long time. Dad was able to laugh at himself for "losing it," because he was winning when it came to his relationship with his son.

The example we present to our teenagers is our most powerful teaching tool, and the good news is we don't have to be perfect. We do, however, have to remember our own human frailties, so that we don't expect perfection from our teens. And perhaps the best model we can give them for accepting human imperfection is to take responsibility for our own transgressions and apologize respectfully.

Letting Them Know We Really Care

We cannot control our teenagers by imposing rules. However, we can influence them through our relationship with them. That relationship begins in infancy and is cultivated throughout our child's life. It's based on all those moments when we were truly there for our kids, and they knew it, deep in their bones.

Those moments are often unpredictable—perhaps it was the time when a family crisis, an illness, or an accident caused us to miss work to be by our child's side. Perhaps it was a special celebration, a holiday, or an award ceremony at school that we made sure to attend. But most of all, it is the sum of all those little moments—driving to school, running errands, cleaning up after dinner, watching a favorite TV program together. Or those last few minutes of the day, as our kids prepared for sleep and we stayed there for an extra few minutes, long enough to whisper, "I love you. Sleep tight."

The parents who know this are the ones always willing to pick up the young teenagers at the mall after the late movie and drive everyone home. They're the parents who get up out of bed at 1:00 A.M. to share a cup of tea with their older teen, home from a school dance and open to talking. They know their kids' teachers and their kids' dreams. And they can even, every once in a while, buy a T-shirt or CD that their teenager will actually like.

If teenagers live with too few rules, they learn to ignore the needs of others

Rules help guide the everyday interactions between people within the family, the community, and the world at large. Family rules teach children how to recognize and respect the needs of others, and let them know what is expected of them. They let our teens know that we care about them and also that we depend upon them. If we don't have enough rules, or if our rules are too lax, we are actually teaching them to ignore our needs to protect, support, and guide them, and to rely upon them as contributing members of the family.

If there are too few rules in the family, it's harder for our teenagers to get in the habit of thinking of the needs of others; boundaries are vague and accountability is doubtful. We need rules for living together as a family so our teens can learn how to consider the needs of others in a natural, spontaneous way.

As their world widens, teenagers have to adjust to and make peace with the legal and social guidelines of their community and accept the limits of individual freedom. When teenagers accept and respect family rules, they are also more likely to abide by the rules of the community. They grow up with an inherent understanding of the importance of respecting other people's rights and needs. This is not always easy for any of us to do. Living in a new global community, we are just beginning to learn how to make international agreements in order to protect the most vulnerable among us and even the planet itself. At every level, rules remind all of us to consider the needs of others. We want to give our teens enough rules so that they can mature into concerned citizens of the community and the world.

Living, Working, and Sharing Together

Many family rules are intended to help keep life flowing smoothly around the house. Often the way meal preparation and cleanup is handled provides a benchmark of how well the rules are helping family members to work together. These rules may not even be obvious, because they're often unspoken and taken for granted within the family. They only become obvious when contrasted with the rules of other families that handle the matter differently. Some rules may be traditions or just habits while others rules define roles and responsibilities. Family members know what to expect from one another and that they can count on one another. The rules help everyone work together so that their needs are met and household tasks accomplished.

Thirteen-year-old Tina is responsible for getting herself up in the morning so she can get to school on time. Before she and her mother agreed on this rule, Tina's mom found herself running upstairs several times each morning to wake her up, or repeatedly yelling up the stairs at her to get moving. This wasn't doing anything to help strengthen Tina's developing sense of independence and responsibility, and it was making her mother really irritable. The rule frees both Mom and Tina from a daily power struggle, and gives Tina the opportunity to exercise and demonstrate greater maturity. It also helps her see that Mom has needs of her own, and things *she* needs to do in the early morning.

Without rules, our teens wouldn't have the benefit of learning how to live and work together with others. Learning to cooperate with others builds a sense of trust within the family and teaches teenagers a lifelong lesson about how intimacy and caring are carried out in practical ways through what we do in our daily lives.

Mom has been struggling with thirteen-year-old Billy over getting him to take responsibility to feed the dog. He is happy to do it when Mom reminds him, and he even thinks of it on his own sometimes, but not reliably. Mom is frustrated that he hasn't fully taken on this responsibility in a way both she and the dog can count on.

"What if I didn't prepare dinner for you and you couldn't get into the fridge by yourself?" Mom asks Billy one day, trying to get him to understand that his dog really needs him.

"I know, Mom. I just forget," Billy protests. But that isn't an acceptable excuse. Billy's responsibility is to remember to feed the dog, not just to respond to his mother's requests that he do so.

Billy and his mom will play this scene out a few more times until Billy truly understands what it means for someone to depend on him. Learning to be responsible for others is a gradual process with inevitable lapses along the way. And, of course, it takes some kids longer than others to learn how to be dependable. Eventually Billy will learn, with his mom's help, to notice the signs that the dog is hungry. One night when he has forgotten to feed the dog, Mom calls Billy into the kitchen so he can see for himself that the dog is lying next to his food dish, looking forlorn. Billy feels terrible, and gets the message right away.

We can't expect our teens to accept a new level of responsibility all at once, and there's no point in getting too upset about it when they don't. We need to remember that this is a learning process that, in one form or another, may take the next decade to master.

Teenagers need coaching to learn how to recognize the needs of others and what their role is in helping to meet those needs. In this case, the family rule, "Billy is responsible for feeding the dog," is about Billy's learning to participate fully in family life, not just helping with the chores. It takes more time and effort for Mom to monitor Billy's taking care of the dog than it would for her just to feed the dog herself, but that's not the point. Mom may occasionally have to remind herself to take a long-term perspective so she doesn't give up, saying, "Oh, it's just easier and faster if I do it myself." Billy needs to learn responsibility, and he needs to feel like a productive member of the family. That's worth the extra effort.

"Please Call Me . . ."

When there are too few rules, teenagers may be confused and uncertain about what their responsibilities are. They may also have a harder time learning how to think about the needs of others and understanding what others need of them. We all need rules for living together as a family. Guidelines teach our kids to be considerate and, we hope, empathic as well.

It's very difficult for our teens to imagine what it's like for us to worry about them—our need to know where they are is much greater than their need to check in with us. But if we don't have rules about their calling us, not only will we have no idea where they are, but they won't learn how to be considerate and responsive to the needs of others.

"Call when you get there." "Let me know where you are." "Call if you're going to be more than fifteen minutes late." These are requests for the courtesy of being kept informed: "Please let me know where you are so I don't have to worry about you." We need to let our teens know that when we say "Please call," it is not about limiting their freedom, but about showing consideration for our need to know they're safe.

Because teens tend to be naturally self-centered, we need to be quite explicit with these requests. "I'll worry about you if you aren't home by eleven, so please call if you're going to be late," is actually not explicit enough. We have to say, "Call me if you won't be home by eleven-fifteen." Sometimes teens are really not sure which is worse: calling and waking you up or coming home late. Since they've never lain in bed wide awake worrying about a child, they don't know. Tell them exactly what you want them to do, and make sure they know that waking you up should be the least of their concerns.

Even if we make this rule clear, it's inevitable that one day we'll hear "I forgot" or "I couldn't get to a phone." Or perhaps more honestly: "I didn't want to interrupt the movie to call you." For parents who are pacing the floor, watching the clock, and trying desperately not to visualize rotating police lights and hospital emergency rooms, a teen's casual response of "I forgot" is often enough to send them off the deep end. It may help to remember at these moments that late-night worrying is part of the initiation into being the parent of an adolescent just as certainly as sleepless nights were part and parcel of being a new parent.

Whether or not our teenagers follow our rules "to the letter," it's still better to have them than not. They do influence the decisions our kids make when they're out of the house. Family rules remind our teens of their connection to us, and of their responsibility to be considerate and call home.

The Courage to Speak Up

It's not always easy to set and sustain rules for our teens. There are times when it may be tempting to just let things go, hoping that they will "grow out of" this stage. However, we have to remember that if we don't speak up when we see unacceptable behavior, we may seem to be condoning it.

Young teenage girls seem to have a special knack for being cruel through social exclusion. They don't generally engage in physical bullying the way some boys do, but since shunning by one's peers is the worst punishment for almost any teen, teasing, ignoring, or whispering about others is every bit as cruel.

One day Dawn's Mom heard a lot of giggling coming out of the den and was glad her fifteen-year-old was having fun with her new friend. Then she overheard Dawn's friend say, "Let's call her up and say we'll see her at lunch tomorrow, and then not show." Peals of laughter followed.

Mom understood immediately what was going on and went in to stop it. Both girls looked up as she entered the room. "I heard what you're doing in here, and I don't like it," Mom said.

"What?" Dawn asked innocently.

"It's mean to make crank phone calls," Mom stated matter-of-factly. "How would you feel if someone did this to you? Can you imagine?"

There was an awkward silence. "Let's talk about it later when you've had some time to think about it," Mom added. She left the room, leaving the door open so she could hear them and they couldn't continue their scheming.

Later that evening, after the friend had gone home, Mom resumed the conversation. Dawn was defensive. "Oh, come on, Mom, we were just playing around. Everyone does it, it's no big deal!"

"It *is* a big deal, Dawn," her mother insisted quietly. "It's never okay to be cruel, and what you were planning to do was cruel."

Mom could easily have ignored this incident, not wanting to embarrass her daughter in front of her friend. Inevitably there will be times when we let some things go that we later know that we shouldn't have. It takes more time, energy, and sometimes courage to call attention to unacceptable behavior, deal with the denial and resistance, and hold firm to what's right. If we want our kids to grow up to be empathic and kind individuals, we have to be aware of what they're doing and be willing to intervene. It may help to think of these situations as opportunities for expressing our values and guiding their behavior. Our values are best translated into guidance when we put them into action.

Rules Mean We Care

Some of our rules are about teaching our teens to be considerate of others, but many of them are actually an expression of our caring for them. "I want you to go to bed at a reasonable hour because I want you to wake up rested and ready for a good day." "I want you to do your homework before you watch TV because I want you to do well in school." "I don't want you out driving late at night because I want you to get home safely."

Teenagers have a tendency to test the rules they're given—it's a natural part of discovering for themselves what's important in life and defining who they are, apart from their families. Part of the challenge for us, as parents, is to wisely discern when to let the rules bend, when to let go of them altogether, and when to hold firm.

Even though teenagers naturally chafe against rules, they still know that our rules mean we care and are one way we support their best interests. Teens who don't have enough rules may feel as if their parents don't care about where they are, whether they've done their homework, or how late they're out. These teens may brag about the freedom they have, but secretly they may wish they had a few more rules to follow.

Jessica and Claire, both thirteen years old, are hanging out at the mall on a Friday night. They have enjoyed going to a movie together, had a bite to eat, and seen everyone there is to see at least twice. They have even shopped a little. Promptly at mall closing time, 11:00, Claire's dad is there to pick her up.

"You want a ride home?" Claire asks Jessica.

"Nah, I'll walk," Jessica says, sounding a bit unsure.

Claire hesitates. She knows Jessica's house is at least a mile away.

"You sure?" she asks again.

Jessica shrugs and says, "I'm fine. You go ahead. I don't really have to be home yet."

Jessica needs more structure and guidance from her parents so she won't be out wandering alone late at night. Without rules to guide her, she is being left to shift for herself and make decisions she is still too young to make. Jessica, like all teens, needs rules that let her know: "We care about you and we want to be sure you'll get home safely."

Claire's dad senses Jessica's uncertainty, and reiterates the offer to take her home. She hesitates for just a second, but she is visibly relieved as she gets into the car. When he drives up to her house, there is no outside light on. Dad waits until he is sure Jessica is inside before pulling away. The message to Claire is clearly communicated by his actions: "I care about you *and* your friends, and I'm willing to go out of my way to make sure you all get home safely." This also shows Claire how to be a good friend, to be concerned about the needs of others even when they're not sure of their needs themselves.

It's sad that some teens have to grow up without their parents watching over them. However, we probably all know kids who are in this situation. Any act of caring and kindness we can extend to them can make a difference in their lives.

Teenagers Want Rules

Teens really do want rules. They will almost never admit this, but it's true. They know rules protect them and help them deal with situations they're not ready to handle. When teens don't know how to say "No" to their friends, they can always fall back on the rules their parents have set for them.

Fifteen-year-old Alexa is carrying a tougher academic load than her friends, who want to hang out on the weekends, including every Friday and Saturday night. Alexa needs some of her weekend time for schoolwork, but she is having trouble telling her friends. One day she actually asks her mother for help in the matter: "Mom, when Alison calls, can you please just tell me, loudly, that I can't go out?"

"Sure," Mom replies, thrilled to help her daughter out. As a working mother, she knows that finding a balance between all the aspects of one's life isn't easy. Sometimes she'd like a convenient excuse to say "No" herself.

Rules help teens feel safer during what can be a dangerous period of their lives. As adults we know what the dangers are—car accidents, substance abuse, STDs, rape, and the list goes on. What parent of a teen hasn't worried about such disasters? Rules help our teens to set limits when they're unable to do it on their own, or even when they're ambivalent.

Respecting Each Other's Privacy

Family rules will need to change over time as children change and grow. Teens have different needs for privacy than younger children do, and parents need to be alert to these developmental shifts. Even siblings close in age may have different needs and want different rules. When this happens, we need to be there to help make sure that everyone's needs are being addressed and respected.

Pam and Sue are just two years apart. Although they are very close, fourteen-year-old Pam has a habit of borrowing sixteen-year-old Sue's clothes without asking, and this is driving Sue crazy. No matter how often Sue complains, Pam continues taking whatever she wants from Sue's closet without asking permission.

When they were younger, Pam and Sue shared everything—toys, books, and clothes. But as Sue becomes more mature she wants to be able to keep her things to herself and doesn't want Pam going into her closet. Sue is asking for a change in the rules: she wants to create a firmer boundary for herself. Although Pam has agreed to this new arrangement, she continues to persist in the old habit of taking whatever she wants from her sister's closet. Finally Sue prevails upon her mother to help.

Since Mom has already spoken to Pam several times about this matter, she now decides to take a different kind of action. She gradually removes an article or two of clothing from Pam's closet every day while Pam is at school. After about a week, Pam begins to notice that things are missing.

"Where are my jeans?" she yells one morning. "And where is my purple sweater?" Mom and Sue are in the kitchen, fixing a quick breakfast. It's Friday morning, and Pam is upstairs having trouble figuring out what to wear to school with her depleted wardrobe.

"Oh, I borrowed them, honey," Mom yells back cheerfully. Sue smiles as she sips her orange juice. Pam rushes downstairs.

"You did *what?*" she asks in disbelief, still in her pajamas.

"I borrowed them," Mom repeats, enjoying the moment. "You were borrowing Sue's clothes, so I thought I'd borrow yours."

Pam looks from Sue to her mother and back again. "Okay, I get it," she says finally. "I'm not supposed to borrow her clothes. Now can I please have mine back?"

Sue and Mom are hopeful that this experience will be the breakthrough Pam needs in order to understand the sanctity of her sister's closet. Mom explains to both girls that she has been remiss in not teaching them about the need to "ask before you take." They all agree, and now Pam understands why it is better to abide by the new arrangement.

Many family rules are about respecting one another's boundaries and belongings. To truly understand such limits, some teens may need to have their own boundaries crossed. Words alone don't always make a strong enough impression for them to put themselves in someone else's shoes. If teens don't learn this kind of respect in the home, they are not likely to be considerate of other people's property out in the world. It's best to learn this kind of consideration within a safe and comfortable home environment.

Modeling Respect for Rules

It's important that our teens see that rules apply to us as well. If we act as if we are above the law, we are teaching our teens to be inconsiderate and uncaring. This is especially true when it comes to rules governing community life. When it comes to being good citizens, we want to be positive role models for our teens.

One of the most common ways our teens see us relating to the laws of the larger community is by watching how we drive our cars. Think about the number of hours your child has been observing your driving habits. No matter what you say about the importance of following the rules, by the time your children are sixteen, your habits as a driver are embedded in their brains. How you relate to other drivers and to traffic laws teaches your teen not only how to drive but also how to relate to the rules of the larger society. After all, the rules for driving are designed primarily for safety, and they serve the needs of us all.

One mother realized, as her daughter was approaching the age for a driver's permit, that she was beginning to give her "negative" driving lessons. "Now, don't *you* do this," she would say, as she zoomed through a yellow light or cut a corner too close. This type of teaching—"Don't do what I do"—is not effective and may also inspire an undesirable cynicism in our kids.

It's more important for our teenagers to see that we respect the speed limit than to arrive where we're going on time. They need to realize that we live with rules, too, and are equally liable for the consequences of breaking the rules—namely a parking or traffic ticket.

Realizing that everyone has rules to follow helps our teens understand that rules are a natural and normal part of living in the world, not just something they have to put up with until they're "free" of the restrictions of home and school. And it helps them see that everyone—teenagers and adults alike—lives with and respects these rules for the greater good of everyone.

Learning from Our Teenagers

There are times when our teenagers are better role models for us than we are for them. This happens more often than you might imagine, especially if you become open to the possibility and are willing to look for right actions in your teenager. Even a very young teen can have moments of unusual maturity and social awareness. Sometimes kids may be more inclined to follow the rules and do the right thing than we are. We want to acknowledge our teens in these instances whenever possible, and praise them when they show such respect. There is no bigger compliment than our saying, "I'm really impressed with you. I learned a lot from the way you handled that."

Soon after a megasupermarket opened in a nearby town, Mom took her thirteen-year-old son, Carl, with her to check it out. The entrance to the store led directly into the bakery section at the exact moment that fresh bread was coming out of the oven. Neither Mom nor Carl could resist: before they placed the warm loaf in their shopping cart, they each tore off a piece of the bread to taste it. What a disappointment! It looked delicious, but the bread was dry and rather bland. Mom was about to leave the loaf on a random shelf in the store, but Carl said, "No, Mom, that's not right. Let's take it back to the bakery and tell them why we don't like it."

Mom stopped the cart and looked at her son with new respect. "You're absolutely right," she said, swallowing her embarrassment over her own lapse in judgment. "That's a much better idea."

Later, when they were in the parking lot heading toward their car, Mom casually remarked, "You know, Carl, I learned something important from you today. Next time something like that comes up, I'll handle my complaints directly."

Carl just smiled shyly, but he heard every word.

Parental Networking

There are many reasons to make friends with the parents of our kids' friends. Not only can we commiserate with tales of the kids' latest transgressions ("You won't believe what she did . . ."), but if the relationship is established, we will feel more comfortable calling them in the middle of the night. We know they'll understand because we're all in this together. Although we can't always be there ourselves to monitor what's going on, we can cooperate with parents of other teens to keep a collective eye on things. At a certain level, all our teenagers are our joint responsibility.

Virginia's parents are going out of town for twenty-four hours. They feel that surely seventeen-year-old Virginia can be trusted to be on her own for such a brief period of time. After all, she is practically ready to leave for college. Before leaving, they tell Virginia that only her best friend, Kathy Thompson, can sleep over.

If you're the parent of a teenager, you can easily guess where this story is going. News of "the party at Virginia's" spreads through the school with astonishing speed. But in this case, there is a twist to the story. Virginia's parents are friends with Kathy's parents, so they let the Thompsons know their plans and ask them to "keep an eye on things." When Kathy's parents drive by Virginia's house at about 11:30 P.M., they're not astonished to find a few dozen cars parked out front and all the lights blazing inside.

The Thompsons take the scene in stride—after all, they remember their own adolescence. When they come in the front door, they maintain a calm, friendly demeanor. As involved parents, they know a lot of the kids who are there. Their primary goal is to make sure no one drives home after drinking, and their secondary goal is to let the teens know the party's over. They stick around until everyone is headed home, and leave Kathy and Virginia to deal with the cleanup.

Let's face it. Our teenagers are better able to outsmart us than we are to know what's going on. We need to work with other parents to form a cooperative network to help watch over the teenagers as a group. It helps if we know the other parents for a number of years. But even if we've never met them, we can still pick up the phone and let them know our concerns. In most cases, they will share those same concerns and will appreciate our having contacted them.

Community Rules

We want our teenagers to grow up with a commitment to participate in and contribute to their community. This means more than just following the letter of the law. It means truly understanding the cooperative nature of community and accepting a level of individual responsibility to support the greater good.

If our teens live with too few rules within the family, they miss out on an opportunity to develop a concern for the needs of others and a community awareness. They may not even realize how their behavior affects other people. Teenagers who are not accustomed to following rules may think "That doesn't apply to me" or "Just one time won't matter" or "I won't get caught." The issues could be anything from shoplifting to trespassing to destroying private property. The possibilities are endless, and even good teens can get into serious trouble thinking this way.

Seventeen-year-old Lawrence and a group of his football buddies organized a late-night prank to move the high school mascot from the entrance of the school to the gym entrance. They meant no harm; they were "just having fun" and enjoying the thought of upsetting the school administration. However, in the middle of the move, the statue began to crack. The boys didn't know what to do. They were afraid that if they moved the statue back, they would damage it further. So they set it down and ran.

It took the principal two days to identify the boys involved. She suspended them and notified their parents. That night Lawrence had to face his father. He knew he was in trouble, but was still viewing the incident as a harmless prank that had gone awry.

Lawrence's father started out by throwing a string of angry questions: "Why did you do this?" "What were you thinking?" and "How could you be so stupid?" Finally, he calmed down. He saw that he wasn't getting anywhere with this approach, and that his son was clamming up. So he tried something new. "You know, that statue belonged to the whole school," he said. "It didn't belong to the administration, and it certainly didn't belong to the football team."

Lawrence was silent. He hadn't thought about it in quite this way.

The point Lawrence's dad wanted to make was not only about punishment or even making reparations, although in this case both were appropriate. He really wanted Lawrence to understand that his actions had an effect on a larger community, that what happened was not just about him and his buddies.

There was a range of responses from the parents of the boys involved. Some treated it as a harmless joke; others took it more seriously and made sure their sons paid the school back through compensatory labor. After talking with his dad and the principal, Lawrence ended up digging trenches for drainage pipes in the athletic field—work that provided hours for him to think about being a responsible member of a larger community.

There is an important lesson to learn here, not only for teenagers but for adults as well. We all need to develop greater awareness and concern for how our actions affect our neighbors and then be able to extend that concern to the entire global community. For we really are all connected: the impact of the fuel we use, the clothes we buy, and the food we eat ripples throughout the world. As we expect our teenagers to learn to be concerned with our needs and the needs of others, we might also ask ourselves whether we are considering the needs of the global community and the planet itself. After all, teens learn their best lessons by watching how we live our lives. Let's make sure the example we provide is one of which we can be proud.

If teenagers live with broken promises, they learn to be disappointed

Although our teens grow in independence year by year, they continue to be dependent upon us. They are not likely to admit that they still need us, but they do. They need to know they can count on us, and that we will live up to our promises. If we break our promises time and time again, they take it personally, feel hurt, and lose faith in us. Although an occasional disappointment can be absorbed and overcome, a regular pattern of breaking promises erodes our relationship with our teenagers. They become increasingly disappointed that they can't count on us, can't believe in us, can't feel safe and secure with us.

We depend on our teenagers, too. Learning how to honor one another by keeping our word is an important part of learning how to live in a family, and how to respect intimate relationships. Parents and teens depend on one another for communication, cooperation, and a million other little things that make life flow smoothly. We all need to know that we can rely on one another to do what we say we will do. Too many broken promises eventually lead to alienation within the family.

Joshua's dad has been promising him that he will make it to one of his basketball games. Joshua is in his last year of middle school and is both captain and high scorer on a winning team. He knows this may be the peak of his basketball career, since next year he will be entering a much larger high school and competing with lots of taller and better players. This is Joshua's season to shine.

But Dad never makes it to a single game. He really means to, but work emergencies always seem to get in the way. They are legitimate emergencies at the manufacturing plant where Dad, as senior manager, is the one ultimately responsible for everything. However, it's also true that work is his clear priority, and too often he makes decisions at the expense of his family. The unfortunate message to Joshua is that when push comes to shove, work is more important to his dad than Joshua is.

After each missed game, Dad apologizes to his son and explains what happened, but eventually Joshua just stops hoping he will come. It's easier that way—at least he doesn't have to waste time searching the gymnasium bleachers and time and time again deal with the disappointment when his father doesn't show up.

Dad's career progresses steadily, and the whole family benefits with a larger house, a nice car, savings for college, and exciting vacations. However, when Joshua goes away to college, Dad wonders how they have become so distant from each other. To Dad, it seems like all of a sudden Josh is just gone.

When parents repeatedly fail to keep their promises, their kids eventually lose faith in them. They learn to live with disappointment, and this often leads to a sense of distance or estrangement. It doesn't happen all at once, but in small, imperceptible increments, so that often the parent doesn't realize what's happening or the significance of it until it's too late. Parents may not see the pattern until their teenager is pretty much grown and has moved on, and even then they may not recognize how they contributed to the distance.

Josh's dad might have avoided this sad outcome by noticing the pattern and how it affected his son. He could have assigned an associate to cover for him at the plant, explaining, "My kid's big game is tonight, and I've got to be there." He wouldn't have had to get to every single game, but enough to make it clear that being there for his son was a priority. This is the kind of commitment that makes a difference in the quality of our relationships with our teenagers.

Can I Count on You?

E motional security is as important to a teenager as it is to a toddler. Even while our teens are pushing us away, protesting that they don't need us anymore—and frequently don't even want to be seen with us—they continue to rely on us for emotional support. Our presence and our dependability lend them the strength and stability they need as they explore the world and begin to develop their own identities. For our teens to make the next, huge leap into the world as independent young adults, they need to know they can count on us in a million intangible ways and that they can depend on us to follow through on our promises.

When we tell our teens, "I'm going to meet with your teacher," "I'll see your performance," or "I'll pick up that book you need," we had better be sure we make that promise a priority. Because it's not really about the teacher, the play, or the book, it's about trust. It's about our relationship with our teenagers and about helping them to establish a secure emotional foundation that they can draw on for the rest of their lives. We want them to enter adulthood knowing that it's safe to depend on loved ones.

Mom had promised to pick up the black tights thirteen-year-old Alicia needed to wear at her spring choral concert, but she forgot. So Alicia was the only one wearing sheer stockings, and she felt terribly self-conscious and conspicuous. She was humiliated and ashamed, and she blamed her mother. As they were driving home from the concert, she fell apart, and burst into tears.

"How could you forget?" Alicia screamed in between sobs.

"I thought you looked just fine," Mom responded evenly.

At this, Alicia became even more hysterical.

"Look, Alicia," Mom said, losing her patience as they reached home, "it's really not that big a deal."

"It is to me!" Alicia managed to cry out as she ran out of the car and upstairs to her room.

Mom hadn't recognized how important having the right clothing was to Alicia, but that's not the point. She had failed to keep her promise, and then had failed to understand why it mattered so much. So Alicia ended up feeling both disappointed and misunderstood.

When teenagers can't depend on their parents to do as they say, they end up feeling all alone in the world. And when teens feel alone, they turn to their peer group with all the intensity of a hunger for family. We don't really want our kids relying on other teenagers in this way. Their friends, some of whom we may not be crazy about to begin with, can't offer the experienced guidance and protection that parents can. Our kids need us, and we need to be there for them. When we disappoint them, we need to realize it *does* matter, apologize, promise to do better next time, and make sure we do.

Keeping Our Promises

Some promises we make are about something that will happen in the future. They may be about privileges that will come with maturity, as in "when you're sixteen you can stay out later on weekends." The promise of future privileges can help younger teens accept their current restrictions somewhat more readily. However, if these promises are not honored, the teenager will feel betrayed, so it's important to be careful what you promise.

Chris's parents had told him he could go to concerts with his friends when he turned sixteen. In the meantime, they drove him to the concerts and picked him up as soon as the concert was over. Four days after his birthday, Chris reminded his parents of their promise. "I want to go to the concert on Friday with my friends," he said. "Ben is driving."

Now Mom and Dad were caught in a bind. They had made this promise more than two years ago, but they hadn't realized *then* how worried they'd be *now* about new teenage drivers. They did understand how much Chris wanted his freedom and they knew they had made an important promise, so they talked with him about their concerns.

"We're not reneging on our promise," Dad assured his son, "but we are concerned about your safety." Chris immediately relaxed. All he really cared about was that he got to go with his friends.

"We just want to know who's driving, what time the concert is likely to be over, and what time we can expect you to be home," Mom explained.

"Oh," Chris said, beginning to understand his parents' worry. He hadn't given any of this much thought. He'd just envisioned himself hopping into the car with his buddies. "Okay, I'll find out," he said.

As the concert date drew near, Mom and Dad made a special effort not to nag Chris about his plans. The night before the concert, he casually told them about the logistics. Much to his parents' relief, it turned out that one of the older kids, someone who had driven to the stadium a number of times before, would be driving. They were still on pins and needles until Chris walked in the door at 1:00 A.M., but they knew that was just something they had to go through, and that at some point they had to let go and trust in their son's ability to take care of himself.

In this case, both Chris and his parents honored their promises, and no one was disappointed. This is how mutual trust and responsibility can grow between parents and teens.

The next morning—or rather, afternoon—when Chris got up, his mother said, "I'm so glad you had a good time and that we can trust you to take care of yourself."

Chris just smiled. "Do we have any orange juice?" he said, yawning.

Changing the Rules Isn't Fair

There will be times when we want to renege on a promise, when we can't believe we ever made the promise to begin with, or mistakenly thought our kid would be far more mature at this age. Whatever the case, we no longer want to honor our word. Unless there is a real risk to life and limb, we need to deliver on our promises for the sake of our relationship with our teens. To renege on a promise our kids have waited for with anticipation is too destructive. We can always view the promise as an opportunity to learn for parents and teens.

Emily's parents had promised her that when she was sixteen they would give her a budget for clothes and other expenses so she could manage her own money. Then when she turned sixteen, they changed their mind, saying, "We don't think you're ready yet."

Emily was furious. "How can I prove to you that I can manage my money myself if you won't even give me a chance?"

But her parents were unmovable.

Frustrated, Emily fell into hysteria. "But you promised!" were her final words just before she slammed her bedroom door.

Emily's parents didn't understand how she could be so upset. They were generous about buying clothes for her, and she always had money for movies and all that junk food she ate. They just didn't want her spending her whole budget in one week and then asking for even more money to get through the month.

Emily's parents may have been predicting their daughter's budgetary abilities accurately, but they had promised to give her a chance, and they needed to follow through on what they had promised. After all, what was the worst that could happen? Emily might be broke before the end of each month and not be able to afford to go out to the movies with her friends.

In fact, this is exactly what happened when Emily's parents finally relented, but it only happened once. After having to stay in a few nights while her friends were at the movies, Emily was sure to make her money last for the next four weeks. And because her parents were calm and clear when the financial catastrophe happened, Emily couldn't pick a fight with them or make it their fault. She had to face the fact that she had mismanaged her funds, and learn from her experience.

Emily's parents were extremely empathic and understanding, but they did *not* give her any extra money. They saw her experience as part of a learning process. Rescuing her with a loan or a few extra dollars would have only interfered with that learning. Instead, they kept their promise and held Emily accountable to her end of the deal. By doing so, they made it clear that the challenge was between Emily and her budget, not between Emily and her parents. Often teens try to turn a conflict within themselves into a conflict with their parents.

While bailing Emily out of the situation she had created would not have really helped her, neither would saying "I told you so," or lecturing her. It's much more effective to hold firm while remaining warm and supportive than it is to respond in an angry, controlling way. We don't have to fight with our teens to enforce limits; we just have to hold the line.

Once a Promise Is Made . . .

Sometimes parents make rash promises because it's the easiest thing to do in the moment. Thirteen-year-old Joseph was badgering his mom about taking him to the sporting goods store. Busy with her own priorities, and overwhelmed by Joseph's nagging, she finally agreed to take him over the weekend. At that moment, she would have promised him almost anything just to get him off her back. Giving in this way can lead to even greater disappointment later. It's better to say "Let's talk about this after dinner" or "Give me time to think about this."

However, Mom had promised him, and Joseph was looking forward to Saturday. He needed new athletic socks, and he also wanted to look over the new skateboard wheels he'd heard about. But when Saturday arrived, Joseph's mom had a whole list of other things she needed to do. If she had thought her schedule over more carefully in advance, she never would have promised to take Joseph to the store, because she knew she had a very full weekend.

When we make promises hastily and under pressure, and then are unable to keep them, our teenagers are justifiably disappointed. Joseph felt bad about not getting to the sporting goods store, but he felt even worse that he wasn't as important to his mom as the list of errands she had to do. Teens take things very personally and Joseph's disappointment was intensified by his hurt feelings.

When we tell ourselves, "I just don't have time to be looking at skateboard wheels," we have to face the fact that this is really a rationalization. Looking at skateboard wheels is not what's at stake here—spending quality time with our kids, and keeping our promises to them, is. Skateboard wheels may not be at all important to us, but they may be a number one priority to our child. And what our children need to know is that they are a number one priority to us. One of the ways we can do this is to give them our time and attention, and take their priorities seriously, too.

It's important to consider how we make decisions about our time, as well as the way we communicate these decisions to our teens. A pattern of promising now and making excuses later can only lead to their disappointment in us.

Suppose Joseph had the verbal skills and the perspective needed to express himself as an adult might.

"You promised you would take me to the sporting goods store today," he would calmly remind his mom.

"I know, honey," she'd say in a rushed voice, "but I have so many other things that have to get done today. Maybe tomorrow . . ."

"I understand you're busy," Joseph would continue. "But these are decisions you make about what's important to you, and I really think your son should at least be on the list of important errands."

This comment would stop most moms dead in their tracks. No longer rushing, Joseph's mom would take a moment to think about what he had said, during which Joseph could pursue his momentary advantage.

"And I'd think that honoring your word would also be important to you."

In most cases, this approach would get Joseph to the sporting goods store and the exciting new array of skateboard wheels. But thirteen-year-olds don't know how to talk to their parents in this calm and rational way. As a matter of fact, when they're stressed or annoyed, many parents don't know how to speak so clearly and calmly to their teens, or to each other either. Most of us react on a more emotional level and say things in the heat of battle that we regret later.

A much more likely scenario in this instance is that Joseph would exclaim in frustration, "You never do anything I want!" at which point Mom would respond indignantly, "How dare you say that! My whole life revolves around you!" and so on, in an escalating spiral, which would leave the relatively minor matter of the skateboard wheels in the dust. At times like this, we really need to stop the emotional fireworks and regain control over ourselves. It's our job as parents to maintain an adult perspective and focus on the issue at hand. When we make promises we can't fulfill, we need to take the initiative to soothe our teen's disappointment and find a creative solution.

Teenagers' Promises

Our teenagers have to learn to keep their promises to us, too. It's easy for them to develop the habit of agreeing to whatever we ask of them simply to get us off their backs, and then conveniently forgetting what they said they'd do. We would, of course, hope they don't learn this from our example.

"I'll never do it again, Mom," sixteen-year-old Nathan promises, with a charming smile and exaggerated sincerity, after he has pulled the family car into the garage with almost no gas in it for the third time in a month.

"And you won't do it this time, either," Mom responds with an equally charming smile. She knows her son would promise her the moon to avoid facing a simple responsibility. "Go back out now and fill up the car."

"But, Mom, I have to—"

"Oh, I'm sure you'll manage," Mom answers, still smiling. "It's only going to take you ten minutes. Now is the time—then we can both forget about it." This conversation is carried out in a light manner, but Nathan knows where the bottom line is, and he heads back out to the gas station.

We don't want to allow our teens to get away with either empty promises or empty gas tanks. It's helpful to be very clear about exactly what our expectations are and to ask explicitly for that behavior. We can't expect our kids to be able to read our minds, and it doesn't help to start an emotional line of interrogation about why they didn't do what we wanted. It's better to "cut to the chase," let them know what we want and when, and then move on.

Stating your expectations and holding firm to them will give your teens the message that they need to honor their word. We don't want them to assume that we'll always be there to pick up the pieces for them. An important part of growing up is to learn to follow through on our promises and learn to match our behavior to our words. This is how our teens develop integrity and become mature, responsible adults.

I Forgot!

Of course, everyone breaks promises at least once in a while— none of us is perfect. It's a consistent pattern of breaking promises we make to our kids that can lead to their deep disappointment in us. If we make a mistake every now and again, we can apologize, explain what happened, and make amends in whatever way possible. Most of all, we can make it a priority not to let it happen again. Simply saying, "Sorry, I forgot," is not enough. It doesn't acknowledge the inconvenience or sometimes the real loss our teenager has incurred by our thoughtlessness.

Anna's mother forgot to send in her financial statement to the college so that her daughter's academic scholarship would be renewed, even after Anna had reminded her on numerous occasions.

"Oh sure, honey. I'll send it tomorrow," she promised. "I've got it almost all ready to be mailed." But she didn't follow through, and the result was that Anna lost the scholarship she needed in order to continue her studies.

This disappointment was too much for Anna to handle. Although she knew her mother was not very reliable, Anna had never imagined that she wouldn't come through for her on such an important matter. Now Anna had to either drop out of school or go into the financial office and explain the problem her mother had caused.

Unable to face either option, she fell into profound feelings of frustration and helplessness. She'd always been a somber, moody teen and this disappointment was too much for her to bear. She was so upset she couldn't sleep or concentrate on her studies. She finally left school with a medical disability—depression.

This story is so blatantly destructive to both mother and daughter, it may be difficult to accept it as realistic. However, it's a true story. And six years later, Anna still has not been able to return to college.

Even older teenagers need to be able to depend on us and know that if we somehow fail them, we will find a way to make it right. In this case, Anna's mother should have gone to the college financial office to rectify the situation herself. It was her mistake, and she should have been the one to make things right. By leaving the ball in Anna's court, she is avoiding her responsibility and overburdening her daughter. This was too much for Anna. And while some kids would have been able to pick up the pieces and go on, it's not fair to ask them to do that.

When the Parent Is the Child

A pattern of broken promises can be a sign of parental irresponsibility. Whether the pattern is due to addiction, workaholism, or just plain immaturity, some parents consistently disappoint their teenagers. Eventually the kids become so disappointed that they either expect very little out of life or they overcompensate, becoming supercompetent and thinking that they have to take care of everything on their own. Neither extreme is healthy.

Brandon had known for a long time that his mother had a drinking problem. It had been just the two of them since he was about ten, and by the time he was fifteen, he had become very experienced at taking care of his mom. He understood that she wouldn't always show up for teachers' meetings even when she said she would, and that she rarely made it to his ball games. He'd long ago given up on her and had learned how to survive pretty well on his own. In fact, he'd taken over some of the roles we tend to think of as parental—preparing meals and paying bills.

In this family there had been a role reversal—Brandon had become the adult in the family and his mother the child. This served Brandon well in many ways. He was mature, handled money well, was responsible with homework, and even held leadership positions at school. But he had none of the easy, relaxed, fun-loving ways that other boys his age enjoyed. Brandon was inordinately serious and even a bit controlling and overly perfectionist. His buddies sometimes complained that he was "no fun."

Someone had to be the adult in the family to make sure that things didn't fall apart completely, and in being one, Brandon sacrificed his adolescence. He went directly from being a child to being an adult and carrying a heavy load of responsibility on his shoulders.

It's almost impossible for teens to maintain such an adult level of responsibility. Eventually they get fed up with it and have to break free. When Brandon left home to go to college, he went wild. He entered fraternity life with the same determination to let loose that he had previously used to hold things together. Now his buddies were putting him to bed after weekend parties, the way he had put his mother to bed after her binges.

Teenagers need to be able to focus on growing up during their adolescent years. They need that time to experiment, make mistakes, and learn from them. While they are doing this, they need dependable and concerned adults watching over them, protecting and guiding them. Teens who are forced to behave like grown-ups when they're not really ready lose a part of themselves in the process. Sometimes, when the opportunity arises, they can regress to the developmental stage they missed and "catch up." Unfortunately, such out-of-sync development often doesn't work out well, and problems can arise. If Brandon is lucky and his fraternity brothers are kind, he'll manage to complete his adolescence safely.

We want our teenagers to be able to create responsible adult lives in which their promises have real meaning. During their adolescence, we represent the adult world to them. We need to show them by our example what it means to keep our promises. Our kids need to see that this way of being works for us in our world so that they will have a model for what it means to be an adult.

In addition, our teens need to know from their own experience what it feels like to be able to count on loved ones to live up to their promises. The sense of security that comes from being able to trust that loved ones will be there when they say they will is part of their emotional foundation. This is the example they will follow as they enter their adult relationships.

Perhaps the greatest promise we make to our kids is when they're born. When we hold them in our arms we implicitly promise to love them and care for them all the way through into their adult lives. We need to keep this promise always in the forefront of our minds, and do what we can to honor and keep it.

If teenagers live with respect, they learn to honor others

Respecting a teen's right to be his or her own person is essential. Remember, exploring who they are and defining their differences from us while still staying connected are the main tasks of adolescents. We don't really want them to become clones of us, no matter how much we might try to influence, shape, or control them. We want them to have the chance to let their own unique qualities emerge and blossom; we want them to find their own voices and be able to express themselves; and we want them to succeed in life in ways that we didn't. In order for them to do this, we need to respect their right to be different from us.

We may agree to this principle in theory, but in actual practice it's not so easy. We may find ourselves perplexed by our teens and the decisions they make. We may feel anxious as we see them become more different from us than we could ever have imagined. ("How can you possibly not want to go to the prom?" or "What do you mean, you don't want to work in the family business this summer?") Sometimes, as we feel ourselves losing control over the decisions they make, we may even fall back on grim parental warnings: "You're making a big mistake," or dire predictions: "You'll regret this one day."

It's difficult to respect our teens' right to be self-determining, especially when we feel strongly that we have the wisdom of experience on our side and "only want what's best" for them. But we really do need to let go of trying to protect them from all the mistakes we made in our youth, as well as new ones they may come up with on their own. Respecting our teens means understanding that they need the opportunity to experiment, make their own mistakes, and learn from them, just as we did when we were young.

This doesn't mean we have to accept everything they do, or that we should abdicate our parental responsibility to set standards, uphold expectations, and define limits for them. It does mean that we need to realize that our teens have their own unique paths to follow through adolescence, and our job is to watch over them and be readily available with support and guidance.

If our teens grow up in a home where there is genuine respect for their own inner beings and the way their lives unfold, they will quite naturally develop the same capacity to honor others and respect their rights. They will know from a place deep within themselves that all human beings have certain fundamental rights, no matter how they look or what their beliefs and customs are—and that an important part of being human is recognizing, appreciating, and honoring those differences among people.

Eventually our teens will even apply this honor and respect to us, their parents. If they've grown up with respect, our teenagers will be more likely to respect us, even as they come to terms with our personal frailties and shortcomings. They will recognize that we are also human beings, imperfect but well meaning, doing the best we can for them. If we have shown respect for them as unique individuals, they will be inclined to do the same for us—and for others—in the future.

Modeling Respectful Interactions

One of the things that makes parenting such a challenge is that we are role models for our teens, twenty-four hours a day, seven days a week. Our kids notice how we treat others, from our bosses and the neighbors to the mailman, the gas station attendant, the grocery clerk, and the waitress. They see us interact with other people thousands of times over the years, and they know our style and patterns of behavior.

No matter what we say to our teens about the importance of respecting others, the old saying "Actions speak louder than words" holds true. If we don't treat people with respect, our teens are not likely to do so either.

Thirteen-year-old Rob hated going out to dinner with his parents. He was embarrassed by the way his dad talked to the waiter, and always felt relieved if they were able to get out of the restaurant without seeing anyone they knew. If the least little thing wasn't to his dad's liking, he would rudely inform the waiter to "make it right."

"Surely you can bring us some more water," Dad would say sarcastically. "Oh yes, and some lemons too, if that isn't too much trouble."

The waiter would remain impassive, and Rob would want to

crawl under the table. There wasn't anything his mother could say; she'd long ago given up trying, and his little sisters just distracted themselves with the toys they brought along.

One day in the school lunchroom, Rob was surprised by his own behavior. A cafeteria server had misunderstood his request and put gravy on his potatoes when he only wanted it on the meat.

"No, not there!" Rob exclaimed rather loudly and angrily.

The boy next to him backed away, and said, "Whoa, chill out, man!"

Rob was really embarrassed. "Sorry," he mumbled, and rushed to sit down. He couldn't believe what he had done.

Our teens can't help but learn from us even when they detest our behavior. It certainly wasn't Rob's intention to take after his father, but the lessons we give through our behavior are powerful ones. Rob was horrified and ashamed to find rude behavior like his dad's spontaneously erupting from him.

If we want our teens to be polite and considerate in their day-to-day interactions with the people they meet, we have to be always mindful of the example we're giving them. Simply telling our teenagers to be respectful of others, especially when we aren't, just won't work. The next time you find yourself feeling frustrated or short-tempered with someone, pause and consider how you would like your teenager to behave in these circumstances. Then take a deep breath, and find a considerate way of responding.

Respect in Relationships

Our teens also need to see us treat our loved ones with respect and at times this may require quite a bit of self-control. We may lose our tempers and verbally attack our spouse for a variety of reasons. No matter how angry we are or how justified in our aggravation, disrespectful behavior is never the right choice.

Our patterns of communication, both constructive and destructive, become the model for our teens. Even if they're hiding away in their bedrooms with headphones on, they still pick up the general emotional atmosphere in the home. Our teens may claim that they don't want to be like us when they grow up, but they are highly susceptible to repeating our behavior, even behavior they hate.

Sixteen-year-old Anita's mother was a screamer. Although she didn't hold a grudge, her first reaction to annoyance was to express her anger loudly, in such a way that it resonated throughout the house. If she was in the kitchen, she'd yell, "Who took the scissors from the drawer?" so loudly and vehemently, that the whole family could hear her, over the sound of the TV, all the way into the family room. She "talked" to Dad in the same tone as well. "Did you take the car in today to get new tires, or did you forget again?" she'd yell at him from one end of the house to the other. This was Mom's habitual way of opening a conversation—loudly and accusingly. Frequently Dad's way of dealing with this was to pretend he didn't hear her.

When Anita had her first serious romantic relationship, this pattern of communication took on new significance. Anita and Phil had been seeing each other exclusively for about four months when they began having problems. Phil was beginning to withdraw and spend more time with his buddies, and Anita was getting upset about it. She asked him again and again what was going on.

Finally, in exasperation, he told her, "I still want to hang out with you, but I just can't stand the way you're always yelling at me."

"What do you mean?" Anita asked in a loud and accusing tone.

"Well, I mean like that," Phil answered succinctly.

"Like what?" Anita asked again. She was completely unaware of how she had sounded to him.

"You yell just like your mother," Phil said.

Anita was speechless. But immediately she knew exactly what he meant, and she was mortified. "I'm so sorry," she whispered.

This was the first step for Anita toward learning a new way to communicate. She knew she didn't want to be loud like her mother, and yet it was the most natural thing in the world for her to do.

Anita can learn to speak to Phil in ways that are more respectful and considerate of his feelings, but it will take time, self-awareness, and lots of practice on her part, and patience and understanding on his.

Our teenagers receive some of the most important lessons about human relationships and communication in the home. This is where they learn how to deal with others. We don't want our teens to have to unlearn our bad habits. We want them to grow up with a constructive model of communication so that they can relate to loved ones easily and naturally, and treat them with respect. We've all learned both good and bad habits from our own parents, and we need to be mindful of what those strengths and weaknesses are. We want to show our kids the best ways we know to communicate with others, to give them a model for positive adult relationships.

Remembering Whose Life It Is

Another powerful way we teach our teenagers how to be respectful is through honoring their right to make their own decisions. This can be especially difficult when we disagree with them, think they're making a mistake, or experience their decisions as a personal loss.

Thirteen-year-old Jeffrey was a pianist with the musical talent needed to become a professional musician, perhaps even a conductor. He had been playing piano for eight years and was already studying advanced music theory. But now that he was a teenager, he had other interests and he also had a mind of his own.

"I want to quit," he told his parents. "This is not really what I want to spend my time doing. I want to play basketball," he added, ignoring the disbelief on his mother's face. "Look, I can palm the ball!" His long fingers stretched easily around it.

"What a shame, to waste all that talent!" his parents said. His mother was the most distraught. She had given up her own dream of becoming a concert pianist in college when she realized how tough the competition was. Without realizing it, her son's musical ability had come to represent a second chance to her. Although she wisely kept her deepest emotions to herself, what she was really thinking was, "How could you do this to me?"

Teenagers can do this sort of thing rather easily, in fact. And when they do, it can be difficult to show respect for their decisions. But no matter how painful it is to us personally, we have to put our own ambitions and desires aside and listen carefully to what our kids are saying to us. In this case, Jeffrey was clearly telling his mother, "Music is not my dream, it's yours."

"If you stop now, you won't be able to continue at the same level later on," his mom pleaded. She realized her son was making a serious decision that would affect the rest of his life.

"I know, Mom," he answered, "but I don't care. That's not what I want to do, don't you get it?"

What was an easy decision for Jeffrey was very difficult for his mother to accept. She sought support by talking it over with her husband, friends, the parents of other young musicians, and finally with Jeffrey's piano teacher. He was also disappointed that Jeffrey had decided to quit studying the piano, but he had been through this scenario before, though with less talented kids. "It's not enough to have the gift," he explained to Jeffrey's mom. "If he doesn't have the passion, drive, and determination, he'll never make it."

It took nearly a year for Mom to make peace with Jeffrey's decision. It was also a mystery to her how Jeffrey could be so happy sitting on the bench and cheering his teammates on during basketball games, but she could see that he was. She knew that this was his life, not hers, so she struggled to respect her son's decision, and eventually she succeeded in letting go of her expectations for him.

Jeffrey was well aware of how hard this was for his mom. Periodically she would ask him if he wanted to return to his piano lessons, and she even invited his old teacher over for dinner one night. Although her own wishes were clear, Jeffrey was grateful that she didn't try to force him to continue in music even though he knew that would never have worked.

Our teens recognize our struggle and effort as parents to honor their decisions even if they don't acknowledge it openly. For we reveal our feelings in subtle and not so subtle ways, especially when we disagree with them. By honoring our teens' right to make their own decisions—especially when it's hard to do—we are really teaching them a much larger lesson: that even when we don't agree with each other, we can still respect each other's decisions. We can honor our loved ones' right to make up their own minds.

This lesson helps them form the foundation for all the future relationships in their lives, including their relationship with us. We want to be able to enjoy a mutually respectful, lifelong relationship with our adult children. There is only one way to achieve that—to let them be who they are, not try to make them be who we wish they would become.

Letting Them Learn from Their Mistakes

What if Jeffrey's decision *was* a mistake and he only realized it years later, with great regret? We want so much to protect our teenagers from pain and suffering, and to have every opportunity. But we can't do it. The reality for all of us, including our kids, is that we have to make the best decisions we can with the information and knowledge we have, and live with the consequences of our decisions. We hope to learn from every decision we make, and when we realize we've made mistakes, we pick up the pieces and move on.

It can be very difficult to stand by and watch our teenagers go through this process of trial and error. But if we constantly try to "save" them from their mistakes, we teach them not to trust their own decisions and we sabotage their ability to learn from their own experiences. We may think we're helping them, but we're hurting them in the long run. There is just no easy, painless way to grow up. Sometimes our teenagers need to learn the hard way, just as we did.

Morgan was one of the oldest kids in her grade and one of the brightest. In her junior year of high school, she decided to go to college on an early admission program, skipping her senior year. Both Mom and Dad were against this idea, knowing how difficult the initial adjustment to college can be. They knew she was ready academically, but they were concerned about her social adjustment.

However, Morgan had her mind made up: she applied and was admitted to the college of her choice. Unfortunately, she suffered throughout her entire freshman year—she didn't fit in with the kids in her dorm, she hated her roommate, and she had trouble making close friends. Socially, she just wasn't ready.

This was a tough lesson to learn, and one that Mom and Dad had tried to protect her from. But ultimately they had realized they had to respect Morgan's decision. And when the outcome they had feared came about, they never once said, "We told you so." Instead, they were supportive and patient with her frequent, unhappy phone calls that whole first year, listening to her and assuring her that in time things would work out.

Respecting our teenagers' rights to make their own decisions often involves a painful letting go. There will always be gray areas where it's difficult to know when to insist that our kids yield to our better judgment and when to allow them to find out for themselves. There are no clear-cut rules to guide us in this matter but it's clear that we must intervene when our teens' decisions involve dangerous behavior. Often we may need to make decisions to overrule them on the spur of the moment, with incomplete information and only our gut instincts to go on.

Fifteen-year-old Serena called her parents late one night to say she was getting a ride home from a party, so they wouldn't have to come pick her up.

"Oh, who's driving?" she asked.

"One of the seniors," Serena answered confidently.

This was not enough information for Mom. "No, Serena, you stay put. I'll be right there to get you."

"But Mom," Serena protested, "nobody else's parents are coming to pick them up."

"That's okay," Mom said, calmly. "I'll take anyone else who needs a ride home, too."

"Oh, all right," Serena replied. She was terribly embarrassed, but she knew she couldn't stop her mom from coming once she'd made up her mind.

Much to Serena's surprise, by the time her mom got there, other parents were also lined up in their cars outside, waiting for their kids. This was a good lesson for Serena—her mom was not so out of line after all.

When our teenagers make dubious decisions based on immature reasoning, we need to actively step in and lend our more rational judgment to the situation. In these situations, teenagers are often relieved to find that sometimes their parents really do know what they're doing, even though that's the last thing they would admit. But they can't be the ones to know which times those are. Making those decisions is on our shoulders.

The better our relationship with our teens, the more information we'll have to make these on-the-spot decisions, and the more likely it is that we'll know when it's appropriate to step in and when it's better to step aside. If we respect their right to make their own decisions most of the time, they'll be more receptive to our asserting our authority, especially when it comes to their safety and well-being. This is yet another reason not to "spend" all our teenager's goodwill toward us on fighting battles that don't really matter, over things like the clothes they wear or the music they listen to.

Respecting Each Other's Beliefs

Learning to honor each other, especially when we have strong differences of opinion, is not always easy for either parent or teen. It can be a real challenge for us to respect our teens' values when they come into direct conflict with our own. It's hard not to take this as a personal affront—after all, aren't we the ones who raised them? And don't their values reflect on ours?

Eighteen-year-old Daniel was thrilled to be able to vote in the upcoming presidential election. Knowing Daniel's political opinions, his father was not happy with this new development, for he knew they were at opposite ends of the political spectrum.

"You'll be canceling out my vote," Dad said in disbelief.

"That's right," Daniel responded, very pleased with himself.

"You can't do that," Dad protested.

"Of course I can," Daniel said cheerfully.

Dad was silent. Obviously, his son was right. Later he said to Mom, "You know, we have a traitor in the house."

From the next room, Daniel yelled, "I heard that!"

Dad yelled back in the direction of Daniel's voice. "Okay, let's hear the reasoning behind your vote," he challenged his son.

Daniel came into the room with his parents, and he was more than prepared to answer his dad's question. Both father and son were history buffs and followed politics closely. The discussion that followed became heated at times, but as Dad listened to Daniel's arguments, he had to admit he respected his thinking process.

"Well, I disagree with all of your conclusions, Daniel, but I'm impressed with the depth of your analysis," he said with a rueful grin. He couldn't resist adding, "But you still can't have the car on Election Day."

"He can take mine," Mom said, smiling. She didn't agree with Daniel's politics either, but she was proud that he was able to think for himself and was taking voting seriously.

Daniel's a lucky teenager—both of his parents respect his maturity and his right to his own opinions. His dad knows how to disagree with him, yet maintain a good father-son relationship and even joke about their differences.

The more central to our lives and the more strongly held our values and beliefs are, the more difficult it will be for us to truly honor our teenager's right to believe differently than we do, and to adopt different values. Nowhere is this more difficult than in the areas of politics and religion, where people tend to hold passionate opinions about what is "right" and what is "wrong."

We may feel that our children's interest in exploring different religions is a personal affront to our cherished beliefs. Of course, the more we resist their right to explore, the more they will be obliged to defend it. No matter how upset we may be by their political and religious explorations, we can still listen to them, take their questioning seriously, and respect their right to reach their own conclusions.

Honoring the Unique Qualities of Each Child

As our kids move through adolescence and their own individual qualities and personality traits become more firmly established, their strongest areas of interest and the ways in which they are gifted become increasingly clear. It is this unique combination of qualities and talents that we must honor, no matter how surprising or unfamiliar they may be to us.

Fourteen-year-old Sherry was into ice hockey in a big way. Where her mother had grown up, there had been no ice hockey at all, much less a girls' team. So when Sherry brought home all her equipment from school, her mother had never seen anything like it. When she put on her padding to play goalie and proudly tromped into the kitchen, her mother barely recognized her.

It wasn't easy for Mom to be enthusiastic about her daughter's latest interest, although she had already spent many seasons watching her compete in team sports. The truth is, she was always the one standing on the sidelines, her heart in her throat, fearful that her daughter would be injured and end up being rushed to the emergency room. Dad wasn't a much more enthusiastic sports fan. Both of them wondered where Sherry's passion and agility had come from—it certainly hadn't come from either of them.

One day, Sherry announced excitedly to her parents, "Our team's up for the state's finals, and I could be nominated for the All-Stars!"

Mom and Dad were caught by surprise. They had both been relieved that the hockey season was just about over, and that their daughter was still in one piece. Now they knew that the season would continue, and even more competitively than before. So to their ears, this bit of news just sounded like more danger. It was hard for them to muster up the appropriate enthusiasm.

Sherry saw their hesitation and interpreted it as a lack of interest. "You could be more excited, you know," she said, sarcastically to cover up her disappointment.

Now Mom and Dad had to explain what their concerns were, and reassure her of their enthusiastic support. They needed to learn how to view Sherry's athletic involvement through *her* eyes and do more than merely tolerate it. Honoring her passion meant realizing what sports meant to *her* and overcoming their own personal concerns about her safety.

We honor our teenagers when we respect and appreciate what they value, even if it goes against our grain. This goes for their music, as well, no matter what we may think of it. It's a good idea to take five minutes to sit down with our kids every now and again and listen to their favorite song, even if it is excruciating for us. This is also a good way of keeping the lines of communication open with them: next to their friends probably nothing is as close to their hearts as their music. If we find the lyrics troubling or offensive, we can talk to our teens about it after we've listened to them. By sharing their music with us, they're showing us they want to stay connected and be understood.

Honoring One's Father and Mother

One of the most common complaints parents of adolescents have is that their teenagers are rude and disrespectful to them. Teens may ignore their parents when they're speaking, answer back, yell, or engage in any number of other irritating kinds of behavior. This is one of the ways teens express their anger at us and blow off steam as well. It's also a great way to distract us from whatever the issue at hand is. We can get sidetracked by reacting to their rudeness, and things can escalate very quickly. Often the real issue is forgotten and never gets resolved.

"Don't disrespect your mother," Dad warns fourteen-year-old Jack, lobbing another attack in this family's ongoing "world war."

"Well, she's being a real A-hole," Jack replies, instantly rising to the challenge.

Now Dad and his son are squared off, with nowhere to go. What was the original conflict about? Does anybody know? Are they going to deal with the real issue, whatever it is, or degenerate into yet another round of name-calling and punishment?

There's nothing to be gained in engaging in power struggles of this kind. Let's be realistic—hard as it is to accept, a certain amount of emotional acting out has to be tolerated during adolescence. It does no good for us to lose our cool when this happens. After all, we're the adults. As much as possible, we should try to keep the focus on the issue at hand and ignore our kids' momentary rudeness. At least we can take comfort in knowing that other parents of teens are going through the same indignant exchanges with their kids.

However, if teens begin to threaten members of the family or others with physical violence, that's another story. Violent or abusive speech or behavior should never be tolerated, and when it occurs it's a clear indication that immediate professional help is needed. This magnitude of problem cannot be handled within the family alone.

We want our teens eventually to be willing and able to honor us, their parents. We have to remember that they have quite a bit of maturing to do before they get to that point; certainly, though, we want some modicum of respect while they're growing up. However, we need to remember that *authentic* respect can't really be demanded, and this is the only kind that really counts in the long run. We can't force our teens to respect us, and attempting to do so will lead at best to stiff politeness, with resentment and disrespect simmering beneath the surface.

The most effective way to teach our teenagers to respect us is by treating them with respect and being respectful in our other relationships. Remember, we are the ones who set the standards for behavior in our homes. As our teens move through their adolescence, they'll gradually come to see us in a different light based on how we behave and who we are. True respect for us will develop and grow over time as our teenagers become young adults and get to know us as people, not just as their parents.

Divorce Is Challenging

One of the most difficult times to model respect for our teens is during a divorce. This is when parents are most likely to behave badly—not just in relation to each other, but toward the children as well. It's such a common problem, there's even a professional label for it—diminished parental functioning. During a divorce, when there's often so much anger between spouses, one of the most challenging tasks is to act in the best interests of the children, including the teenagers.

How parents treat each other during the divorce process and in the years that follow teaches children of all ages more about respect and honor than a million lectures on the subject. These lessons are especially relevant for teenagers, who are either just waking up to the thrill of romantic involvement or beginning to organize their own lives around intimate relationships.

The challenge for divorced parents is to respect each other by cooperating as co-parents and to honor each other by doing their best not to diminish each other in their children's eyes. If there are problems with the way the ex-spouse is parenting, our teenagers will eventually figure it out and will come to their own conclusions about how to relate to that parent. In the meantime, we need to bite our tongues and refrain from trying to sway them to one side or another. Asking kids to choose sides puts them in an impossible situation emotionally, and isn't fair to them. Admittedly this is far easier said than done, but the more our teens are caught in the middle, the more difficulty they will have adjusting to the realities of divorce and maintaining good relationships with both parents.

Divorce has been called a crazy time, and the temporary insanity can last far longer than the legal process. Sixteen-year-old Brian's parents had been divorced for a few years when his mother accused his father of breaking into her house while she was on vacation. This was very upsetting to Brian, who didn't know what to think. A police report was filed, detailing a list of items missing from the house—an old tool box, a picture frame, and boxes of his dad's old financial records which had been forgotten about and left in the attic. Nothing of material value was taken. Both parents hired attorneys and went to court over the matter.

"Who else would take your dad's old junk?" Mom asked Brian. "She's crazy," Dad said to him calmly. Poor Brian was caught in the middle, unwilling to believe that his father would stoop so low as to break in and enter his mother's house, and equally upset to think that his mother would think so ill of his dad.

A few months later, at Christmastime, Brian and his mother were decorating their usual size Christmas tree and ran out of ornaments. The tree looked bare to them. They stared at it together and then at each other, slowly realizing what this meant.

"He took Christmas tree ornaments, too. I just didn't know it until now," Mom said. Brian said nothing. But when he visited his dad's house over vacation, he noticed the missing ornaments hanging on his dad's tree. He didn't know what to say or do. He knew it wasn't really his battle, but it clearly affected him and his relationship with his father, who still insisted he was innocent. Brian knew now that he couldn't really respect or trust his father. But he couldn't side completely with his mom, either, because then he'd feel disloyal to his father. In the end, Brian lost respect for both of his parents. It seemed to him that their anger with each other was more important to them than his emotional well-being. Hadn't they considered how their behavior would affect him?

No matter how intense the animosity surrounding a divorce, it's absolutely essential for both parents to keep in mind that teenagers will learn critical lessons about relationships from the way their parents treat each other through this difficult process. Admittedly it can be very hard to keep to the high road, especially in the heat of battle. However, we have to make every effort to consider the impact our words and actions have on our children. What we do during difficult times will determine whether or not we deserve our teenager's deep and abiding respect. It is this kind of fundamental respect that influences the nature of our lifelong relationship with our adult children.

Kids Need Heroes and Heroines

Teenagers need heroes and heroines in their lives—role models to respect, be inspired by, and emulate. They need to know that ordinary people "just like them" can persevere, accomplish their goals, and be honored by the community. This gives them hope, and a sense of purpose and direction.

Unfortunately, the most readily available "heroes" in our society tend to be stars from the movies, TV, music, and sports. But these heartthrobs are not always the best role models, to say the least. They appear on the scene fully packaged, glamorizing sex and money, and often representing a rather shallow set of values. It's much better for teens to have people they know as their role models. Then they can see the steps their heroes have had to take along the way to their success, how they overcame obstacles, and how they persisted in the face of discouragement.

When Jasmine was growing up, her teenage cousin Savannah took care of her most afternoons while her mom worked. Jasmine went everywhere with Savannah and her friends. Unfortunately, a few of the friends had babies while they were still in high school. Even though these teenage pregnancies were a strain on both the young mothers and their families, there were always fun showers and celebrations with loads of presents and excited congratulations to welcome the new babies. In the midst of one of these parties, Jasmine turned to her cousin and asked, "Don't you want to have a baby of your own, Savannah?"

Laughing, Savannah answered her with a hug. "You're all the baby I want right now. I'll have my own babies after I graduate from college and can really take care of them myself."

Jasmine never forgot those words as she watched Savannah work her way through college. Because Savannah had to pay her own tuition, it took her six years, not just four. But she never complained, and she kept at it. When Jasmine was a teenager, she attended Savannah's college graduation ceremony, and by then she too knew exactly what her own goals were—she wanted to be just like her cousin! The feeling of pride she felt as she watched Savannah walk across the stage and hold up her diploma triumphantly was an inspirational moment that helped carry her through her own struggles to get her degree.

We can also be on the lookout for other local heroes. With some extra thought and effort on our part we can find examples of men and women who embody the values we want to instill in our teens.

Don't be discouraged if you don't get an enthusiastic response out of your teen when you do this. Do it anyway. Provide him with examples of positive role models close to home who are being honored.

"Remember your third-grade teacher, Mr. Thompson?" Mom asked fifteen-year-old Caleb one day.

"Yeah, sure, what about him?" Caleb asked, mildly curious.

"Well, he just received an award for being a Little League coach for twenty years. Here's his picture in the paper."

"Oh yeah, I remember him."

No matter how blasé their response, never doubt that small doses of such information do make a positive impact on our teens. The cumulative effect of these stories is a far more effective and pleasant way to influence them than by trying to lecture them about values. We want to make sure our teens are hearing some messages that will counteract, or at least balance, the enormous impact of the pop culture that constantly surrounds adolescents. Highlighting positive models close to home can help our teens identify real heroes and heroines who will inspire them in ways we value.

Being There for Our Kids

The whole point of adolescence is to grow up. These years are a transition between childhood and young adulthood. Our teenagers have to come to terms with their unique gifts as well as their realistic limitations. As they move through adolescence, our influence wanes but never disappears. We want our teens to become adults who can respect themselves, know what they believe in their hearts, and take the steps to live out their own dreams for themselves. In our complex world, this is quite a challenge.

Sometimes we may feel as if we're parenting in the dark, without quite knowing what's really going on in our kids' lives. Fortunately, most teens work their way through the potential minefield of adolescence and come out on the other side of it intact. (Just think for a minute about some of the things you did that your parents never knew about.)

There will always be some aspects of our teens' lives that we know nothing about. We can't control that—our teenagers are too good at keeping secrets from us when they want to and feel they need to. However, we can always encourage them to respect themselves by listening to their own needs, taking care of themselves, and feeling good about what they do for themselves.

Our teens face an almost overwhelming number of difficult decisions every day—about how they behave, what they think and believe, who they hang out with, and what they tell us, their parents, about it all. The choices they make will have a profound impact on the kind of people they become. We want our teens to take the time to reflect on the decisions they're making in their young lives and on the kind of person they're becoming. This is the best way for them to have the chance to grow into self-respecting adults who are able to weather the challenges of adulthood.

If teenagers live with trust, they learn to tell the truth

W e can take it for granted that our kids will do at least some of the things most normal teenagers do. They will likely test their limits, lie, be outrageously emotional, experiment with drugs and alcohol, fall in love, eat junk food, be almost unbelievably self-absorbed, come home late, ignore us, explore their sexuality, drive too fast, fight with us, get tattoos or body piercings, smoke cigarettes or marijuana, forget to call, get bad grades, waste their money, listen to terrible music, cheat in school, dye their hair, start a business, go on road trips—and in general live these years passionately and sometimes recklessly.

We want them always to feel free to tell us the truth about what they're doing, because that gives us our best chance to protect them, to the extent that this is possible. Yet we know our teenagers will not always tell us the whole truth. Teens are secretive almost by nature. Part of their becoming independent is about *not* sharing everything with us. We want to respect their right to have their own private lives, yet we also want to be sure that they're safe. So we have to rely on their ability to discern between when they should tell us about something and when it's okay to keep a secret.

For our teens to be able to do this, they have to feel safe enough to trust us with the truth, especially when they're making critical decisions. They need to know we won't panic, embarrass them, or become punitive or controlling. Grounding them for a decade won't work. We simply have to rely on their willingness to trust us. We have no way of knowing what they're up to, unless we hire private detectives to follow them around, and if that's what it comes down to, we've already lost them. We need to be able to trust them and they need to be able to trust us.

When they do trust us and confide what's really going on in their lives, we must first acknowledge them for having the maturity to tell us. Then we have to live up to their trust. Often we won't be happy about what we're hearing, but we have to remind ourselves that we'd rather know than not know what's really going on in their lives. We need to put aside our own fears and upset feelings, and help our teens to think through the situation they're in and how best to handle themselves. When our kids come to us with their problems, we can look at it as an opportunity to teach them how to engage in effective problem solving—how to determine what's really going on, explore various options, choose the best course of action, and then reflect on what they've learned. If our teens don't feel safe enough to trust us with the truth, they'll miss the guidance we can give them as they learn to solve the problems of everyday life.

Fifteen-year-old Luis was hanging out with Katherine at her house one day when he told her about how he had seen their mutual friend Rebecca smoking cigarettes. Later in the afternoon, Katherine casually mentioned this to her mother, and Luis got upset with her.

"Why did you tell her?" he demanded as soon as they were out of earshot. Luis's opinion was that all parents were like enemy spies.

"Oh, my mom won't say a word," Katherine assured Luis. "I can tell her anything."

"What did she say?" he asked. Now he was curious.

"Not much. She wasn't surprised," Katherine answered. "She just wanted to know how I felt about cigarettes and smoking, and all."

"Oh," Luis answered. He knew that he wouldn't have been able to have any such conversation with his mother, that she would have just yelled at him about the kind of friends he had.

Katherine and her mother enjoy a high level of trust in their relationship. Mom didn't panic over the news that a friend of her daughter's was smoking. She didn't "play cop," getting on the phone to call the girl's mother, nor did she assume that Katherine would also start smoking. She simply took the information in stride, and gave Katherine the opportunity to talk it over with her calmly.

There are limits to this level of trust and confidentiality. If Katherine had confided in her mother about something that was immediately life-threatening—a friend who had talked about committing suicide, or someone who was involved in serious substance abuse—Mom would need to take action, first letting Katherine know that it was her responsibility to do so. When teenagers trust us enough to tell us the truth about a dangerous situation, they're also trusting us to take action to protect them and their friends.

The more our teenagers trust us, the more they will let us in on their lives, and the more likely we will be able to intervene when necessary. If our kids can't trust us with the truth, we won't have a clue about what's really going on in their lives. Kids can be experts at concealing the facts, and that's just what they do if they feel it's the only choice they have.

Luis and Katherine's friend Rebecca didn't have the kind of trusting relationship with her mother that Katherine did with hers. When she came home one night, her mother met her at the door, took one whiff and said, "You reek of cigarette smoke."

"I know, Mom," Rebecca agreed. "It was awful. Almost everyone at the party was smoking."

"Were you smoking?" Mom asked, directly and specifically.

"Oh, no. I was just glad to get out of there," Rebecca lied, looking her mother straight in the eye.

"Oh, good, " Mom said, relieved. Perhaps on some level she suspected Rebecca was lying, but she had no real proof and so had to let it go.

Our teens can be experts at deceiving us. We can ask them the clearest and most direct questions possible, and they can look us straight in the eye and lie. Unless we have built a relationship with them in which they know they can trust us with the truth, we will have no idea of what's really going on.

Can You Handle the Truth?

If we really want our teens to be honest with us, we have to be prepared for the times when they do tell us the truth and it's hard to take. We may be surprised by the seriousness of situations that they are able to describe in a matter-of-fact way. At these times we need to keep our cool, and remember that their willingness to tell us the truth about a difficult situation means that they want us to help them handle it.

Driving home from the grocery store one day, Mom offhandedly asked her fifteen-year-old daughter, Kelsey, "What do you hear about drug use at school?"

Kelsey answered quite truthfully, "Oh, there's everything from heroin to ecstasy."

Mom wasn't totally prepared to hear this news, and she certainly wasn't prepared for Kelsey's nonchalant tone. She knew intellectually that there were drugs at every school, but it was upsetting to hear about this reality, coming from her own daughter.

She tried to maintain her calm, saying, "You know I don't want you trying any of that stuff."

"I know, I know," Kelsey said, beginning to tune her out.

"But what's most important to me is that we can always talk about it," Mom added. "Whatever you've done, I want you to know you can always come to me."

Now there was an awkward silence. Mom had no idea what Kelsey was thinking, but she waited patiently.

After a long pause, Kelsey said, "Well, you know that party I went to a few weeks ago? One of the kids there was taking drugs, and she had a bad reaction."

"What happened?" Mom asked in a concerned tone of voice. This led to an open discussion about drugs—from how to say "No" to what to do in an emergency. If Mom had panicked or gone into lecture mode, Kelsey would have clammed up immediately. Just by starting the conversation with a statement of her position on drugs she had almost lost her daughter. It was her clarification that honest communication was the most important thing to her that kept the conversation going.

Mom can't rely on Kelsey not ever to try drugs. The chances are about fifty-fifty that she will experiment with something somewhere along the way. In this conversation, Mom is building the trust necessary for Kelsey to be able to tell her the truth, no matter what she does. This may turn out to be a lifesaving precaution later on.

We have to be realistic—we can't control our teenagers' behavior. But it's still our responsibility as parents to clearly and firmly state our position on the issues that loom large for adolescents. It's even more important, though, to develop and maintain the trust necessary for truthful, open communication and for our genuine connection to our teenagers and their world.

Our First Priority Is Their Safety

Our first priority is our teenagers' safety. Just as we gradually came to trust that our young children would always look both ways before crossing the street, we eventually have to trust that our teens will know how to take care of themselves in a variety of dangerous and unpredictable situations.

We all worry when our kids go out with friends, take the car, come home late, or forget to call us. And the unfortunate truth is, we have a lot to worry about. Adolescence is a dangerous time. However, we don't want to stunt our teens' healthy growth toward independence, so we have learn to trust that they will make rational decisions. The problem is that this learning process takes time, and before our teenagers grow up they will almost inevitably make some terrible decisions, just as we once did.

Late one Sunday afternoon, thirteen-year-old Ritchie bounced into the house. "Guess who brought me home!" he asked his dad, barely containing his excitement.

"Who?"

"Sean's older brother, that's who," Ritchie proudly announced. "In his new jeep!"

"Oh," Dad said, slowly realizing the potential for trouble.

"It was great! We had the music all the way up, and I got to ride shotgun!"

Knowing Sean's older brother's habits, Dad asked, "Was there any beer in the car?"

"Oh, no," Ritchie replied. "He left the beer at the house."

"So, he had been drinking?" Dad continued calmly.

"Yeah, but he just had one beer. I saw the can in the kitchen."

"But how do you know whether that was his first beer or his fifth?" Dad asked.

Ritchie looked a little put out. "Aw, Dad, it was just two miles. And the jeep is brand-new," he answered, with that initimitable and deeply flawed adolescent logic.

"Well, I'm glad you got home safe and sound," Dad said. "You were lucky."

"Lucky?" Ritchie asked, still not understanding.

Dad looked at his son and put on his most serious face. "You got into a car with a driver who'd been drinking," he said. "Accidents can happen even on a two-mile drive, and in fact most accidents *do* happen within a short distance of people's homes."

"Aw, Dad . . . ," Ritchie began.

"No," Dad said, stopping him. "You know how 'designated drivers' work?" Dad changed the subject to catch his son off guard. Ritchie looked puzzled, but stopped defending and listened, curious where his father was going with this. "They don't drink at all 'cause it's too hard to tell whether someone's had one drink or five, whether it's safe for them to drive or not," Dad explained.

Now Ritchie was beginning to understand. Still he repeated, a bit more lamely this time, "But it was a new jeep."

"I know it was, son," Dad said, patting Ritchie on the shoulder and saying again, "I'm glad you got home safely."

Ritchie knew the rule about "no drinking and driving." He just didn't know that the situation he had just been in fell into that category. He was simply too young and inexperienced, and didn't realize that no drinking literally meant no drinking at all. We have to remember that our teenagers' brains work differently from ours and they need help learning things we take for granted. Yelling at him or punishing him wouldn't have taught him anything, except not to be so open and honest with his parents in the future. Instead, Ritchie's dad helped him understand how to apply the drinking and driving rule in real life so he could make better decisions in the future. This will serve him well as he moves beyond adolescence and faces the drinking-and-driving issue again and again.

What we really want is for our teens to get through adolescence safely, in one piece. They need our help to learn how to make sane, rational decisions about their own safety. It won't help to tell them to avoid situations that we know they will almost certainly find themselves in. If we do that, they will be tempted to cover up rather than ask for our advice about what to do if they happen again. And, unfortunately, our teenagers' ability to think rationally and maturely doesn't develop soon enough to handle the complex situations typical of adolescence. As parents, we have to start at the very beginning of adolescence to help them to learn how to think through situations and come to the best decision for themselves.

Confidences and Confidentiality

When our teens do tell us the truth about what's happening in their world, we are likely to learn information about other teenagers that places us in perplexing or awkward moral and social dilemmas from time to time. For example, what do we do if our teen tells us another kid is shoplifting or drinking too much at parties? Although these are signs of trouble, and not insignificant matters, they are not clearly life-threatening. How do we know when it's right to be discreet and maintain confidentiality, and when it's right to call the other kid's parents and inform them of a serious problem?

If we have maintained open and honest communication with our kids, we will face this dilemma more than once during their teen years. These are complex situations, and each one needs to be eval-uated on an individual basis. There are no simple solutions, and we may not feel entirely comfortable with the decisions we make. How-ever, when we find ourselves in this kind of dilemma, it is actually a good sign, for it means our teens trust us enough to let us in on the real complications in their lives and are willing to let us help guide them through it all.

Haley, a senior in high school, was going to the prom with her boyfriend, Dylan, with whom she had had a serious relationship for over a year. Haley told her mother she was going to be sleeping over at Carol's house, but actually she and Dylan had made reservations at a local hotel, where they planned to spend the night together af-ter the prom.

When Haley's mother mentioned to her daughter that she was

going to call Carol's mom to confirm the sleepover arrangements and thank her, Haley panicked. Carol, who trusted her mother to understand the situation completely, however, assured Haley that her mom would "cover" for her.

Carol's mother was very unhappy about being put in this position, and calmly explained to her daughter why this presented a conflict for her. "So you want me to lie to Haley's mother?" she asked Carol.

Suddenly Carol began to see that the situation was not quite as simple as she had previously thought. "Well, I didn't think about it like that," she said.

"What would I say to Haley's mom when she calls the morning after the prom and wants to speak to her daughter?"

Carol hadn't thought this far ahead. "Tell her we're still asleep?" she tried halfheartedly. But she could see this wasn't going to work.

Now mother and daughter looked at each other and laughed, "Now what are we going to do?" Mom asked.

"I don't know," Carol admitted.

The most important relationship for Carol's mom is the one with her own daughter. She wants to preserve Carol's trust in her and the honesty between them. However, she doesn't want to lie to Haley's mother. Furthermore, if her own daughter were in this situation, she knows she would not want another parent to lie to her.

By not overreacting, and by being able to discuss the situation calmly with Carol, Mom taught her how to think about the way things are likely to unfold and to recognize the moral dilemma involved. By honestly facing a complicated situation together, they became a team. As they continued to discuss it, Mom asked Carol to consider how she got into this situation in the first place, reminding her gently but firmly that she put both of them in an awkward position by saying that she would lie for Haley.

There was a lot for Carol to learn in this situation, and if the whole thing had turned into a heated conflict between her and her mother, she would never have had the chance to reflect on her own responsibility in the matter, or the moral questions involved.

"This is really Haley's problem, not yours or mine," Mom said. "You'd better let Haley know that I won't cover for her." She knew that Carol's intentions to help her friend were good, but she wasn't willing to lie to another mother about the whereabouts of her child. Carol understood why she was wrong to get herself into this situation, and she knew that her mother was right not to lie to another parent.

The real conflict to be worked out here is between Haley and her parents. By insisting on telling the truth, Mom helps Carol extricate herself from a complicated situation and also provides Carol with a good model of conscientious and responsible behavior to follow.

We will all face comparable situations with our teens—situations that raise complex issues that can't be solved simply. We want our teens to develop the ability to think through such situations and to consider all the possible outcomes and their meanings, and to weigh what is most important and identify what they think is right. The best place for them to learn how to do this is at home.

The Importance of Not Interrupting

If we want to encourage our teenagers to talk to us, we need to create a receptive atmosphere in the home. We want them to feel free to share their concerns with us, to let us know what they're doing, and, in general, to use us as their sounding boards. To create this kind of open atmosphere we have to be readily available to them and listen to them when they feel like talking.

It often seems as though our teens most want to talk with us when we're either very busy or half-asleep. We may be rushing out of the house or just settling into a nice nap when they decide to open up an important topic of conversation. Whenever possible, we need to set aside our own agenda and be available for these conversations. We have to be able to catch our kids when their mood is right for opening up. Teenagers learn quite quickly when their parents are too busy for them, and when they do, they take their thoughts, questions, and stories elsewhere, usually to their peers. We want to do everything we can to encourage our teens to talk to us about what's most important to them even if that means being inconvenienced.

Once our teens do begin to talk with us, we have to listen carefully. This means listening both quietly and patiently. It's okay to ask a few questions, but not so many that the conversation begins to feel like an interrogation. We also need to refrain from jumping to conclusions, assigning blame, or overreacting emotionally before our kids have finished talking. We have to give our teens time to tell their stories their way, to find the right words to express how they're feeling, and to let us know what's really happening in their lives. If we can learn to sit quietly and listen, our teens will fill up the empty space with their thoughts, feelings, fears, and aspirations. That's much better than our filling up the silence with lectures and unsolicited advice.

"I was driving home, and this guy was in the car next to me at the light," sixteen-year-old Michelle began. "Then he pulled along side, honking, and waved me over. I pulled over—"

"You did what?!" Mom interrupted sharply, terrified at what might have happened. "I told you never, ever to pull off the road!"

Dad joined in with Mom, immediately threatening to withdraw Michelle's driving privileges. "You shouldn't be on the road alone at night anyhow. Clearly you're not responsible enough."

With this kind of response, how likely do you think it is that Michelle will continue to tell the rest of her story honestly? She was trying to talk with her parents about a situation that concerned her, but now she was faced with the more immediate problem of dealing with hysterical parents.

"You know who it was?" Michelle smiled, confidently. "It was Billy, from my old school."

"Oh, Billy! How is he?" Mom asked. "Where's he going to school now?" She had always liked Billy.

Unfortunately, it wasn't really an old schoolmate, and even if it had been, Michelle's parents should not have been so easily distracted from the real issue, which was their daughter's safety. Their hasty overreaction to Michelle's story had interrupted the important discussion that needed to take place. They needed to walk through the steps of appropriate decision making in such a situation with their daughter: "What could you have done instead of pulling off the road? What would you have done if the guy had pulled a weapon on you? What was your escape plan?"

Teenagers still have a long way to go developmentally when it comes to analytical thinking and problem solving. We can't expect them to be able to think like grown-ups. This is one of the reasons we want them to trust us enough to talk things over with us—so that we can give them another perspective, and the benefit of our greater life experience and maturity. If Michelle's parents had listened to her story all the way through, they could have helped her understand the seriousness of the risk she had taken and explore alternative courses of action with her. Suppose they had been able to listen to her whole story, before responding.

"This guy got out of his car and walked over to my window. He was a lot older than I thought he was," Michelle continued. "I didn't know whether to roll down my window or not."

"What did you do?" Mom asked, holding her breath. These are not easy stories for parents to hear. They're like our worst nightmares come true.

"I rolled down the window partway, but I kept the car in drive just in case," Michelle answered. Telling the story, she began to have a sinking feeling as she realized the potential danger she'd been in.

"That wouldn't have been good enough if the guy had a gun," Dad said matter-of-factly.

There was a momentary pause, and then Michelle continued. "We just talked for a few minutes. I guess he thought I was older, but I told him I was just a junior in high school. Then he drove away, and I came right home."

"Did he follow you home?" Mom asked anxiously.

"Geez no, Mom," Michelle answered, impatiently, realizing that she hadn't even considered that possibility until now. All three were quiet for an uncomfortably long minute.

"I guess I was lucky, huh?" Michelle finally admitted.

Teenagers can only hear so much from us at one time. Mom and Dad would be wise not to overdo their reaction to the situation and discuss all the possible dire consequences at once. Michelle needs time to digest the fact that she made a bad decision and was just lucky that things turned out the way they did. Mom and Dad need the chance to calm down, to remind themselves that their daughter is both safe and, hopefully, wiser than before. Over the next few days, Mom and Dad can initiate some conversation about the incident, checking in with Michelle to see if she is willing to talk further. They can ask her, "Knowing what you know now, how would you rather have handled this situation?" This kind of question helps teens to be prepared for similar situations in the future. Most important of all, though, is that our teenagers know that they can tell us the truth and we will listen to them.

When Kids Lie

Almost overnight, lying and telling half-truths, misrepresenting the facts, avoiding questions, manipulating, and distracting become highly developed skills in our teens. They want desperately to feel independent well ahead of their being truly ready for the accompanying responsibility. Lying helps our teens feel as if they have their own lives, separate from their parents. In a way, it allows them to "play" at being independent when they're really not. Even though almost all teens are expert liars, sometimes we can still catch them at it. After all, we're not only more experienced than they are, but we were once teenagers ourselves.

It's helpful if we don't take it personally when we do catch our teenagers lying to us. Often, there is no significant betrayal involved. Teenagers just want to keep parts of their lives to themselves. What is important is how they make decisions about what to tell us honestly and what to lie about.

"That's a great sweater. Where'd you get it?" Mom asks sixteen-year-old Max.

"At the mall," Max answers.

How is Mom to know it's not at their local mall, but at the one an hour away where, theoretically, at least, the girls are prettier? While Max's answer is not exactly a lie, it isn't exactly truthful either. This is not the sort of half-truth to go to battle over with our kids. After all, it doesn't involve any high-risk behavior. The main thing it does is give Max a feeling of privacy and autonomy about his own life, which is something he craves.

Max is trying to stretch his independence. If he had asked for permission to go the mall an hour away, his mother might have said, "You don't need to go there. They have all the same shops right here." But Max did need to go there—he needed to go for the adventure, if nothing else. He needed to go to that mall in order to develop confidence in his ability to navigate a wider world and to feel competent in it.

As our teens tug at us, asking for more freedom, we often hold on to them, trying to keep them safe. Rarely does our timing synchronize so perfectly that we're gently letting go as they're gradually becoming ready for greater independence and responsibility. Normally it's more like a stressful tug of war. In the course of this process, we need to accept the fact that occasionally our teens will lie, or at least fudge the truth, in order to gain more freedom. As long as they're not in real danger, we need to live with these misrepresentations and half-truths, knowing that they're a normal part of adolescence.

However, when teens lie to avoid getting caught and punished for wrongdoing, it's another matter. Sometimes they don't want to face disappointing their parents, or they may just not want to be hassled or to take responsibility for their actions. This is a different kind of situation, and we have to deal with this kind of lying differently. Sometimes it's not lying, but an almost complete lack of communication, that is the signal. If our teenagers have stopped talking to us, or if most of our conversations consist of "How was the . . . ?" followed by a curt "Fine" and an abrupt change of subject, we can be sure they're not telling us the truth about their lives. It's also suspicious if all their stories sound too good to be true, and they seem to be avoiding all the normal ups and downs of adolescence.

When fourteen-year-old Cassie's best friend, Sandy, was caught shoplifting, Cassie's parents assumed that their daughter was likely to be doing the same and just hadn't been caught yet. They debated whether to search her room first or talk with her about it. They decided to be completely straightforward and direct with their daughter.

"We're worried about whether you might have been shoplifting, too, along with Sandy," Dad said, initiating the conversation.

Cassie opened her eyes wide. "No, I haven't. Why would you even think that?" she protested.

"Well, the two of you go everywhere together," Mom pointed out. "Did you know what she was doing?"

"Well, yeah, I did, but that doesn't mean I took anything," Cassie answered somewhat sullenly.

"How about we all go up to your room and take a look around?" Dad said. He stood up, and Mom was right beside him.

Cassie panicked. "You can't do that!" she said.

Her parents looked at her sadly. "Oh yes we can," Mom said calmly.

And so the truth came out. Cassie's parents found an inordinate number of CDs in her closet and a huge stockpile of makeup products. Although Cassie promised she would never do such a thing again, her parents knew not to trust her words. They knew that they all needed help to deal with this situation and get Cassie back on a positive track.

When parents catch their children in a pattern of lying, accompanied by other high-risk behavior, it's important to immediately seek professional help. These problems seldom go away on their own, and trying to pretend they will can only lead to more serious trouble in the future. There are times when the best thing we can do as parents is to admit that we need help dealing with our teens.

Staying in Touch with Other Parents

Teens have a way of telling their parents that they're only doing "what everyone else is doing," and insisting that their parents are the only ones to enforce certain restrictions put on their activities. However, when parents get together and compare notes, they often find that their concerns and rules for their kids are quite similar. We parents have to share information with other parents to help one another figure out the best way to protect all the kids in the community while they go about the difficult business of growing up.

Fifteen-year-old Mark's parents had heard about a party that had taken place while the parents were out of town. There was a lot of drinking and the house had been trashed.

"Were you at that party last Saturday?" his parents asked.

"No, I was over at Joe's," Mark said. "It was mostly older kids at that party."

Mark's mom was still suspicious, so she made a few phone calls to other parents. Sure enough, she heard through the grapevine that both Joe and Mark had been seen at the party, though briefly.

Mom and Dad confronted Mark with this new information. "We heard that you and Joe were at the party the other night," Mom said.

"Who told you that?" Mark asked incredulously.

"That's not important. What's most important to us is that we know where you are, and that you are honest with us," Mom said.

Mark protested, "But we didn't know where we would be. The party was down the street from Joe's house. All we did was just walk over to see what was happening. I can't call you every minute."

"That's true," Dad acknowledged. "But you can tell us the truth later, when we ask."

"I thought you'd yell at me if I told you," Mark grumbled.

"What's really important to us is being able to believe what you tell us because it's true."

"A lot of situations like this are going to come up in the next few years," Dad added, "and we want to know we can have honest talks with you."

If Mark's mom and dad had gotten caught up in their anger and disappointment, made threats, or laid down heavy punishments for Mark's behavior, they would have missed this opportunity to let him know that it's safe for him to tell them the truth, and always better to do so.

We need to have enough mutual trust that we will be able to have conversations that go beyond the surface and address the really important issues that arise during adolescence. We can't know what our kids are up to every minute or control them from our increasingly remote position. Our best means of influencing our teenagers is our ability to have honest conversations with them.

You Can Count on Me

We especially want our teens to be able to trust us in cases of emergency. We want them to know that they can call us at any time, from any place, and that we will come pick them up, no questions asked, without fear of repercussions.

How do we define "emergency" with our teens? Well, we should let our teens know that an emergency can be any time they or their friends feel uncomfortable or unsafe. These situations may involve drugs, alcohol, sex, violence, bad driving, illegal activity, or any combination of the above. And we need to remember that males are as much at risk as females for finding themselves in dangerous situations. If we want our teens to be able to say "No" to high-risk behavior and get themselves out of harm's way, then we have to be willing to support them 100 percent when they turn to us for help. When they are faced with the choice of proceeding with a potentially dangerous situation or calling us, we don't want them to think, "I can't tell my dad about this, he'll kill me!" We want them to know beyond the shadow of a doubt that their well-being and safety is always our greatest concern.

Ever since she was thirteen years old, Maria's parents had told her, "If you are in a bad situation, we will always come and help you, no matter what. Don't be afraid to call us, ever." Maria's mom also felt strongly that all the parents should look out for all the teenagers. So she added, "And if need be, we'll take care of any of the other kids, too. In fact, you tell your friends they can call us any time in an emergency if they can't reach their parents."

Maria did call her parents one night to come get her at the local mall. She was only fifteen at the time, but she looked eighteen. Some older boys were following her and her girlfriend around, and the girls were feeling uncomfortable. Maria's call came just as her parents were sitting down to dinner. Without hesitation, her dad left the table and drove right over to pick the girls up. They didn't really discuss what had happened that night, but a few days later Maria talked to her mom about the incident.

"At first, the guys seemed nice, and they were really cute," Maria said. "We talked to them for a while and then they wanted to take us to a party."

Mom mumbled, "Uh-huh," and remained quiet.

"We said we didn't want to go, but they wouldn't leave us alone even when we told them to go away," Maria said. "We got scared."

"You were right to be scared," Mom said. "You should always trust your instincts in a situation like that."

Maria nodded soberly.

"I'm glad you called us," Mom said. "Even if you'd told one of the security guards, they're not a lot of help in that kind of situation. It was much better to get out of there. You made a good decision."

Emergencies don't always have to be catastrophic events that occur in the middle of the night. They can occur any time our teens feel they are at risk. We want our teens to trust their own instincts when they feel unsafe and to call us immediately. By coming to their aid when they do call, we are letting them know that we care about them, we trust their judgment, and we trust them—all things they need to know.

Being Honest with Themselves

We want our teens to grow up to be truthful with us, but it's even more important that they learn to be honest with themselves. We want them to be able to face themselves, without denial or distortion, and to be able to reflect truthfully on who they are in the world. Their ability to be honest with themselves will form an important part of the foundation they need in order to make mature choices about how to live their lives.

Tracy was nineteen and returning to college for her sophomore year.

"This is the first time I'm going back to school feeling like I can really be who I am," she told her mother as she finished loading up the car.

Her mother was taken aback by her daughter's statement. "What do you mean?" she asked.

"Well, I don't have to be like the other kids at school, do what they do, keep up with them in any way. I can be whoever I want to be," Tracy explained.

Her mother looked at Tracy in a new light. "You're growing up. That's what that means," she said after a pause.

"Finally, huh?" Tracy laughed and gave her mom a big hug. Mom hugged her back, thinking but not saying, "That's for sure."

If teenagers live with openness, they learn to discover themselves

One of the most important ways our teenagers discover who they are and who they want to become is by seeing themselves through our eyes. They need to bounce ideas off us and see our reactions. And whether or not they admit it, our engaged presence and our interest in their ideas are absolutely essential to them as they experiment with new roles, beliefs, and interests and as they seek to form their own adult identities.

There will inevitably be disagreements during this process, but our general perspective and way of understanding the world continue to form an important part of our teens' inner foundations. They may question or challenge us, and they may rebel, but our standards remain important to them. It is, in fact, by questioning our rules, standards, and opinions that they find their way toward deciding what they really believe, and the way they will choose to relate to the world.

Being open to our teenagers means, first and foremost, being available to them. This includes spending both scheduled and unscheduled time with our kids—just being with them, and being open to what *they* want to talk about or do. Sometimes we have to make a conscious effort to put aside our own "agenda"—rushing to get our errands done, asking how they're doing at school, or telling them how to behave. We have to make time to just "hang" with our kids and follow *their* lead in a conversation. Admittedly, older teens are often too busy with their friends and their own activities to have much free time to spend with their parents. This is one good reason to develop the habit of spending time together early in adolescence. If they can enjoy being with us, if they feel affirmed and understood by us, our teens will make the time to spend time with us, no matter how crowded their schedules.

We have to strive to be open-minded with our teens, and avoid making snap judgments or losing patience with them. Our teenagers are in the process of discovering themselves, which means they are in a constant state of flux. They'll change their minds tomorrow about what they said today without a second thought, so often there's no point in getting upset over their sometimes dramatic proclamations. When they've said something particularly outrageous, try staying open to the idea, and see how long it takes them to arrive at a totally different position on their own.

There will be times when it's not so easy to listen with an open mind to our teens' thoughts and feelings. Teenagers seem to have a sixth sense for saying precisely the thing that's going to upset their parents the most. It's almost as if they're testing us to see whether we can really and truly accept them, whoever they are and however inappropriate their remarks. Our natural reaction in these instances may be to become defensive, argumentative, or controlling. When this happens, we need to take a deep breath, calm down, and decide how we really want to respond to our teens. We don't always have to agree with them, but we do have to remain consistently open and available to them. Just as when they were smaller, they need to know, deep in their hearts, that though we may not agree with some of their ideas or actions, we always accept and love *them.*

Besides being open-minded with our teens, we also need to be openhearted. This involves more than just passively accepting our teens' thoughts and feelings, or respecting their right to self-expression. They know when they're being humored, and they don't like it. True openness allows us to truly enjoy our teenagers, to take pleasure in them. So much is written about the conflicts and challenges of parenting an adolescent, and for good reason. However, we also want to encourage parents to open their hearts to their teenagers and be able to *enjoy* these years—to delight in their teens' process of questioning everything, their exploration of their new independence, and their discovery of themselves.

In the midst of all the emotional storms of adolescence, it's easy to lose sight of the fact that it's actually a privilege for us, as parents, to be able to witness and participate in this roller-coaster ride. We want to be open to our kids' day-to-day experience of discovering who they are as they grow into their adult lives. Most of us remember only too well how hard those years are. We can help our kids, not by telling them what to do or by trying to protect them from the difficult experiences they will inevitably have, but by being there for them emotionally—often just in the background, but always ready with a listening ear or a warm embrace when it's needed. The more open-minded and openhearted we can be with our teens, the freer they'll feel to explore their deepest thoughts and feelings with us. We don't really want to miss out on these last years of living with our kids. We want to know who they are and be an important and positive presence in their lives. But we will only be invited into their hearts if we honestly open ours to them.

Being Available Means Listening Without Judging

We want to hear stories from our teenagers' lives; we want to hear what they're thinking, how they're beginning to understand themselves and others; we want to hear their questions, doubts, and concerns as well as what's exciting and funny to them. If we are open to them, and create an atmosphere of true interest in what they have to tell us, they will share their world with us.

"Guess what happened in science lab today?" fourteen-year-old Giselle said eagerly. Her mother had just walked through the door after a tough day at work. She put down her things and hugged her daughter. "Come tell me about it while I grab a cup of coffee," she said.

"We had a fire in chemistry!" Giselle nearly exploded. "You should have seen the flame from Wayne's experiment! It almost reached the ceiling, and then the whole room filled up with smoke. It was *awesome*!" Gabrielle recounted as she followed her mom into the kitchen. "The fire trucks even had to come."

"Wow," Mom replied, wondering where the science teacher had been during all this excitement.

"We missed the next period because of the fire, and that was math. And I wasn't really ready for the test—boy, did I luck out!" Giselle continued.

Even though Mom was really tired, she was tempted to begin a parental lecture, and she would have been quite justified in making at least two important points: one, the threat of fire should be taken seriously, and two, Giselle should have been prepared for her math test.

When we find ourselves about to use the word "should" it's a clear tip-off that we're about to go into lecture mode. And even if we think what we're doing is "sharing" with our kids, or imparting our wisdom to them, the problem is that teens don't really listen to us when we lecture them. They hear "should" and their mind instantly goes somewhere else.

Giselle's mother knew this, so instead of lecturing, she replied, "I'm glad they got the fire under control right way. How did they get it out? What happened when the fire trucks came?"

Being open to our teens' experience means focusing on how *they* see the world, not the way we do. We may not think of a smoke-filled science lab as being "awesome," but kids do. We can be open in our response to such a report, refraining from lecturing with our kids, and at the same time guiding them gently toward a more mature perspective. Giselle's mother didn't contradict, criticize, or lecture her daughter, but she did introduce an adult perspective to the conversation by taking the threat of fire seriously. Then she followed up Giselle's story by asking her what happened next. Only much later in the conversation did Mom return to the subject of the postponed math test, by saying, "Well, I guess you've got a second chance to prepare for that test. How much time do you need to study?"

Often it may seem as though our teenagers most want to talk with us when we're stressed out, doing something important, or it's the middle of the night. However, it's best to welcome as a top priority our teenagers' sharing with us *at any time,* even when it's inconvenient for us. By being open and available to them most of the time, we encourage our teens to let us in on their world.

Being Open to All the Possibilities

Our teens come up with lots of ideas, most of which don't become realities. They're mentally trying out various possibilities, often just enjoying the fantasy or testing out how we'll react to various kinds of notions. By imagining and beginning to plan out an adventure, they are testing their wings, experimenting with their independence, and thinking about how they would actually carry their ideas out.

Two fifteen-year-old boys are planning to drive cross-country the summer after they get their driver's licenses. A sixteen-year-old girl wants to climb Mount Everest. A thirteen-year-old girl spends many hours practicing dance routines and singing along to her favorite music, telling her mom she wants to audition as a backup singer. A fourteen-year-old boy wants to go into the most undeveloped area of Guatemala to deliver medical supplies. It's so easy for us to panic when our teenagers tell us about their dreams. Immediately we see all the things that can go wrong. But being open to our kids doesn't mean telling them all the potential problems with their plans, or even sharing our fears about potential disasters with them. We need to respond delicately when they tell us about their dreams, respecting the inspiration underlying their often unrealistic schemes.

The parents of the future backup singer may not be thrilled with their daughter's aspirations, but can still say, "Everything begins with a dream." This statement is relevant to her fantasy about a music and dance career, and it also applies to anything else she may aspire to do in her life.

If we're lucky enough to hear about our teen's plans and dreams, we'll notice that they just keep coming up with new ones. We have to be careful not to discount their ideas just because they keep changing. Teens try on new ideas the way they try on clothes— to see how they fit, what they feel like, what the reaction of others will be. This kind of exploration is one of the ways they learn about themselves and how to develop ideas for their future. We don't want to discourage this process by focusing solely on the problems inherent in every new idea.

Every once in a while a teen will come up with an idea that he will continue to steadily develop, year after year, as he matures. Fourteen-year-old Stewart wanted to hire a helicopter to fly medical supplies to a village in Guatemala. His church had "adopted" the village, and he had learned a lot about the people who lived there, what their lives were like, and what their most crucial needs were. By the time he was sixteen, Stewart realized that simply delivering supplies wasn't a solution to all their problems and he also understood how difficult and possibly dangerous it would be to do. When he got to college, he realized that what the people in the village really needed, even more than medical supplies, was a waste management system. By the time he graduated from college, he had helped raise the money for twenty-five composting toilets, to be donated to the village. Stewart flew down to help install them with other members of his church and, although his parents were a bit worried about their son's safety, they were also very proud of him.

Stewart's parents had been open to his idea from the beginning, but they didn't take it seriously until years later, when they saw how determined he was about helping the people in Guatemala. Their openness to his interest from the beginning, however, had given Stewart permission to continue to develop his plan.

We can't predict which of our teenagers' dreams will mature and develop into realities. But we do need to be open to all of their ideas, no matter how far-fetched they seem at the time, so that we don't discourage them from dreaming. If we are there, really listening, we give them the opportunity to refine their plans and make them more realistic. As they talk about their plans with us, they begin to hear and see themselves in a new light. They discover who they really are in dialogue with us. It's a privilege to be part of that process.

Respecting Their Developing Philosophies of Life

It's inevitable that at some point during adolescence our teenagers will assume philosophical viewpoints diametrically opposed to ours. It helps to be prepared for this moment by seeing it as part of our teens' separation from us and one of the ways they discover who they are. We don't want to take it as a personal insult or mistakenly assume that they'll always feel this way.

Fifteen-year-old Sandra was studying economics from a global perspective, and she was beginning to view her father's career as a corporate executive in a new light.

"You've wasted your life, Dad," she announced out of the blue one Sunday afternoon. "You sold out for money."

Dad was speechless. Nobody had ever spoken to him this way. He was especially insulted because he was proud of how well he'd provided for his family, and Sandra, especially, had benefited with lots of nice clothes, exciting vacations, and summers at expensive horseback riding camps.

But he recovered quickly. "Does this mean you don't want us to buy you a car next year?" he asked.

Sandra blanched. "Well, no, but . . ."

"But what?" Dad asked, pushing his advantage.

"Oh, never mind," Sandra said, and walked out of the room.

Dad might have won the first round of that disagreement, but he lost the opportunity to explore with his daughter how she saw the world and how she was beginning to see her life. He could have responded in a variety of other ways that would have left the door open for further discussion. For example, he might have said "Ouch, that hits home!" or "How did you come to that conclusion?" or even, quietly, "What do you plan to do differently in your life?" These responses, if stated neither defensively nor aggressively, would have allowed Sandra to explore what she really thinks and feels with her dad, instead of closing off communication with sarcasm.

We also have to consider the possibility that her initial statement to her father was simply intended to shock him, with the sole purpose of getting his attention. It may have been a fifteen-year-old's clumsy attempt to connect with her dad. Unfortunately his immediate reaction was a negative one, simultaneously defensive and aggressive. It shut up his daughter, but it also closed the door to important communication.

When our teens challenge us in this way, we want to try not to make them "wrong," and us "right," but instead to engage them, connect with them, and rise to the challenges they present us with. We can only do that if we're open to whatever they say, no matter how personally threatening or even insulting it may be. Sometimes we may have to put our first reactions aside, and make an effort to understand their point of view, try to see things through their eyes.

This doesn't mean we have to always agree with our teenagers. We can accept their right to hold to their own viewpoints, while maintaining our own. But the minute we try to control our kids' thoughts or to persuade them to think more like us, we disrupt the conversation. Our teens are extremely sensitive to any attempts to control them, and immediately tune us out, withdraw, or engage us in arguments. This is the situation Sandra's dad found himself in. Now he had to figure out what he could do to open up the conversation again. He waited about an hour, giving both of them time to calm down, and then he approached her.

"Okay, I'm ready now to entertain the possibility that I've wasted my life," he began, with a slight smile. This was not quite a full apology, but at least he was letting her know that he knew he hadn't been exactly open to her in their previous conversation.

Sandra looked at him warily.

Understanding her hesitation, he continued, "What's the matter with wanting to provide for my family?"

With that invitation, Sandra was ready to engage again, and now she confronted him with some tough and challenging questions. Dad listened to Sandra as she spoke about her concern for the plight of people in developing countries, the environment, and the inordinate profits some people, including her dad, were making.

Dad listened carefully to everything his daughter had to say. Of course, none of the points she was making were new to him, but he didn't want to make the mistake of not listening to her again. By being open to her concerns and taking her questions seriously, Dad knew he was not only helping her develop her own critical thinking process, but he was also nurturing their relationship. And though they didn't change each other's minds, they did engage in a respectful dialogue about a meaningful topic.

Valuing What Our Teens Value

Being open to our teenagers means being ready to learn from them—being interested in the music they like, what they're reading, and who their friends are. We must be willing to enter into their world and be receptive to, or at least curious about, what's important to them. This means that we also have to be open to teen culture, much of which seems designed to offend us. What we need to remember is that just a few decades ago our own teen culture was equally dismaying to our parents. The worrisome question "What's this world coming to?" is asked by every generation of parents as their kids go through adolescence. As adults we need to have some perspective on this situation, and realize that teenage rebellion is a natural part of the process of growing up.

Our interest in their world must be genuine, however, for teens are experts at being able to discern hypocrisy. If we only pretend to be interested in their lives, they'll view it as condescending or phony. We must truly be able to value whatever our teenagers value. After all, this is the larger lesson—to be open and receptive to whatever is important to someone you love, even if you have no interest in it yourself. When we show interest in our teens and their world, they learn an important lesson about caring and generosity in relationships.

One evening, fourteen-year-old Erica had her music blaring out of her bedroom window. Her mother was sure that the neighbors could hear it, and she was embarrassed.

"Turn that thing down!" Mom yelled at her, through the door. No response. She repeated herself, yelling at the top of her lungs.

Erica opened her bedroom door and asked her mother, "Did you say something?"

Mom charged into the room and turned off the CD player. "There," she announced and took a breath. "How can you stand that stuff?"

We all know how important popular music is to teenagers. It's a central part of their culture and an important way they communicate with one another. Teens listen to music together in their bedrooms or over the phone; they go to concerts; they download music from the Internet, they trade CDs, and make personalized tapes with specially selected songs as gifts for each other. In their yearbooks, they quote from popular hit songs at least as often as they do from poetry or literature.

Erica's mother doesn't have to actually like the music her daughter listens to, but she does need to be open to it. She could just as easily have said, "Erica, you have to turn that music down a little or it's going to disturb the neighbors." She could have suggested that Erica listen with headphones, so that she could enjoy the full effect of the music without bothering others. She might even have asked, "What are you listening to?" If Mom had spent a few minutes listening, and then asked to see the lyrics from the CD cover, she would have shown Erica that she was interested in understanding what the songs meant to her.

To be able to communicate with our teens, we need to learn about their true thoughts and feelings. We have to have some understanding of their world, from the music they listen to to their favorite movies. This is relatively easy to do—all it requires of us is that we suspend our critical judgment and remain open. Leafing through teen magazines, reading an article here and there, or watching videos with our kids and talking with them about what their favorite parts were, or just being warm and friendly to our teenagers' friends will open up opportunities for meaningful conversation and sharing. Since so few grown-ups value what teens think, most kids will open up to parents who express genuine interest in them and their world.

A Time of Intense Feelings

One of the reasons music is so important to teenagers is that it helps them express the intensity of their feelings. We may think that their feelings are "just due to hormones," and that they will eventually calm down, but from the teenagers' perspective, their feelings are the most real part of their world.

We need to be open to and accepting of our teens' full range of emotions, from the highs to the lows. Whatever they're feeling in the moment is always the most important thing to them. Discounting or minimizing their feelings will only keep them from sharing with us. We want them to talk about their feelings with us so that they can gradually learn to understand themselves better.

"Don't you have a French test to study for?" Mom asked fifteen-year-old Paul, who was whispering into the telephone one night.

"Hold on a sec," Paul said into the receiver. Turning to his mom, he said, "Don't worry, I'll study. I'm busy right now." He gave his mother an intense look which she didn't quite understand, but she nodded and went back to the living room. She interrupted her son's conversation a few more times that evening, but Paul stayed on the phone, talking intently, for a couple of hours. The next day, Mom asked how the French test had gone.

"It was pretty hard," Paul admitted.

"It might have been easier if you'd studied for it instead of sitting on the phone all night," Mom said.

"Yeah, but . . ."

This is a critical point in the conversation for Mom. If she continues to press her point about the importance of studying, she'll miss the opportunity to discuss her son's emotional life with him. And at this point, his emotional life is far more important to him than his grades in French are.

"I was talking to Lara last night because she was so depressed," Paul explained. "She said she wanted to die, and that I was the only one she could talk to. I couldn't hang up!"

"That's pretty serious," Mom agreed. "What happened?"

"Well, I got her to calm down," Paul said, obviously proud of himself. "But I'm still worried about her."

"Me, too," Mom said. "Now I understand why you stayed on the phone for so long. I think this is too much for you to handle on your own."

"Yeah." Paul sighed, relieved that his mom understood. "I'm wiped out."

As Paul went through the story of Lara, he began to realize how stressed he was by the whole thing. He took a second look at his decision to stay on the phone rather than study, and gradually came to the conclusion: "Once was enough. I don't want to go through another night like that. It's too scary for me. What if she doesn't calm down next time?"

Mom nodded quietly in agreement. "I wonder if there's someone else she could talk to."

"Well, maybe a counselor or something," Paul reflected.

"You know, I really need to talk to her parents about this," Mom said. "We can't just do nothing. Her parents need to know what's going on so they can help her."

"I know, I know," Paul mumbled, not happy about how Lara would react to this news. "But let me talk to her first."

Mom didn't simply dismiss the situation as adolescent melodrama. She instantly shifted her focus from the French test to a matter that was obviously more urgent. By doing so, Mom shows her son that she understands the importance of his feelings, and also that parents can be counted on to help when things get tough. Paul needed his mom to say, "This is too much for you." He wasn't able to come to that conclusion on his own, even though he certainly felt like it. Both her presence and her mature perspective are a relief to Paul. He doesn't have to continue to wade through an emotional crisis that is far too difficult for him to handle or take on more responsibility than he should. He needs grown-up help and support, and so does his friend.

Paul would not have been able to have this conversation if he felt his mom didn't understand him and what's important to him. In general, teenagers won't let us know what's happening in their lives if they don't feel that we're open to them and their experiences. When this happens, they not only miss out on having our help in difficult situations, but they also lose out on the chance to learn about themselves by talking things over with us.

Sometimes our teens will hear themselves in a different way just by talking through their thoughts and feelings with their parents. They can begin to sort out their confusion by explaining to us what's going on and how they think and feel about it. However, if we over-react, panic, try to control them, take over, or worse yet, criticize them early in this process, they'll clam up immediately. We need to listen to the whole story and remain calm throughout. Asking occasional questions, just to clarify what they're saying, will keep the conversation flowing smoothly. Our primary role is to listen so our teenagers can reflect on their own thoughts and feelings, rather than have to deal with our reactions to what they're telling us.

Is It Possible to Be Too Open?

We can strive to be open-minded and openhearted with our teens, but we don't need to be *totally* open and honest about absolutely everything. We don't need to volunteer detailed information to our kids about our history of drug use, our sex lives, or our unresolved feelings toward an ex-spouse. In fact, these are the classic topics *not* to be discussed.

This doesn't mean that we lie to our teenagers, especially as they're likely to be too sophisticated to believe a total denial. However, it does mean that we are very selective about what information we give our kids and at what age and level of development. Our first consideration is the effect our example will have. For example, we might say to a thirteen-year-old, "Yes, I experimented with marijuana, but not until I was much older than you and then not for very long," whereas with a seventeen-year-old, we might say, "Yes, I smoked dope, but after a year or so, I just lost interest in it and stopped." These are subtle decisions that parents must make based on their own comfort level and their sense of what's best for their teenager.

Our teens may want to hear some stories from our adolescence, but they certainly don't need to be overwhelmed with full disclosure. Nor do we want to burden our teens with our old problems from childhood or from failed marriages. These types of stories can be discouraging or even depressing for our kids, and may leave them feeling that they have to take care of us emotionally or get away from us to protect themselves.

The point of sharing our experiences with our teens should be to teach or support them—to let them know we can understand what they're going through because we have gone through similar experiences. Talking about the mistakes we made and what we learned from them can be funny, and helpful, too. But we do always need to consider what kind of a role model we're presenting to our teens.

Our openness about ourselves should be an invitation for our teens to sort through their own thoughts and feelings, not listen to ours. An important part of the job of being a parent is to support and encourage our kids as they develop and mature. It's not their job to support us by listening to our problems. Even though our teenagers are not children anymore, they still need us to be their parents, not their friends. Becoming friends with our kids can only happen later, after they begin to establish themselves as mature adults, independent in their own lives.

"You won't believe what Dad just told me," fourteen-year-old Janice said to her mother as she hung up the phone.

"What?" Mom asked with a sigh, wondering what unpleasant surprise was coming next from her ex-husband.

"He's not coming to my graduation," Janice answered. "He's going to be on vacation."

"Well that's just like him, isn't it?" Mom replied with irritation. "He only does what he wants to do for himself. He hasn't changed a bit. Still just as selfish as ever . . ."

At this point, Janice will either run from the room in tears, scream at her mother, or fill in as her mother's therapist. None of these is a good option. Mom may think she's being open with her daughter, but she's really dumping her old frustrations with her ex onto her daughter. This isn't fair, and neither parent is really being open to Janice's needs—they're both acting in ways that are self-absorbed and harmful to Janice.

Janice's mom could have said, "I'm sorry to hear that," and resisted the temptation to vent her unresolved anger with her ex. It's hard enough for Janice to deal with her own feelings about her dad not coming to her graduation. She doesn't need the additional burden of dealing with her mother's anger toward her father.

By simply saying, "I'm sorry," Janice's mom would acknowledge her daughter's hurt feelings and leave plenty of room for Janice to continue to express herself. Mom doesn't really have to say much more than that—perhaps a well-timed question here and there, as Janice begins to talk. At some point, she might ask, "What are you going to say to Dad about this?" Questions of this nature would help Janice to consider how she wants to respond to her father. Although the situation is an unfortunate one, Janice has to learn to deal with her disappointment and move on. Her mother can be helpful in this process if she stays focused on Janice's needs and not her own.

Modeling Openness

We have to remember that the most powerful impact we can have on our teens is the model we give them by our own example. Our teenagers can learn from watching us how to marshal their inner strength and resources to meet the challenges they face. Life is not always easy, and we want our teens to have realistic expectations about what it may bring, as well as the resilience to rise to the occasion when they are called upon to do so.

Marilyn's mother had broken her ankle in the snow and it was taking a very long time to heal. In the spring, she started going to a special exercise class to recover full use of her leg, but the process of healing was slow and discouraging. Fifteen-year-old Marilyn watched her mother force herself to do the exercises at home, even though it was obvious that doing them was painful.

"Does it hurt?" Marilyn asked one day, as her mom was lying on the floor stretching her heel to the ceiling.

"Yup," Mom groaned.

There was no need for lectures here. The reality of the situation spoke for itself. Watching her mom work hard and persistently to gradually heal her ankle will leave an indelible impression on Marilyn. Seeing her mom struggle through this injury and persevere will serve as a valuable example for Marilyn to draw on when she faces similar challenges in her own life. We want our teens to have a model of responding to life with courage and perseverance.

It's okay to be open with our teenagers about how we sometimes struggle with changes in our lives. When we are under stress our ability to be flexible is a powerful example for our teenagers to see. Certainly our kids will encounter even greater changes and at a faster rate than we can even imagine. Learning how to adapt to new circumstances will be essential for them.

Ryan's dad wasn't prepared for the rate of change that he was confronted with during his career. When he was laid off from his job, he came to the rude awakening that he had become obsolete. His computer skills were out of date and needed to be completely upgraded. This was a major crisis point for him, as technology wasn't his strong suit.

Dad could have maintained a stoic facade and not talked about the employment crisis he was facing. Instead he talked about it freely at home, expressing his disappointment in the company for letting him go after decades of loyal service, as well as his worries about the family finances. It took him about a week to get over the shock. Then he signed up for some computer classes.

At first Dad had great difficulty with the new technology. It seemed as if he had to throw out everything he ever knew and learn things all over again with a totally different system. He even asked Ryan for some help at the beginning. But gradually he began to pick up speed, and eventually he became quite proficient. By the end of his course, he was even able to show Ryan a few new things on the computer. In the meantime, he began looking for a new job. After almost a year, he found a better job than the one he'd lost.

Ryan watched his dad throughout that year. He saw everything he was going through, and he also saw that his dad did not lose hope even when he was most discouraged. Ryan could not have received a more powerful lesson about adaptability, perseverance, and faith in oneself. Because Dad was open about what was happening in his life, Ryan felt more willing to talk openly about some of his own disappointments and struggles. He also didn't have to worry silently about what the family's fate would be—he knew his dad wasn't hiding anything important from him.

Even though they may appear to ignore us or live in a different universe, our teens are still learning from us. The more open we can be with our teens about our own experience of life, the more they will share what life is really like for them. They will learn that everyone has good times, not-so-good times, and some downright challenging times. The issue is how we, parents and teens alike, deal with these times. In the process of sharing with one another how we live our lives, our teens will be best able to discover who they are and who they want to become.

If teenagers live with natural consequences, they learn to be accountable

Simple as it may seem, most adults are still working on fully understanding the concept of natural consequences. Let's be honest: if we all had completely mastered the rules of cause and effect, we would all be the perfect weight and have great retirement plans.

We may intellectually understand the relationship between our behavior and potential outcomes, yet still not act in entirely rational ways. So why should we be surprised when our teenagers act without regard for the consequences of their actions? Learning to make wise decisions is a long-term process of maturation, and most of us are still involved in that process, too. We all realize the importance of accountability long before we are able to behave in ways that are consistently accountable.

If we think of learning to be accountable as a long-term developmental process, then we can more clearly see that our role as parents is to help nurture our teenagers' learning, rather than to control, discipline, or punish them for their shortcomings. Also, this process is one that begins in early childhood and continues throughout their entire lives. Young children begin to learn about natural consequences when they leave their toys in the driveway and the toys are run over or stolen. And just as it's difficult for us to allow our young children to learn the "hard way"—by experience—it may also be difficult to allow our teenagers to face the natural consequences of their actions. But sometimes that is the best way for them to learn.

Fifteen-year-old Sonia was treasurer of her ninth-grade class. The kids had raised a few hundred dollars with bake sales in order to fund an end-of-the-year dance. When she needed to give the faculty advisor the financial report, she panicked, and confided in her mother.

"I borrowed about fifty dollars from the class treasury a few months ago. I thought I'd be able to pay it back but I haven't, and now they're going to think I stole it."

Recognizing the seriousness of the situation, Mom responded, "You took money that didn't belong to you. That *is* stealing."

"You're not supposed to make this worse," Sonia replied impatiently. "You're supposed to help me!"

"How do you want me to help you?" Mom asked, suspicious of where this conversation was going.

"You can loan me the money, so I can pay back the school, and I'll pay you back by baby-sitting," Sonia said.

"Hmm. That may get you out of trouble this time, but it's not good for you in the long run," Mom answered. "I don't want you to think you can get out of this so easily. You need to face the music on this one."

"What do you mean?" Sonia asked.

"I think you need to tell your advisor exactly what you've done. Take full responsibility for your mistake and decide with him how to handle this and replace the money."

"No way!" Sonia replied sharply, frightened and adamant at the same time.

"I'll go with you if you want, but you created this mess and you're the one who has to find a way through it," Mom said. She was at least as adamant as her daughter.

Sonia and her mom went around and around on this one, but Mom wouldn't change her position. They talked about how Sonia had arrived at the decision to "borrow" money from the treasury and how she had rationalized to herself that this would be okay. Furthermore, Mom told Dad about it later that evening, even though Sonia didn't want him to know. Mom had insisted he needed to be included and kept informed about the situation. Dad was equally concerned and also volunteered to go with Sonia when she met with her advisor.

"I don't need both of you there," Sonia protested.

"Okay, but let me know what happens," Dad said.

Sonia practiced with her parents exactly what she would say to the advisor—how sorry she was, the fact that she knew it was her responsibility, and that she'd never do it again. She spoke to him the next day after school, while her mom waited outside his office in the corridor. When Sonia and the advisor came out of the office, Sonia looked greatly relieved. They had worked out a plan for Sonia to pay back the class treasury with her allowance and baby-sitting money and had agreed that the whole situation would be kept confidential, just between the two of them. Sonia also had to promise not to run for class treasurer again for at least a year.

"So what did you learn from all this?" Mom asked on the drive home.

"Handling the treasury is harder than I thought," Sonia admitted. "And more serious."

"You're really responsible for that money," Mom agreed. "Dad and I couldn't just rescue you by bailing you out. You have to learn to face the consequences and be accountable for your actions. You understand that, right?"

Sonia nodded. It was a tough lesson, but she did understand.

In this situation, Sonia was literally accountable for the missing money, which she had to pay back in full. This was a concrete way for her to make amends for her behavior. Being accountable means more than just saying "I'm sorry" when we do wrong. We have to teach our kids to take full responsibility for repairing any damage or pain they may have caused through their actions.

If Mom and Dad had protected Sonia from embarrassment by giving her a loan, she would not have had to face the natural consequences of her action. This may have encouraged her to think that she could get away with it again, and it would have fostered an unhealthy dependency on her parents at a time when she should be becoming more independent. The natural consequence of her action was having to admit to her advisor what she had done, and be held accountable by him.

Sometimes our job as parents is to send our teenagers to deal directly with the people who will hold them accountable. Our teens take on responsibilities that don't directly involve us. When they make mistakes of this kind, we have to resist the urge to protect them or make excuses for them, and thereby hinder their learning process.

Modeling Accountability

One of the ways we can model accountability for our teens is in the way we handle our own financial affairs. Probably the most common natural consequence of fiscal irresponsibility is debt. If we spend more money than we earn, we end up in debt. This may appear to be merely a simple and straightforward statement of fact, but a large percentage of parents today are uncomfortable with the amount of money they owe. The truth is, as a society, we have developed some unhealthy financial habits, and the model we are providing for our children is not always the best one.

Even though our teens may not know the exact details of our financial standing, they'll be sensitive to tension and concern about money pressures in the household. They'll notice if there are frequent phone calls from bill collectors, or if there are an unusual number of bills arriving in the mail. Knowing that their parents are stressed and worried about money, without knowing the details, can make teenagers anxious. Our kids need to know that we're in charge of our lives so that they can feel safe and secure.

"Who was that on the phone?" sixteen-year-old Marta asked her parents one night. "And why do they always call at dinnertime?"

Mom and Dad glanced at each other, not quite sure what to tell their daughter. Finally Dad said, "That's the credit card company. We've hit our limit and can't charge anything else."

"We've set up an arrangement to pay it off," Mom assured Marta. "It will take about a year or so."

"A year!" Marta exclaimed.

"Yes," Dad said. "We got ourselves into this mess, and now we have to work our way out of it."

It was upsetting for Marta to learn of her parents' credit card debt, partly because she knew it meant she'd have to cut back on her spending, too. In addition, it was sobering to realize that her parents had made some mistakes and now had to deal with the consequences. Marta had to grow up a little to adjust to the reality of her parents' failure to properly manage their finances.

Mom and Dad made the best of a difficult situation by emphasizing that they were taking responsibility for their debt and would slowly but surely pay it off. They didn't tell Marta to learn from their mistakes but instead shared with her how they were learning from this experience. They explained to her what they would have to eliminate from the family budget in order to become debt-free. So when they canceled the cable TV service, Marta knew why, and accepted that it was part of their overall plan to become more fiscally responsible.

Avoiding Power Struggles

As our kids move through adolescence, it becomes even more important that they learn to predict what natural consequences are likely to result from their behavior. We want them to be able to prevent problems before they begin, especially as the risks become more serious.

Elijah has always been a very active child who becomes hyper when he eats chocolate—which, of course, he loves. His parents have always controlled the quantity and choice of sweets Elijah eats, but now that he is thirteen, they are no longer able to do so.

One night the family is having frozen yogurt for dessert. Elijah wants to crumble chocolate cookies on top of his—and he thinks that not one, not two, but four cookies would be about right. Dad is furious. "No way! Two cookies is enough. You know you'll be wired all night with that much chocolate. You won't be able to concentrate enough to write your report for school." An argument ensues, with Dad escalating his attempts to control Elijah, and Elijah escalating his insistence on his right to make his own choices about both his dessert and his homework.

Even just a few months ago this would have not been a major point of conflict. Elijah might have grumbled at his father's interference, but he would have acquiesced. Now those days are gone. With the onset of adolescence, his developmental task has shifted from following his parents' directives to learning how to make decisions for himself. Elijah needs to learn the natural consequences of eating too much chocolate, especially when he has homework to do.

Just as our teenagers are beginning to explore their independence and are facing some of the most serious risks of their lives, we parents have to shift away from trying to control them to encouraging and supporting them as they learn from their experiences. For thirteen-year-old Elijah, right now the issue is about his eating habits, but in five years the decision may be about safe sex or driving in an ice storm, and in five years his parents won't necessarily be there to tell him what to do. The irony and the difficulty for the parents of teenagers is that at the same time we are becoming increasingly worried about their safety, we have decreasing control over their behavior. No wonder adolescence is such an anxious time for parents!

In this instance, Dad could have taken a totally different tack, one that was more about Elijah's learning from experience than about controlling his behavior. "Okay, go ahead," he might have said as Elijah began to pile on the cookies, "but let's see what happens as you start to work on your homework." Then later in the evening when Elijah was having trouble doing his homework, Dad could help him understand the natural consequences of eating too much chocolate and help him decide how he wants to handle himself in the future.

The Beauty of Natural Consequences

One of the most difficult challenges in being a parent is being sufficiently flexible. We finally find a routine or approach that works, only to discover that our kids have changed and we need to develop a whole new strategy. If we are not flexible, however, and simply persist with "old" methods that no longer work, we will grow increasingly frustrated, feel as if we're banging our heads against a wall, or assume that our kids are unreachable. As our kids grow and develop, we need to change and grow, too. This is especially important—and especially difficult—during the quicksilver changes of adolescence.

As Elijah's dad came to realize, a direct confrontation with a teenager is almost always a losing battle. They have far more energy than we do for the fight. Furthermore, it's embarrassing to find ourselves arguing intensely over something as silly as whether a thirteen-year-old should have two cookies or four. If we persist in trying to control our teenagers, we are likely to find ourselves caught in the role of cop, not parent. And our teens will usually find a way to outsmart us anyway, no matter how punishing or controlling our edicts.

The beauty of natural consequences is that they flow from the teenagers' own behavior; they are not punishments imposed by us. If they stay up too late, they're tired the next day. If they don't do their laundry, they won't have their favorite clothes to wear when they want them. They cannot avoid their own responsibility in these matters by blaming us or engaging us in a confrontation. The real battle is an internal one, with themselves.

When Todd was younger, the rule had been "twenty minutes of trumpet practice before you can watch TV." When Todd turned thirteen, his mother noticed that she was beginning to spend more time and energy enforcing the rule than Todd was spending practicing. She even found herself setting a timer to ensure he completed the full twenty minutes. Then it dawned on her that he wasn't really practicing for his lessons but was simply playing pieces he'd learned last year. She realized that her tactics weren't working, and that "the trumpet wars" were beginning to have a negative impact on her relationship with Todd.

"The new rule about music practice is that there is no rule," Mom announced to Todd one day. "If you want to keep taking lessons, you've got to do at least a minimum of practice time. We can decide together what that means. The rest is up to you."

Somewhat surprised by this abrupt change in his mother's attitude, Todd was almost defensive. "Well, I want to go out for marching band in the fall—they're the only band that travels with the team."

"That's great," Mom responded. "Then I'm sure you'll want to keep up with your practice."

Some teens would respond to this situation by taking responsibility for their practice time. Other teens—and we all know them well—wouldn't pick up the trumpet again until the week before the auditions for marching band. Todd's mother has to be resigned to stay out of it, whichever way Todd chooses, and he in turn has to accept the natural consequences of his action or inaction. It's now Todd's business, a matter between Todd and the director of the marching band. Mom has wisely removed herself from the struggle.

If Todd's mom had continued supervising his practice, it's easy to imagine how the "trumpet wars" could have escalated. Teens naturally resist a parent who's controlling and pressuring them, even when they actually want to do what the parent is insisting they do. With his mother's continued nagging, Todd might have lost his focus on his desire to join the marching band and instead gotten caught up in rebelling against his mom. Then he would have missed out on the larger opportunity to discover whether he had the self-discipline needed to be selected for the band.

Allowing Our Kids to Make Mistakes

We have to recognize the limits of our ability to influence our teenagers. We can give advice and direction but the rest is up to them. Still, it can be difficult for us, as parents, to watch our teens *not* plan ahead, knowing the negative consequences that await them. But there are times when we need to let them learn from their own mistakes. At least we can hope that such hard-won lessons will make a difference as our teens face the future and more important life choices.

Fifteen-year-old Alison was very excited about the possibility of being an assistant counselor at her old summer camp. She knew there were lots of kids interested in the position, and that she should call for an interview early, but she didn't do it. When she finally did, all the jobs were filled.

Totally crushed and overwrought, Alison cried to her mother, "I can't believe it! How could they have filled up all the positions so early?"

Mom remembered telling Alison early in the spring that she should call the camp and express her interest. She had even nagged her about it, and warned her that there were only so many positions, and a lot of kids to fill them. Then she decided to let the chips fall as they may. So Mom had been expecting this crisis.

Perhaps the most important thing she did at this point was to be empathic, and refrain from saying, "I told you so." It may be awfully tempting to be self-righteous in these moments and to let our kids know just how smart we are, but that doesn't help them. There are some experiences every generation has to go through themselves. Teens are more likely to learn from mistakes they see on their own than the ones we point out to them. This also allows them to preserve their sense of dignity, which is very important for them. After all, they're already living with the consequences of their behavior and they don't need to be embarrassed or shamed on top of that.

"I know how disappointed you are," Mom said.

"No you don't!" Alison cried, and ran from the room sobbing.

There wasn't much Mom could do at that moment but give Alison some time to calm down. About an hour later she knocked on Alison's bedroom door. "Can we talk?" she asked.

"Okay," Alison said sorrowfully. She was sitting on the bed, looking dejected.

"I have some ideas of other things you can do this summer. Are you ready to hear them?"

"I guess so," Alison replied. "But it won't be the same."

"No, it won't," Mom agreed, "but what else can you do?"

So Alison and her mom explored various alternatives together. As a matter of fact, Alison's mother was also terribly disappointed that Alison wasn't going to be able to work at the camp. Watching her daughter procrastinate and lose out on a wonderful opportunity had been difficult for her, but Mom kept her own feelings to herself. She knew Alison already had enough to deal with and she didn't need to deal with her mother's disappointment in addition to her own.

Knowing When to Intervene

There are times when it is our parental responsibility to intervene, stopping a downward spiral into disastrous natural consequences. We don't want our teens to become so discouraged that they can't learn from their mistakes and take constructive action.

Fourteen-year-old Scott's grades were going progressively downhill. When his mother met with his teachers, they told her he rarely turned in his homework. She was shocked to hear that, as she knew he actually worked hard on his assignments. When she asked Scott about this, he just shrugged and mumbled vaguely, "Sometimes I forget it. Or I can't find it. I dunno."

Mom quickly became exasperated. "Don't you know you're getting marked down for that?"

Scott shrugged again and stared at his hands. He seemed to have an uncanny fascination for them at the moment, and that only made Mom more frustrated.

"Let's talk about this later," she said, realizing that she was too upset to continue. She knew she needed to calm down and reapproach the situation, but then what? Should she punish Scott for getting bad grades? Should she check to see that his homework was in his book bag every morning? Or should she let the natural consequences of his behavior unfold? She knew that he wouldn't be able to play sports if his grades fell below a certain point, and that that would be a big disappointment for him.

Some teens are not able to learn from natural consequences as easily as others. When this is the case, as it is for Scott, who had major problems with his organizational skills, it's not helpful to let them continue on a downward path. Scott was already doing his best. He didn't really understand how it was happening that he couldn't keep track of his homework. He was already experiencing the natural consequences of not turning in his work, and he still didn't know how to make things better. He wasn't being lazy or uncooperative—he needed help with organizing his life.

Scott knew that he was having trouble in school, but he didn't know what to do about it. Punishing him for his bad grades would only make him feel worse about himself than he already did. Trying to take over for him wouldn't work either. Even if his mother were to put the homework into his backpack herself, it wouldn't help him develop the skills he needed for his life in the long run, and it might not even guarantee that the papers would be delivered into the teachers' hands. For teens who have problems with organizational skills, mysterious things often happen somewhere between home and the classroom, and somehow the work just doesn't get handed in. Parents are sometimes surprised to find weeks' worth of carefully done homework stuffed into their teens' school lockers.

Scott needed help with learning how to organize himself and keep track of his work. Mom can intervene in what would otherwise be a downward spiral by finding that extra help for him. With teenagers, it's usually better to let a professional provide help than try to do it ourselves. This avoids setting up the natural resistance many teens have to their parents telling them what to do. Perhaps Scott's teachers could refer him to the learning specialist at the school, who could help teach him better organizational and study skills.

Staying Connected

The consequences posed by sexual activity and alcohol and drug use present a particularly troublesome area for parents. We certainly don't want our teens to have to learn the hard way when serious risk to their health and safety is involved. But we also have to accept the fact that we won't be able to intervene at the point when these very important decisions are being made. Our teens will be with other teenagers, far away from our protective reach. Our only hope is to stay well enough connected with our teens that we know what's going on in their lives and can talk openly with them about the decisions they're making and what consequences may ensue.

There's no point in telling a sixteen-year-old girl who's deeply in love that aside from moral issues, the natural consequence of sex may be contracting a sexually transmitted disease or becoming pregnant—or both. She already knows this, and still, much to our dismay, she may not even consider these facts as she progresses toward engaging in sexual intercourse. We need to have talked with our teenagers for years prior to this about the importance of love, the nature of sexual relationships, and the consequences of sexual activity. We need to have sat with them through endless TV shows and movies, discussing what we saw together. They need to fully understand our values and our hopes for them—for the way they treat themselves and allow others to treat them now, and what they want for their future.

At the point when we do have specific concerns about our teenagers, it's best to express them in a straightforward manner: "I know this is a serious relationship. I understand what it's like to be young and in love. I just don't want you to get pregnant."

Don't be discouraged if your teen breezily reassures you, "Don't worry, I won't." At this point you need to press for more specific reassurances. "I'm glad, but what are you doing to be sure?" or "I want to know what you're doing to prevent pregnancy."

This is not a time to be judgmental or to lecture our kids about the virtues of abstinence or waiting until marriage. Of course, we can always restate our preferences and our values, but we also need to be realistic about the pressures in our teenagers' lives. It helps if we already have an open, trusting relationship with our teens in which communication flows freely. But sometimes we just have to do the best we can with what we've got because of the risks involved for our teens.

The more our teenagers see us as a resource—a source of helpful information, guidance, and support—the more likely they'll seek our advice as they make the decisions that will involve serious consequences for them. If they see us as primarily critical, controlling, and likely to panic or judge them when they confide in us, they'll make these potentially life-changing decisions on their own and we won't even know about them until it's too late.

Creating Their Own Futures

Understanding how a chain of events or reactions occurs is the first step in our teenagers' integrating the concept of cause and effect into their daily lives. This allows them to begin to plan more effectively and also to feel that they can be in charge of themselves and their lives. They're learning that, to a great degree, they actually can direct the course of their lives, beginning with small concerns and eventually leading up to the important matters of planning their career paths and their adult lives. As adults, we may not remember how much is involved in learning how to plan ahead—we may have come to take this process for granted. But our teenagers need to learn these skills in order to plan the steps that will create the future they envision for themselves.

Joseph's high school held a winter cotillion every February. When he was in the ninth grade, Joseph had no interest in it, but the following year he knew exactly which girl he wanted to ask to the dance. However, by the time he got around to asking her, she had already accepted another invitation. Like most girls, she was a bit more sophisticated in these matters and she let Joseph know she was really disappointed that he hadn't asked sooner, because she would rather have gone to the dance with him.

Joseph had learned the hard way how much planning ahead needs to go into certain kinds of social events. This thought frankly had never occurred to him, and he hadn't let his parents in on his plans, either. His parents hadn't really noticed how Joseph was maturing, even though to an outsider it would have seemed fairly obvious. They had no clue that their son was interested in going to the cotillion, and even less that he had his eye on a specific girl.

We have to consciously try to see our teenagers as others see them, so that we stay abreast of their development and realistic about their growing up. Otherwise, we get "stuck"—seeing them at a certain age and missing out on how much they're changing and maturing. It can be hard to realize that our kids are ready for greater responsibilities or new and different activities, such as dating.

The weekend of the dance arrived, and Joseph was moping around the house. "What's with you?" his dad asked, still not realizing what had happened, but aware that Joseph was upset about something.

"Ah, nothing," Joseph muttered.

Undeterred, Dad continued, "Why aren't you going out with the guys tonight?"

Joseph wouldn't say anything, but he did continue to hang around the room, so Dad persisted with his attempts to understand his son's unusual moodiness. He didn't say anything particularly brilliant or magical, but he also didn't give up on the conversation. Finally Joseph told him what had happened.

Suddenly Dad saw his son in a whole different light. "I'm sorry to hear that," he said, and then added almost as an afterthought, "So, have you asked her out for another time?"

Joseph looked blank. "Well, no, I haven't," he said.

"Hey, that's the whole point of this." Dad laughed. "You're supposed to learn from your mistakes."

"Well, I guess I could," Joseph said slowly. "I mean, she sort of said she wanted to go out with me."

Dad smiled. "Yeah, she did. So I guess you could go ahead and ask her."

With his dad's help, Joseph was learning how one thing leads to another. He needed this extra coaching to understand fully that there was good news in the way the girl had responded to him and not to miss another opportunity to ask her out.

We have to remember that natural consequences are not necessarily punishments. They can also be logical outcomes flowing from our actions or, in some cases, our inaction. Learning how to influence the course of events, and adjusting our plans as one thing leads to another, is an essential skill in living a successful life.

Accepting Accountability and Making Amends

Understanding how natural consequences work includes more than just behaving in ways that are likely to lead to favorable outcomes. Accountability means taking full responsibility for the impact of our behavior when we have failed, too, and doing whatever it takes to make things right. This is what it means to make amends for our behavior, and sometimes we have to search for the best way to accomplish this.

Fifteen-year-old Krishna was captain of his school's track team. Part of his responsibility as captain was to put the boxes of water bottles on the bus before they left for out-of-town track meets. One day he forgot. He had a million excuses for why he had forgotten, but the bottom line was that the track team wasn't going to have their water bottles at that meet. The coach didn't realize the bottles were missing until they got to the stadium, and he had to go on an emergency run to find water. This placed an extra burden of stress on the team right before an important competition.

Krishna felt terrible about letting his teammates down and disappointing the coach. He felt he didn't deserve to continue to captain the team. Even though he apologized to everyone, he still felt just awful about it. That night his mom asked him how the track meet had gone.

"Fine," Krishna answered tersely.

"Just fine?" Mom asked. She wanted to hear the usual detailed report. "How did the relay team do?"

"They won."

Mom looked at Krishna. "What's the matter with you?"

"Nothing."

"Nothing?" she repeated.

After a substantial pause, the story came out. Mom could see Krishna's eyes well up, but he wouldn't allow himself to cry. It would have been so easy for her to console him, accept his excuses, and lift the burden of guilt from his shoulders. Or she could have dismissed the whole thing as "no big deal"—after all, the team had gotten their water eventually, and they did win the meet. Or she could have heaped extra blame on him, asking, "How could you be so irresponsible?" But she didn't do any of these things. She held him accountable, and acknowledged the importance of the situation, without making him feel worse than he already did and without minimizing his feelings.

"This is a tough one," she said thoughtfully. Krishna nodded. "What do you think you can do to make sure this doesn't happen again?"

Krishna shrugged. "I don't know."

"Well, think about it," Mom insisted. "That's one way you can make it up to the team and the coach.

The next morning Krishna came downstairs with a form he had designed on the computer. It listed all the equipment and supplies that needed to go with the team on the bus. "This checklist will ensure that I never make the same mistake again," he announced.

"That's a great idea," Mom said. She looked over the list and then added a note of reality in her response: "This will certainly make it easier to be sure that everything the team needs is on the bus before you go."

Holding our teens accountable means finding that balance point between consoling them and blaming them, between taking them too seriously and minimizing their feelings. Just as we don't want to make excuses for our teenagers' mistakes, we don't want to heap criticism on them when they're already down.

We also want to encourage our teens to find a way to make amends when they have done wrong. Is there anything they can do to make the situation better? Our job as parents is not just to make our teens feel better—that may be tempting at times, but it's only a temporary solution. We need to encourage them to figure out what will help ameliorate the consequences they have set in motion, and to take constructive action. Our teens will naturally feel better about themselves as a result of making amends. And they will develop the confidence that comes from knowing they can fix things even after they've made a mistake. This helps them to be less fearful about failing and more confident about living up to their responsibilities.

When Tragedy Occurs

Unfortunately, it's not always possible to make amends—some consequences cannot be ameliorated. These are the tragedies of the teen years, and the thought of our teens being involved in such a tragedy is every parent's worst nightmare. However, these are precisely the same natural consequences that all teens say "won't happen to me."

Tragic natural consequences seem to occur most often in cars. One minute a teen is driving along just fine, and the next minute, before he knows what has happened, he's been in an accident. "It happened so fast," they say. "I don't know how it happened." When this occurs, there is a very efficient system of accountability already in place that will teach our teens the consequences of their actions, as long as we don't interfere. Traffic fines, the suspension of driver's licenses, insurance rate increases, auto repair costs, and even jail sentences will all impress a teenager with just how serious a matter driving is. In these cases, we must be very careful not to try to rescue our kids from the consequences of their actions, but let them face them to the full extent.

In some instances teenagers may also have to face the fact that their behavior, knowingly or unknowingly, intentionally or unintentionally, led to permanent damage or even someone's death. No longer can those teens enjoy the belief that they are invincible; they somehow have to learn how to live with the consequences of their actions. This is a very sad way to learn accountability, and we, as parents, need to stand by our teens without protecting them so much that we interfere with this important learning.

As parents, we've probably all heard of a tragic car accident involving teenagers; we may even know someone personally who was involved. It seems that the end of the school year, around high school graduation, is an especially risky time for teenage drivers. We can warn our kids about the dangers, check their tires and brakes, give them drivers' education classes, and enroll them in MADD (Mothers Against Drunk Driving). We can promise to pick up them and any of their friends, at any time, anywhere, with no questions asked and no scenes. We can take away the car keys from teens who are at our house and whom we know have been drinking or doing drugs. We can give our kids safe cars to drive—cars without a lot of pickup and not capable of very high speeds. We can make sure that we go for a ride with them every once in a while, to see how they're driving. Yet we will still worry, because we know we can't protect them 100 percent.

Most important, we can be available to them, giving them generous amounts of our own time, energy, and attention. A warm, open relationship between parents and teenagers really does give our teens the strongest possible foundation for making wise and safe decisions.

Parental Accountability

As parents, we have to face up to the natural consequences of our own parenting behavior. For instance, we know that the more available we are to our teens and the more involved we are in their lives, the more likely they will be to confide in us, consider our suggestions, know what our values are, and come to us for help when they need it. Our investment of time and energy during our kids' adolescent years can make a lifelong difference in the quality of their lives.

We need to keep in mind the simple realities of cause and effect, and not put our teenagers in super-fast cars or allow them to drink alcohol and then go out with their friends. We must be sure to fully inform our teens, both male and female, about how to prevent pregnancy and help them find access to birth control if and when they need it. We want to be sure they know the dangers of going out with people they don't know very well, or drinking to excess, and talk with them about what to do if they find themselves in a frightening situation.

We know we can't control our teenagers, but we should never underestimate the amount of influence we still have over them. It's our responsibility to give them the very best preparation for adulthood we know how to provide. We must never forget that our most powerful message for our kids is the way we live our own lives.

If teenagers live with responsibility, they learn to be self-reliant

R esponsibility is one of the hallmarks of maturity. We've encouraged it in our children since they were little, and we've nurtured their developing sense of responsibility with every passing year. Now that they're teenagers, we want them to develop an inner sense of responsibility so that they can do what's needed and what's appropriate in any situation, according to their own set of values. And we want them to choose to do what's right even when it's inconvenient or hard for them to do so.

As teens mature, their sense of responsibility informs a wide-ranging array of behaviors, from how they handle money to how they handle their personal relationships. Often, as they begin to show greater responsibility, they also gain greater freedom and privileges. "Yes, you can take the car, if you pick up your sister at her girlfriend's house—at four o'clock sharp!" "Yes, we can get a dog—but you must help feed, walk, and clean up after him." Our teens' sense of responsibility will influence whether their day-to-day lives flow smoothly or career from one crisis to another.

Our teenagers have to learn that being responsible means seeing things through from start to finish, especially when others are relying on them. They may be slow to realize that their actions affect others, or that others depend upon them. Participating in group projects at school and team sports are a couple of ways they have the chance to work together with others toward goals that are greater than just meeting their own individual desires. Group participation teaches teens to be responsible for one another as well as for themselves.

Because we want our teens to develop the inner integrity that is an essential part of being a responsible person, we have to ask whether we ourselves are providing them with a model of integrity by living up to this standard. After all, how many adults consistently behave in ways that are truly responsible—both to themselves and toward others?

We can't force our teens to be responsible by merely telling them to be responsible. That internal need to be responsible has to arise from within them. It has to *feel* right to them. When faced with a difficult decision, a child who has been raised to think and act with integrity is more likely to think, "This is the way we do things in our family," and then to draw the strength to do what's right from that inner knowledge.

As our teenagers progress through adolescence, they will increasingly need to rely on themselves, often without our ever knowing the details of what they're up to. The more their sense of responsibility is internal, self-directed, and independent of us, other authorities, or even their peers, the more self-reliant they will be. A strong sense of self may in turn lead to increased ability to work with others and to know when to ask for advice, guidance, support, or information.

Going to School Is a Teen's "Job"

School is usually the first place, outside the family, in which kids learn to be responsible for themselves and to others. In school, their responsibilities increase year by year in both number and complexity. As adolescence dawns, school often becomes more challenging—the tests are harder, teachers give more homework, and the papers are more extensive and require more long-range planning. Not every teenager is ready for the greater academic responsibility that comes with middle school. Some kids adjust easily, while others have more trouble.

One day Mom got the kind of call from the assistant principal that all parents dread. Thirteen-year-old Warren had handed in a term paper that had been downloaded from a website. He hadn't even bothered to rewrite any of it—it was word-for-word plagiarism. The school's punishment was that Warren would receive a failing grade on the paper and two weeks' detention. Mom, however, insisted on adding to the consequences.

"I want you to write your own term paper now," she said at the meeting, with the vice principal and teacher present.

"Aw, Mom," Warren protested, "don't you think this is enough? I admitted the whole thing."

"No, I don't think it's enough," Mom said. "You missed out on the experience of writing your own paper. I want you to know that you can succeed at this assignment."

"That's a great idea," the teacher agreed. "You can even use some of your detention time in the library to work on it."

Warren knew when he was outnumbered.

"This is not a punishment," Mom continued. "Admitting your mistake is not quite the same as fulfilling your responsibility. And I want you to know you can do the work you were asked to do," she repeated.

"If you run into problems, just let me know," Warren's teacher added. "I'll be glad to help."

Mom was right to insist that Warren complete the assignment. She didn't want him to miss an opportunity for building the confidence in his own abilities that he will need as his classes become more challenging. He needs to learn now that he can rely on himself to do a good job with his school projects. Having confidence in his own work will build his sense of self-reliance and hopefully decrease the chance of his plagiarizing again.

Notice that Mom kept the focus on constructive and positive action. She didn't dwell on the fact that he had plagiarized, or ask him why he did it, since there is really no acceptable reason for such behavior. Nor did she punish Warren by taking away privileges at home. This issue was primarily a matter between him and his teachers. Mom's insistence on holding Warren to his academic responsibilities shows him that she supports the school's response to plagiarism and also that she believes in him and his abilities.

Our teenagers' primary responsibility in life is their performance in school—meeting the academic demands and requirements in order to succeed. Our teens have to learn to be responsible within the school setting. We can support and encourage them as they do so, but they need to learn, gradually, how to manage their schoolwork on their own. We can help them do this by being interested in what they're doing in school, talking with them about what they're learning, and valuing the importance of education.

Teaching a Work Ethic

Our teenagers learn about the world of work initially through our example. For years they've observed how we approach our jobs, whether we work at home, on the road, or outside the house. They've watched us get up early in the morning to meet deadlines or stay up late to do reports; they've seen what it takes to work hard on a day-to-day basis. This is the strongest model of a work ethic we can give them. Our teens are also aware that we all have parts of our jobs that we don't like or are uncertain about. We go through disappointments, anxieties, successes, frustration, and surprises. Our kids know when we're stressed at work. It doesn't hurt to talk about it in ways that can be helpful to them.

"I'm really worried about the presentation I have to give at work next week," Mom mentioned to fifteen-year-old Janine while driving her to a friend's house one day. "I'll have to work on it over the weekend."

"Does that mean you won't be able to take me to my dance class?" Janine asked, thinking of herself first, as any normal teenager would.

Mom smiled. "No, I'll be able to do that."

After a pause, Janine realized what her mom had just shared with her. "I've never heard you say you were nervous about something at work before."

Mom laughed. "I get anxious about presentations. Everyone gets nervous at one time or another."

"Like when I had to give my history report in front of the class?" Janine said.

"Right. You were nervous, but you did real well."

"So will you, Mom."

"I know the material. I just have to trust myself," Mom replied.

"Maybe you should run through your talk out loud like I did," Janine suggested, feeling very grown up to be making this suggestion to her mother. "It helped me."

"You know"—Mom paused thoughtfully—"maybe you're right. I haven't done the talk and the slides together yet."

For the most part, our teens take our work habits for granted. Yet our example leaves an indelible impression on them about what it means to be an adult with a strong work ethic. They notice how we handle our professional responsibilities and they learn from us, even though it may appear that their primary concern remains with themselves. Janine's first thought was to make sure that her mother's extra work wouldn't interfere with her schedule, but she quickly moved on to understanding the parallel between the way her mom was preparing for her work presentation and the way she had prepared for her history report.

The way we handle our challenges at work provides our kids with a valuable example of what responsiblity looks like in day-to-day life. Allowing our kids to see our anxieties and insecurities, and how we manage them, is a powerful lesson. We all face challenges at work. Part of learning how to be self-reliant is finding the inner resources to rise up and meet those challenges.

It Takes Time!

The more our teens practice being responsible in a wide range of situations, the more confident they will be that they can count on themselves. This is what it means to be self-reliant—to be able to trust that you will be able to find a way to do whatever needs to be done.

Becoming more self-reliant and independent doesn't mean our teens have to do everything on their own. As they need us less, they separate from us very gradually, yet remain connected to the family. They even begin to understand that they have a responsibility to be considerate in their relationships with family members. This means they learn to think of the others' feelings and be more responsive in their relationships with parents and siblings. This is quite an achievement in teenagers' development—to learn that they can separate and become more independent while remaining connected and responsive.

Mom had been nagging sixteen-year-old Krista for a week about buying a birthday present for her little sister. Mom knew Krista's school and extracurricular activities kept her so busy that there was no way she'd have time to go shopping. Krista just kept telling her that she had everything covered.

The night before her sister's party Krista came to her mom. "I'm all set with the present, but I forgot a card. Do you happen to have an extra?"

"An extra card? Sorry, no," Mom responded. "What did you get her?" She was amazed that Krista had managed to come through with a present in time for the party.

Krista held out a box with a highly coveted and difficult-to-find doll in it. "I ordered this over the Internet," she said, smiling. "I used my new credit card."

"You know, the stores around here were out of that," Mom said, impressed.

Krista beamed. "I know."

Krista was able to manage a very busy schedule, yet still find just the right present for her little sister and do it on her own. Of course, she forgot the card, but this didn't matter to her sister, who was thrilled with the doll. Meanwhile Mom was adjusting to a new level of maturity in her older daughter, a sense of competency and reliability of a whole different order.

During adolescence our kids seem to change overnight. Usually the joke is that they go from being twelve-year-old angels to thirteen-year-old monsters. But our teens can also transform themselves into civilized human beings in a gigantic developmental leap. What makes it difficult to deal with is that it's usually not a global transformation. They can be impressively self-reliant in some ways while still very dependent upon us in others; they can be highly responsible in one area while totally irresponsible in others.

So even though Krista appears to be more responsible in this situation than her years would indicate, it's an uneven maturity. She can remember to get her sister a birthday present, but her bedroom is an unholy mess, and her mom is sure that a new type of mold must be growing somewhere in a pile of dirty clothes. But Mom chooses to ignore this disaster-in-the-making, knowing that Krista will eventually catch up in this area of responsibility. She certainly doesn't clean up Krista's room for her—she knows that would interfere with Krista's learning how to take care of her own things as she develops more self-reliance, and Mom trusts that she will do so in time.

Practicing Day-to-Day Responsibilities

A delicate dance goes on between teenagers and parents through-out adolescence. We want them to become more self-reliant, yet it's difficult to know when they're ready and able to take over certain responsibilities. They want to become more independent, yet they also still enjoy being catered to and fussed over. How do we time things so that our letting go of them is more or less in sync with their growing capacity to be responsible?

This dance gets acted out by teens most frequently around standard household tasks, from making their own breakfast to do-ing their own laundry. Different families can have quite different timetables—some eight-year-olds start the morning coffee for their parents, while some sixteen-year-olds are still being served break-fast every morning. One thing is sure, though—if we wait for our teens to volunteer to take over their own household tasks, we could be waiting for a very long time.

When Mom decided it was time to let thirteen-year-old Alicia take care of her own laundry, it was a disaster. Alicia went through everything in her closet and drawers and then began to wear her dirty clothes again. Mom couldn't stand this, so she resumed doing the laundry for Alicia. A year later, with a firmer conviction, Mom de-cided it was time for Alicia to take care of her own laundry, no mat-ter how she handled it, and this time Mom held firm.

"School pictures are tomorrow and I don't have anything to wear," Alicia complained one night.

"Oh?" Mom responded noncommittally.

"Couldn't you just wash this one shirt with your stuff? That way it'll be dry in time for tomorrow."

"I'm not doing my laundry today," Mom answered, trying hard not to get caught up in a fight over laundry. This was really Alicia's problem, and she didn't need to be involved.

"I don't see what the big deal is," Alicia said, and huffed out of the room. An hour or so later, Mom heard the sound of the washing machine starting up.

Mom held firm, but it wasn't easy. It would have felt much better to rescue her daughter and wash the shirt for her. This scene goes on in most households with teenagers, whether the issue is washing clothes, fixing breakfast, or changing the sheets. These battles begin in early adolescence, and go on into young adulthood. At some time, though, the parents will stop doing their kid's chores for them, and the teens will take over, becoming more responsible in the process.

Sometimes we may feel as if nothing we do works with our teens. No matter what we say to encourage them to be responsible, we are met with resistance. At this point, we have a choice. We can keep knocking our heads against a wall, or we can back down gracefully. Generally our teens have more energy to resist than we have to insist. If the issue is not over truly dangerous matters or a serious moral issue, then it may be wise just to let it go. We don't have to win every round with our teenagers. In fact, it can sometimes be more important to lose a few.

Our Teens Can Surprise Us

Our teenagers' behavior at home may bear no relationship to their behavior out in the world. Their process of maturing can be quite uneven as they save their most resistant, irresponsible behavior for us. It's not uncommon for parents to be surprised by how a teacher sees their teen. They may even ask, "Are we talking about the same kid?" We may be the last ones to know that our careless, sloppy teens have become competent in ways we'd never imagined.

Mom and Dad maintained a vigilant style of supervision over sixteen-year-old Nicole. They really didn't think Nicole was mature enough to take care of herself without their help. To them, she seemed to be more dependent than most teens, needing her parents' support and advice even about little things, for instance which pair of jeans to wear. What her parents didn't realize was that at sixteen Nicole, like most other kids her age, was facing serious decisions about drugs, sex, and alcohol. For most teenagers, opportunities to indulge in these things are everywhere—at school, parties, or hanging out with friends at the mall. This is just normal life for teens, but parents may not realize that their kids have had to grow up quickly to handle these issues.

One night at a party, one of Nicole's friends drank way too many shots of vodka and then passed out behind the sofa. He didn't just fall asleep, he was out cold. There were grown-ups in the house who were checking on the kids now and then, but they didn't really know what was going on. Nicole was the one who realized there was a serious problem, and she took immediate action. She called 911 to report an emergency, gave the address, described the boy's color, his breathing, and what he'd been drinking. The ambulance arrived quickly and took the boy to the emergency room, where he was treated for alcohol poisoning.

Nicole made a very responsible decision and she basically acted on her own. Many times in such a situation, teens will turn to each other and decide together—"Oh, it's all right, he'll be okay"—especially if it means they can continue to party and avoid getting into trouble with their parents. Nicole listened to herself and did the right thing, even though she knew it meant the party would be over and some of the kids would be in trouble.

Afterward, Nicole downplayed the importance of what she had done. "I knew that getting help right away was the most important thing, so I did it," she explained.

Nicole's parents didn't know whether to be horrified about the situation, or proud of their daughter for being a hero. They were truly surprised that it was Nicole who had taken charge. How could this be the same kid who habitually slept through the alarm in the morning, frequently forgot to put gas in the car, and still lost her wallet on a regular basis? But this is exactly how teens are— dependent and forgetful in many ways and responsible and mature in others. As parents, we need to be careful not to underestimate our teenagers and the complex challenges they face, no matter how young they may seem to us at home.

Balancing Greater Responsibility with Greater Freedom

As our teenagers get older, we have to give them progressively greater freedom, even though we know the serious risks that are a normal part of adolescence. We need to hold gently to the ties that bind them to us, so they can continue to tug on the line checking to be sure that we're there for them. Yet our hold has to be loose enough to allow them gradually to venture further and further out into the world, beyond our reach. This is true figuratively as well as literally as our teenagers' world becomes larger and more distinct from ours. We aren't always going to know exactly where they are or what they're doing. We have to learn to let go even as we hold on to them, so that we remain available to them when they do need us. This is the paradox of parenting an adolescent.

We begin to give them greater privileges when we see that they can handle them. We are reassured when they call home as promised, letting us know where they are and who they're with, so we give them greater freedom. As we watch our teens succeed at solving more complex problems and negotiating more complicated arrangements, we begin to trust that they are finally achieving a new level of independence and self-reliance. Having said all this, we have to admit that our teens will inevitably come up with ideas that strike cold fear into our hearts.

"You know what Eddie and I want to do next summer?" said seventeen-year-old Chris, approaching his parents in midwinter. "We want to go on a road trip."

Mom was too stunned to respond. Dad asked, "Where to?"

"I don't know. Maybe west, maybe north. That's the whole point. We'd explore," Chris answered proudly, adding, "We can camp out. It won't cost us much."

This didn't reassure his parents. They were thinking of the thousand and one things that can go wrong on a road trip, especially for a couple of teenagers. Although they didn't want to discourage their son's budding independence, Mom and Dad were not enthusiastic about the plan.

"I was hoping you'd make some money for college next summer," Mom said, desperately trying to think of some way to dissuade him without putting forth open resistance.

"I thought about that," Chris replied. "I'm going to work at the sausage factory again this summer and I figured I could work extra shifts. That way I could earn enough so that I could take off the last two weeks before school started."

"And what car are you planning on taking?" Dad asked.

"Eddie's brother's going into the army next summer and said we could use his car."

"You've been planning this for a while, haven't you?" Dad acknowledged.

Chris smiled happily, nodding.

Mom and Dad told Chris they'd like to talk it over for a few days, while they tried to get used to the idea. Finally they came up with a plan that would prepare both them and their son for this new level of independence.

"We're willing to support you with this idea for a trip," Dad explained. "But we want to know that you'll be able to take care of yourself on the road. So first we want you to learn how to change tires, replace the belts, and do minor repairs. You can start this weekend by helping me change the oil on my car." Dad was a pretty handy mechanic himself, and he looked forward to teaching his son a few things about the car.

"That's it? You mean you'll let me go?" Chris didn't know whether to be shocked or elated.

"That's it," Mom affirmed, and added, "Have Eddie come over this weekend when you work on the car so he can learn, too. The more both of you know, the better off you'll be."

The balance between freedom and responsibility plays out most dramatically for teens when it comes to car privileges. When our teens start driving, by definition we loosen the parental strings. Perhaps this is why getting a driver's license is often considered an initiation rite in our culture. A true initiation rite, however, functions as a bridge between childhood and adulthood by preparing the teen to take on adult responsibilities. Obtaining a license to drive means gaining more freedom, but it isn't necessarily linked to learning the adult skills necessary for self-reliance.

The plan Chris's parents came up with made the road trip into an effective initiation rite. Learning some basic auto mechanics would actually make the boys safer on the road. Throughout the rest of the winter and the spring, Chris and his dad spent many hours in the garage working on the family cars. This was a practical way of increasing Chris's self-reliance and wonderful quality time together as well. One day Eddie's brother even brought his car over for a tune-up, and together Chris and his dad made sure it was road-worthy. By the time summer rolled around, Chris was ready for the trip, and so were his parents. And both families were able to enjoy the boys' mounting enthusiasm as they planned for their adventure.

The World of Work

A first job can also serve as an initiation rite for teenagers. Whether it's lawn mowing, baby-sitting, or flipping burgers, holding a job teaches teens many of the skills they will need to enter the adult world—showing up on time, working conscientiously, dealing with others, and generally being responsible.

It's not that this is the first time teenagers realize that others depend upon them. But it's the first time others outside the world of family, school, and sports depend upon them, and that makes all the difference. To "forget" to do the dishes at home is one thing, but to forget to do something on the job is a much bigger deal.

When Caitlin turned fourteen, she began baby-sitting on weekends for a neighbor who worked as a nurse. One Saturday afternoon Caitlin showed up thirty-five minutes late. She'd been on the phone with a boy she liked and had lost track of the time. As soon as she arrived, the neighbor, who was extremely distraught, rushed out of the house. Caitlin was a bit miffed that the neighbor was so abrupt, but she settled in with the toddler and the time flew by.

When the woman came home from work that night, she was direct with Caitlin. "You arrived very late this afternoon," she said.

"Oh right, sorry about that," Caitlin responded amiably.

"Well, your arriving late made me late for my shift at the hospital. I can lose my job for that. I have to be there on time so I can get the report about the patients from the nurses who are leaving. They were angry that I wasn't there and they had to wait for me. And all this happened because you were late today."

Caitlin was shocked. She hadn't thought of all that and didn't know what to say. Of course, Caitlin's mother frequently complained about her lack of responsibility, but her complaining had nowhere near the effect on Caitlin that this situation did. "I'm really sorry," she said much more soberly, now that she understood the impact of her carelessness. "I won't let it happen again." And she didn't.

First jobs give teenagers the chance to receive feedback about their behavior from grown-ups other than their parents. If it's negative, as in this case, they will often receive it more objectively and respond with less resistance to the criticism. If it's positive, the feedback may mean more to them, since they know it's not "just" coming from Mom or Dad.

Sometimes our teens need to leave home to learn the lessons we have been trying so hard to teach them for years. This is one of the reasons why it's so important to have other adults involved with our kids. Faced with the anger of her neighbor, Caitlin had to accept responsibility for showing up late and she knew, without anyone specifically saying so, that if she wanted to keep on baby-sitting, she would have to make sure she got there on time in the future.

There's a lot for our teenagers to learn through these early work experiences. If they can learn to accept the responsibility now, they will have an easier time later, when the success of their adult careers will depend upon how responsible they can be.

Handling Their Own Money

Families differ in terms of how they regard the money that a teenager earns. In some families, the teens' income goes directly into the family budget. In others, it goes into savings for college, and in some families, the money belongs solely to the teen, to spend as he or she wishes. No matter how the money is allocated, the very fact of earning money helps adolescents develop greater self-reliance.

As soon as our teens begin calculating how much money they'll earn for working X number of hours, they begin to understand in a concrete way the relationship between time and money, and what their purchases really cost them. This begins to alter their perspective on spending money, especially their own.

"You know that computer game I want?" fourteen-year-old Sean said to his mom. "I just realized I'm going to have to mow *eight lawns* to earn enough money. That'll take me all weekend!"

"Did you factor in the cost of gas for the lawn mower?" Mom asked, knowing that he hadn't.

"Uh . . . no," Sean said, realizing immediately that it might take him even longer than he had thought. "I might not want it that badly."

Earning their own money to pay for their purchases does wonders for teenagers' rampant consumerism. All of a sudden they don't need to buy every new fad that comes along. As long as their parents are buying, they tend to want all the newest things, immediately. When they're spending their own money, teenagers can become much more discriminating, and conservative in their spending— even downright thrifty. They learn not to expect so much to be given to them automatically, and they also come to appreciate more what they do receive from their parents.

Making Major Life Decisions

As our teens mature, they will begin to face major decisions— about college, jobs, marriage, or lifestyle—that will greatly influence the way the rest of their lives unfold. Sometimes we won't like the choices they make. However, part of accepting and recognizing their entry into adulthood means living with our own frustrations and disappointments as they make these decisions. This is when we really have to learn to let go.

It can be helpful to us, as parents, if we have the support of other parents of teens as they go through the same process. What's most important is that our teenagers have our support as they begin to follow their own dreams. This may involve putting aside our own expectations for them. As difficult as it may be to let go of our hopes for our kids, we have to respect their right to be responsible for their own life decisions. We also have to accept that we did the best we could, and that their lives are now shifting into their hands. We can remain available and supportive and still manage to give them advice, whether they want it or not. But as long as they are responsible and self-reliant, they have the right to choose the path for their own lives.

If teenagers live with healthy habits, they learn to be kind to their bodies

The longest relationship in our teenagers' lives will be the one they have with their own bodies. Their bodies have to last them for many decades and the shape they're in will in many ways determine the quality of their lives. Healthy habits established early will benefit our children over their entire lifetimes. Given this long-range perspective, we have precious few years to influence our kids to take good care of themselves. The primary way we can do this is through example— by taking good care of ourselves.

From the time our children are very young, they need to see us living a healthy lifestyle—taking the time to exercise and to prepare healthy meals, as a regular part of day-to-day living. Probably the biggest obstacle to our doing this is our rushed and overcrowded daily schedules. How many of us are able to plan even thirty minutes a day to devote to taking care of ourselves in some way? Perhaps if we realized how important our example is to our children, we would be more motivated to maintain healthy habits.

There is a strong connection between healthy lifestyle, personal vitality, and good self-esteem—the more health-conscious our teens are, the better their energy level will be, and the better they'll feel about themselves. This dynamic can begin anywhere in the cycle, but it's definitely all related—the better their sense of self, the more likely they'll take care of themselves; the more they take care of themselves, the better their self-esteem will be, and so on.

Feeling well and feeling good about themselves can help sustain our teenagers through the difficult social storms of adolescence. We want our teens to develop a healthy sense of themselves, not be dependent on peer pressure or popularity contests. We want them to treat their bodies with kindness and respect, no matter what everyone else is doing. To take care of themselves in this way, they need their parents to model healthy habits and kindness toward themselves and one another.

Yvonne's family had always gone on vacations that were physically active. They skied in the winter and camped and hiked in the summer. During the year Yvonne's dad refereed for a community basketball league, while Mom swam competitively in master's classes. Yvonne and her three siblings were on a variety of sports teams and, although the family schedule was complex, someone from the family was almost always present to cheer the kids on.

When Yvonne was about fourteen, her parents noticed that she wasn't hanging out with her old group of friends as much as she used to. It seemed she was either home, at soccer practice, or with one or two of her closest girlfriends. Her parents didn't know whether to be worried that she was too isolated, or relieved that she wasn't spending all her time at the mall with the other kids.

"Do you miss spending time with Cheryl and Melanie and that group?" Mom asked. "You used to be together all the time."

"I see them at school," Yvonne answered noncommittally.

"They were both such good athletes," Dad said. "I wonder why they quit the soccer team."

"They're into other stuff now," Yvonne explained. "All they do is hang out at the mall and all they care about is boys."

"Oh." Dad was nonplussed.

"I'm happy with what I'm doing," Yvonne added. "I don't need to hang out with those kids."

Dad gave his daughter a hug. "I'm honored that you're still willing to hang out with me," he said, smiling. She grinned.

Yvonne has a strong, supportive family foundation upon which she can build a healthy lifestyle, not only in terms of her physical activity but also in her social independence. She's defining her own path through adolescence, based on *her* values and interests, not on what would make her fit in or be more popular. When Mom and Dad checked in with her about her social life to make sure she wasn't feeling left out, they found out that the reverse was true. Yvonne isn't interested in aimless hanging out. She has a few close friends who share her interests, and she's happy with that arrangement.

If we're worried about how our teenagers are spending their time, we may need to take a look at our own allocation of time, resources, and interests. Establishing a healthy lifestyle requires a significant investment of time and energy every day. We do this in our own way by following our interests, and by finding some kind of physical activity to practice on a regular basis, whether it's competitive sports, yoga, martial arts, or just walking. The strongest message we can give our teens about how to be healthy and take care of themselves is through the example we set for them in the way we live our lives.

Listening Is Essential

Hopefully we've been talking with our kids about health issues since childhood, and as they've become teenagers, we've done a lot of listening. "Health issues" for teens cover a wide range of topics, including all the biggest issues we worry about for them—drugs, sex, and alcohol—as well as the less urgent but equally important issues, from brushing and flossing their teeth to eating well and exercising.

It's very difficult to start conversations about health issues if we wait until our teenagers are sixteen. If they haven't already experienced us as being able to listen to them and understand their perspective long before then, they're not likely to pay much attention to us at this point. We have to establish ourselves as a credible source of health information as early as possible in their lives. And we have to do this in a way that encourages them to feel safe enough to talk with us and to trust we won't respond to whatever we may hear by being punitive or hysterical, but rather available, calm, and helpful.

We have only limited influence over our teenagers' behaviors. At this point in their lives, no amount of lecturing, threatening, or punishing will have much effect. We can't control what our teenagers will do on impulse when immersed in their adolescent world. And we are rightfully most concerned, even fearful for our teens' safety, when it comes to the potentially dangerous combinations of drugs, sex, alcohol, and driving.

The amount and the nature of the influence we will have on our teenagers is directly dependent upon the quality of our relationship with them. If we have an open, supportive, trusting relationship, our teens are more likely to adopt our values and listen to our advice. The best way to nourish and develop such a relationship is through open communication, with us doing most of the listening and them doing most of the talking. We should consider this balance in every conversation we have with our teens. (We can even count the minutes for each side if that helps us remember.) And don't forget, if we're lecturing, our teenager is much more likely to be counting the minutes than to be actually listening to what we're saying. When it comes to giving advice to teenagers, less is emphatically more.

Sometimes we forget that it's okay to have moments of silence in our conversations with our teenagers. If we can learn to quietly wait out those pauses, our teens will have the chance to fill them in. We will only know about their lives—what they're doing, how they're feeling, what they're thinking—to the extent that they're willing to share with us. Our job is to make it as easy as possible for them.

When Mom heard troubling rumors about the dance that had been held at the middle school over the weekend, she decided to ask fourteen-year-old Tyler about it.

"I heard some kids were asked to leave the dance last Friday," she said by way of an opening.

"Yeah," Tyler answered. "Bruce and Sherman got kicked out for drinking."

Mom waited. She wanted to hear more, but she didn't want to turn the conversation into an interrogation.

"You know, it wasn't really fair to kick them out," Tyler said, after an unusually long silence.

"How so?" Mom asked.

"Well, other kids were drinking, too," Tyler answered. "It's just that Bruce and Sherman were more obviously drunk."

"So they got caught," Mom said.

"Yeah."

After another long pause, Tyler added, "Betsy was just as drunk. She got sick in the bushes outside. No one seemed to notice that."

"Hmm, doesn't sound like much fun," Mom said, keeping the urge to lecture her son under control.

"No," Tyler agreed. "She looked pretty bad, too."

In this conversation, Mom gives Tyler plenty of time and space to share with her what he knows about the dance. She doesn't jump right into lecture mode and cut him off. Tyler's mom has long ago made her position on alcohol use clear, and she doesn't need to repeat it endlessly. That kind of repetition is a turnoff for our teens and discourages them from even entering into a conversation with us.

Mom lets Tyler know she's aware of the kind of things that go on at school dances, and that she'll listen to him tell her about it without lecturing him. The message he gets is clear—it's safe for you to talk with me about alcohol. I'll listen to you, and I won't panic.

During adolescence our kids will be making potentially life-altering decisions. If they trust us, they'll feel safe enough to talk with us about those decisions. We want to be clear about our own personal values and guidelines and continue to model a healthy lifestyle for them by our own behavior. We also need to be good resources for accurate health information and to be open to whatever our teens are willing to tell us about their lives. It helps if we humbly remember how little control we have over them, and that we are dependent on their willingness to allow us into their lives. What we really want for our teens is for them to be able to take care of themselves, and to be kind to their bodies throughout adolescence as well as the rest of their lives.

Talking About Alcohol

The drinking age in this country is twenty-one. But many teenagers start experimenting with alcohol long before that. Every family has their own position on alcohol use, whether they abstain entirely, drink moderately, or overindulge. Our position is that teenagers need to understand that individuals vary remarkably in response and tolerance to alcohol and that if they choose to drink they need to learn how to safely handle their own individual response. We want them to feel that they can talk with us so they can learn from any experience they have. Many teens reach the legal drinking age with little or no guidance from home or clear information on drinking limits. If they choose to drink, they need to learn what their limits are—what they can drink, and how much they can drink, without getting sick, acting stupid, or blacking out. They need to learn how to drink socially without getting into trouble, and they need to know how to set up safeguards and backup plans for times when their decision-making abilities may be impaired. The chances of date rape or acquaintance rape increase substantially when alcohol is involved, so when teenage girls go to parties, they should have a close girlfriend who will not leave them alone with anyone and will make sure they get home safely. This is as serious and as important a matter as it is to have designated drivers.

The way most of us learn about our limits with alcohol is by testing them. Most parents who drank in their teens have vivid memories of becoming violently ill after drinking too much as a teenager. This seems to be part of the learning process. If our goal is for our teenagers to learn how to handle their response to alcohol, we have to accept the fact that they're going to have some tough lessons along the way. Our goal should be to keep them as safe as possible while they are going through this learning process.

Of course, if our teens are getting drunk every weekend, then they're not really learning. They're indulging in self-destructive behavior, and quite possibly developing a serious chemical dependency problem. If this happens, we have to talk with them about their behavior. If there are signs of other problems as well, like falling grades or other behavioral problems, we may need to seek professional help for our teens.

One of the reasons we want communication to be open with our kids is so that we can recognize developing problems as soon as possible. We want to catch our teens before they get too mired in problems of this nature, so that we can help guide them along more constructive pathways. In order to do that, we have to talk to them about drinking in very specific ways. For instance, we want our teenagers to understand that drinking to the point of a blackout—when they can't remember what happened while they were drinking—is a very serious and dangerous matter. It means that they drank to obliterate themselves, not just to get high and have a good time. Blackouts are considered one of the signs of alcoholism. And it goes without saying that if our teens are not conscious of what they're doing, they take the risk of exposing themselves to all kinds of potential dangers. However, some teenagers see blackouts as a normal part of drinking and somehow part of the fun. We need to be sure that our teens know that having a blackout is a warning signal, to be taken very seriously. And as with most high-risk issues, we need to give them this information long before we think they'll encounter it.

Generally, our teens are exposed to or involved with high-risk behaviors much earlier than we imagine they will be. Thirteen-year-old Carmen is only in the eighth grade but she has the following conversation with her mother after coming home from a sleepover at her friend's house.

"Did you have fun?" Mom asks as she is preparing dinner.

"Yeah," Carmen answers nonchalantly.

"What did you do?"

"Watched videos," Carmen says.

Mom waits quietly to see if Carmen would add anything.

Carmen continues. "Someone brought a bottle of wine."

"Did you have some?" Mom asks in a straightforward and calm manner.

"No."

Mom doesn't know whether to believe Carmen or not, but she thinks that the most important thing is that Carmen was willing to tell her about what had happened.

"You know your dad and I don't want you drinking wine with other kids. If you're curious about it, you can have a little wine at dinner with us tonight. And by the way," Mom adds, "thanks for letting me know about it. It's important for us to be able to talk about these things."

Carmen's mom is calm and practical about her daughter's early experience with alcohol. She doesn't ask which kid brought the wine, and she doesn't scold, warn, or lecture. She lets her daughter know that the best place for experimenting with alcohol use is safe at home with her parents.

Many parents would not be so open-minded or liberal with their teens. Some might even have punished Carmen or attempted to restrict her friendships, and prohibited her from drinking. And that might work, but it would only work temporarily. At some time during her adolescence, Carmen is almost sure to experiment with alcohol. It's best if she does it at home, or at least is able to talk with her parents about her experiences. We need to keep this realistic, long-range perspective in mind as we decide how best to respond to our teens' exposure to alcohol use.

If Your Teenager Drinks

There are no set answers about what to do if our teenagers come home drunk, or at what age to allow drinking if ever, or how much drinking and partying are okay. Parents make decisions about these matters based on their own personal values and, we hope, based on an understanding of and communication with their own kids. Policies about alcohol will work better as guidelines if they are made jointly with teens, rather than simply imposed upon them.

Discussions about alcohol need to continue throughout adolescence, because our teens' social lives are changing rapidly. We especially want to know how our teens perceive binge drinking—consuming a large quantity of alcohol in a short period of time. This is a far more dangerous way to experiment with alcohol, and we want our teens to be able to talk about it with us. There can be very strong peer pressure to indulge in binge drinking and our teens need our understanding and support to be able to make their own independent decisions and not cave in to peer pressure when they are confronted with it.

Late one Saturday night, sixteen-year-old Bradley was attempting to tiptoe into the house without waking his parents, but he was drunk and kept banging into things. His parents were up and waiting for him. They took one look at him and decided to do nothing—that night. "No point talking to him now," Dad said, and Mom agreed.

Early the next morning they found Bradley fully dressed and asleep on the living room sofa. At first Mom tried to be quiet so she wouldn't disturb her son, but then she realized she was only pandering to bad behavior. So she bustled around in the kitchen in her usual way, banging pots and pans, and turned on the TV. Dad joined her just as Bradley was beginning to mumble and move about.

"How're you feeling, son?" Dad asked in his heartiest voice, knowing full well that his son was not feeling well at all.

Bradley didn't answer, but headed straight for the bathroom, and then went back to sleep in his room. Many hours later, after a shower, Bradley joined his parents.

"Feeling better?" Mom asked.

"Yeah," Bradley answered. "What time is it?"

"It's three o'clock," Dad said. "You lost most of the day."

"You were pretty drunk last night when you got home," Mom said.

"Yeah."

"Is this the first time you've gotten drunk like that?" Dad asked.

"Yeah," Bradley said, holding his head.

"Who drove you home?" Mom asked, showing Bradley that her first concern was about the combination of drinking and driving.

"Barb drove—and she didn't drink anything," Bradley reassured his mom. "She took a bunch of kids home. You should've seen Tom—he was really wasted."

"That's wonderful of Barb," Mom said. "Please thank her for me and I'll thank her myself the next time I see her."

Bradley looked at his mom as if she was crazy, but this was Mom's way of letting him know she wanted to stay connected to him and his friends, and to let them know she understands what's going on and is willing to recognize and appreciate mature behavior. When Bradley's mom saw Barb after school the next week, she remembered to thank her for taking care of Bradley and their other friends. Barb was both surprised and pleased.

Bradley and his parents continued this conversation later that afternoon, while Bradley helped himself to some coffee and toast. Neither Mom nor Dad overreacted to what had happened. They knew that most teenagers get drunk some time or other during adolescence, and that this was not a regular pattern for Bradley.

As a matter of fact, they were taking advantage of this prime opportunity to talk with him about responsible drinking behavior. Still suffering the effects of his hangover, Bradley was more open than usual to receiving advice, and was not just running out the door in pursuit of his busy schedule. His parents had had some errands planned for the afternoon, but they postponed them in order to be around when Bradley woke up. They didn't want to miss this window of opportunity for an important conversation.

After a while, Dad asked Bradley, "So, what'd you learn from this experience?"

Bradley thought before answering. "I learned I can't drink that much beer," he said, finally.

"How much beer do you think you can drink?" Mom asked.

"About three bottles," Bradley answered.

They went on to discuss other variables involved in drinking— how much food he had in his stomach, how quickly he drank the beers, whether other kids were pressuring him to drink more or faster. As a result of this discussion, Bradley saw the experience of having gotten drunk as part of the process of learning how to manage alcohol. This is precisely what his parents wanted for him. The way they handled the situation is a good example of how we can influence our teenagers through our relationship with them by maintaining open communication.

Above all, we want our kids to be willing to tell us what's really going on in their lives. When they don't talk to us, it's usually because they don't want to deal with our going off the deep end or trying to control them. Most teenagers would actually like to be able to talk with their parents about everything and anything as long as they don't feel their parents will become hysterical and controlling when they do. Our kids know they're dealing with difficult issues, and they are likely to be both confused and worried about some of the situations they're encountering. If we don't panic and overreact, if we are patient and give them plenty of room to open up, they are more likely to let us in on their lives and to listen to us.

Two Tons of Steel at Sixty Miles an Hour

More than anything else, we want our teens to survive adolescence. This means that sometimes we need to keep our focus on behaviors that may be life-threatening and let most of the other stuff go. We have to accept that there is going to be a certain amount of junk food, mindless TV, computer games, and just plain wasted time in our teenagers' lives. But the limits we set for them have to be clear—we need to let them know that we cannot accept behavior that endangers them. If we have to choose between trying to ensure that they eat five fruits and vegetables a day and that they drive carefully, the choice is obvious.

Driving a car is the most potentially dangerous thing most of our teenagers will do. Although we will do most of the teaching and practice driving with them, we still want our teens to attend a driver's education class. They'll learn driving tips that they wouldn't pay attention to if we were the ones giving them, and the things they learn there may someday save their lives or the lives of others.

We also want to be sure our teens get their learner's permits as soon as possible. This will give them the maximum time needed to practice driving with us in all types of weather conditions and on all types of roads before they go out on their own. The more practice time and the greater the variety in their exposure to different kinds of driving we give them, the safer they'll be when they're driving on their own.

Teens can easily take for granted the risks involved with driving. By the time they get their licenses, they've already been waiting for years, and by now they're sure they can drive better than we can. Just think of all the hours they've spent in the car. Yet they don't fully realize the potential destructiveness of two tons of steel barreling down the road at high speed, or fully understand how one tiny mistake or a moment's inattention can lead to a fatal collision. With their adolescent sense of immortality and their lack of driving experience, it's no wonder the accident rate is high for teenage drivers.

Given this reality, wearing a seat belt, whether they are in the front seat or the back, is actually one of our teenagers' most important health habits. Wearing seat belts has now become such a strong cultural norm that it usually isn't a point of struggle between parents and teenagers. However, teenagers are still tempted to pile a bunch of kids into a car without regard for how many people can really fit safely, or whether everyone will have a seat belt. We want

our teens to resist the pressure to stick together by cramming everyone into one car. If we have talked about it in advance, our teen may
be the one to say, "No, that's not gonna work. We need another car."

As our teenagers start learning how to drive we'll be amazed at
the amount and the volume of criticism, warnings, and uncontrol-
lable outbursts of fear and panic that will inevitably leave our lips.
Rest assured, this is standard behavior for most parents of a new
driver. However, we want to be sure to balance such negative comments with positive feedback as much as possible.

Mom was taking fifteen-year-old Tommy out to practice driving
with his new learner's permit. As he settled behind the wheel and
automatically buckled up, she said, "I'm so glad you're in the habit
of wearing your seat belt."

Tommy, who was concentrating on starting the car, shifting his
foot from brake to gas, and backing up out of a narrow garage, didn't
acknowledge her comment, but he heard it. Don't be disheartened if
your teen ignores your supportive statements. Say them anyway,
and trust that they do, in fact, register.

As they drove around town, Mom continued giving Tommy positive feedback. "That was a great defensive maneuver you just did."
"You were really careful at that intersection." "Good job, letting those
people cross." Of course, she also let slip a few shrieks along the
way, a couple of times couldn't help placing her hand on the dash-
board, and couldn't refrain from shouting a couple of times, "Slow
down!"—but that's to be expected. Sitting in the passenger seat with
our teens as they practice driving is a white-knuckle experience for
all parents. However, the more we do it, the better they'll become at
driving.

One of the most important issues to take a clear stand on is the matter of driving under the influence of either alcohol or drugs. We need to be very clear with our teens that this *should never happen*—whether they are drivers or passengers. Our message will be most effective if we are coming from a caring, loving position rather than threatening, scaring, or trying to control them. We must remember that our teenagers only listen to us when the communication is open. This is the hallmark of a quality relationship and the best assurance that what we say will have an impact on their behavior. Also, we need to be willing to discuss exactly what we mean when we tell them not to "drive under the influence." For instance, what if they had one drink three hours earlier? What if they don't know whether or not the driver had anything to drink? Talking through and exploring potentially ambiguous situations will help our teens feel prepared when they are confronted with them and have to make on-the-spot decisions without our help.

Is Just Saying No Really Enough?

Of all the health issues that confront teens, parents may worry the most about drugs. This may be because of our own history of experimentation with drugs in the past. We know we were just plain lucky to escape without major problems, and we don't want our teens to take the same risks we did. We may be fearful that our teens will suffer brain damage or addiction if they try anything at all, or we may be concerned about the illegality of most drugs. Or, we may be worried about the things that can happen to kids when their judgment is impaired by drug use. Whatever our greatest fears are, many of us are primed to overreact. The problem is that overreacting doesn't help. To be effective, we need to be both calm and credible when discussing drugs with our teens.

Some of our kids will know more about drugs than we do. If we overstate the case, saying, "All drugs lead to addiction," or "If you use drugs, your brain will fry," they are likely to discount everything we say. Most teens, even thirteen-year-olds, are likely to know someone who has used drugs and is still okay, at least as far as they can see. If our teenagers think that we don't know what we're talking about, they won't listen to anything we say.

If we wait for our teens to bring up the issue, we'll be way too late. A wide variety of drugs are readily available to any interested preteen. We have to initiate conversations about drugs early and often as they mature. Simply repeating a slogan like "Just say no" is not really helpful. When we have these discussions, we need to reflect on our teens' level of maturity, and make our comments relevant to the experiences they're having now. Preteens may have access to Ritalin or other stimulants used to treat ADHD. Glue for sniffing and marijuana are also readily available to preteens. As our teenagers move through middle school, a wider range of illegal drugs emerge on the scene, from crack cocaine to ecstasy to heroin. Even while our teens are relatively young, the whole panoply of illegal drugs is present. It's critically important that we be able to listen to our teenagers so we can understand what's happening in their world, and also so they will feel safe enough to talk to us about their lives.

When thirteen-year-old Nick casually mentioned to his mom that one of the kids in his class had been kicked out of school, her first reaction was to feel a bit of panic.

"Who?" she asked. "What for?"

"Garrett," Nick answered. "I didn't really know him that well. He was selling dope."

If Mom had panicked at this moment (and we could all under-stand why she might), she would have ended the conversation and had no clue what her son was thinking. If she had gone right into lecture mode, Nick would have pretended to listen and then proba-bly would have decided never to confide in her again about this sort of thing. Mom knew it would be wiser to ask a few questions and be open to hear her son's reactions to the situation.

"Wow," Mom said, consciously taking a deep breath. "How's the school handling this?"

"They're going to have an assembly tomorrow on drug educa-tion," Nick answered.

"What will happen to Garrett?" Mom asked.

"I don't know, but he's not allowed back in school. I heard he may go to a military academy."

"His whole life is changed now," Mom said. "This is pretty serious."

"I guess it is," Nick agreed.

"Let me know what they say in assembly tomorrow."

The next day Mom followed up with Nick by asking about the assembly.

"They talked about how strong the marijuana is nowadays, that it didn't used to be like that," Nick explained.

"Yes, I've read about that," Mom said. "It's seventeen times more potent than it was when I was a teenager."

"Wow!" Nick said. He was impressed, both with the dramatic in-crease in the strength of marijuana and that his mom was clearly keeping up on things.

"Did they talk about ecstasy, too?" Mom asked.

Nick told his mom more about what had been covered in the as-sembly, and they had a real conversation about drug use. In this conversation, Mom wisely established herself as someone with up-to-date information about drugs and as someone who is able to talk about them calmly. Nick knows she doesn't want him to experiment with drugs and now he also knows he can talk with her about it.

In this example, Nick's mom had the easy role. Garrett's parents have a far more serious challenge. Sending their son to a military academy may or may not be the best response to this situation. There are so many variables involved that there is no one solution guaranteed to work if we discover or suspect our teenager is using drugs. Sometimes it's very difficult to know whether our teens are just engaging in light experimentation and will be okay, or if they're getting into deeper and deeper trouble. If they're sinking into serious problems, they will lie to us about their drug use, which makes it even harder to know.

These are extremely difficult, complex issues. It's always best to seek professional help from someone experienced with both teenagers and drug-related problems. Even then, there are no guar-antees. Some parents and teens struggle with drug problems for years. It can be a long, tough road where setbacks are considered normal and a cure doesn't exist.

Talking, and most of all listening to our teens, are the best pre-vention. We nurture our relationship with our kids this way, making sure that they know we care about and support them. Probably the healthiest habit our teens can have when it comes to drugs or alco-hol is the habit of talking with us about these health issues and let-ting us know what's going on in their lives.

Nicotine: The Most Common Drug

The most common drug addiction among teenagers is to nicotine. Even just experimenting with cigarettes can lead more quickly than we may realize toward a serious nicotine addiction. Within just a month of experimentation, our teens can develop a physical dependency that is very hard to shake.

What can we say to our teens that they don't already know about the health risks of smoking? They know as much as we do, yet they still light up to look cool, fit in, relax, or lose weight. The peer pressure to try smoking can be so intense for teens that it overrides all the health warnings, and cigarettes can be openly shared without concern for the legal problems that arise with other drugs. Sharing a smoke even creates a sort of adolescent bond among kids that gives them greater security and confidence.

Some of us have the additional problem of our own addiction to nicotine. If we've stopped smoking, we can share our struggles and solutions. If we still smoke, we can admit we're hypocrites but that the truth is that we wish we'd never started. We can work on quitting and even if we fail, at least we're giving our teens a real life example of how difficult it is to quit as a deterrent to starting. Don't be afraid to be open about your addiction to nicotine. Sometimes we can be a model of what *not* to do. Whether we smoke or not, the message is the same: "Don't smoke. It's much easier never to start than it is to quit."

The Truth About Sex

The more informed our teenagers are about sex, the better their decisions about engaging in sexual activity will be. Being informed means more than just understanding the basic mechanics of reproduction and hearing dire warnings about sexually transmitted diseases (STDs) or the risk of dying from AIDS. Being informed means knowing how to say "No" to sex, how to discuss contraception with sexual partners, and how to use a condom. It also means understanding sexual intimacy as part of a loving and committed relationship, rather than as a contact sport.

We don't want our teens engaging in any sexual behavior in a casual way. Some teens regard oral sex, and even anal sex, as being in a separate category from vaginal intercourse, and rationalize to themselves that this type of sexual contact isn't really sex. With this mind-set, they can be promiscuous while remaining technical "virgins." In some areas, this has led to a near epidemic of casual sex and the accompanying STDs.

We don't want our teens to develop the habit of using any form of sexual behavior in a casual or exploitive way, manipulating others, or allowing themselves to be manipulated. We don't want any teens, male or female, taking advantage of each other, trading sexual favors, or pressuring each other for sexual contact. We don't want teenage girls, in particular, to feel they have to perform oral sex in a misguided effort to feel popular or liked. We don't want our teens to feel pressured by their peers, older teens, or even adults to do anything they're not ready for, or to feel threatened in any way.

We all live in a sexually stimulating culture. Our teens are surrounded by sexually explicit media through music, videos, and the movies. Unfortunately, most of this imagery displays sex for sex's sake—not as an intimate part of a loving, committed relationship. We want to be sure our teens also see examples of sexual intimacy as an expression of love in order to balance the extensive media input.

Hopefully we're in a loving relationship, rich with warm, spontaneous expressions of affection that can serve as a model for our teens. Even if we're not, we can at least notice and mention the examples from TV and the movies that do depict such a loving closeness.

Ultimately, we want our teens to mature both psychologically and sexually so that they can enjoy sexual intimacy in a loving relationship. We hope they'll be able to communicate, and trust their partner with highly personal information about what pleases them both emotionally and sexually. To be able to communicate in this intimate way, our teens will need to learn about their own sexual responsiveness. And one of the best ways to do this is by self-stimulation.

Most teens explore their bodies as part of learning about themselves, and this is a totally legitimate part of the blossoming of their sensuality and sexuality. Yet talking about masturbation remains a taboo in our culture, though it seems we can now talk about most everything else. Being able to include the topic of masturbation as we talk with our kids about sex is a way of acknowledging that this is a healthy part of becoming a mature sexual being.

Admittedly it's not easy to raise these subjects with our kids, and there's a lot to talk about. But we do want our teens to learn far more about sex than just how not to get pregnant or how to avoid getting an STD. We want them to learn how to enjoy and appreciate their sexuality as a natural and integral part of a loving relationship, and to be able to choose a partner who will be as caring and kind to them as they know how to be to themselves.

Conversations about sexuality, like those about alcohol and drugs, need to begin early and continue throughout adolescence. Teenagers go through many stages as they discover themselves. Their attitudes and questions about sex will change as they grow older and mature. We want to continue to be a helpful resource and a positive influence for them all along the way. This means we need to keep listening to our teens so that we can talk about what's relevant to them at their current stage of development.

"You've been spending a lot of time over at Melanie's recently," Dad observes casually to his sixteen-year-old son.

"Uh-huh," Mike responds.

Now Dad doesn't know what to say—a dozen awkward comments go through his mind, everything from "I hope you're using condoms" to "Why don't you two hang out over here sometime?" He pauses, and says nothing.

"I'm off, late for practice," Mike says, and heads out the door.

And that's about it for this conversation. It may seem as if nothing was accomplished, but at least Dad let his son know that he's aware of where he spends his time and that he's interested in what's going on. This little snippet of conversation helps to keep the door open, making it easier for Dad to follow up later by asking, "How's Melanie?" in a day or so.

We want our teens to know we're interested in them and want to know how they're doing. Now if Mike does someday want to talk with his dad about Melanie, he doesn't have to start from scratch.

"You know Melanie?" Mike asks his dad a few weeks later.

"Sure," Dad says.

"Well, she dumped me."

"What happened?" Dad asks, and a slightly longer conversation ensues during which he is able to ask quite naturally, "How involved were you with her?" and "Are you hoping to get back together?"

By staying connected with the unfolding story of our teens' lives, we let them know we are available and concerned about their well-being. We want them to know that we recognize the seriousness of the decisions they face as a normal part of adolescence. We realize our teenagers are taking charge of their lives in more and more important ways, and we want to stay connected to them and know that they're taking good care of themselves. We need to make sure we touch base with our kids pretty much every day, even if the conversation is only a brief one.

Accepting Homosexuality

Teenagers know when they're "different," and they know the social costs of being different. To go through adolescence with one's sexual identity a secret or a point of internal conflict is extremely painful. In fact, a significant percentage of attempted teenage suicides involve homosexual teens. These teenagers desperately need our acceptance and support; they need to know that we love and care about them.

Some parents have difficulty accepting that their teenager is gay. A few parents will even reject their own children. This is always a tragic loss for everyone involved. Homosexuality is not a "lifestyle choice," but an inherent part of who they are. Gay teenagers need extra expressions of love and support from their families to help compensate for the social isolation they may feel as a result of the prejudice and lack of understanding that still exists in the world regarding homosexuality.

The kinder we can be to our teens who happen to be homosexual, the kinder and more caring they will be able to be to themselves. This will influence their decisions regarding sexual behavior and the risks they take. For some, this may mean the difference between a healthy lifestyle and life-threatening illness.

Dad was aware that his fifteen-year-old son, Jeremy, was somewhat effeminate. He always had been a sensitive kid and recently seemed even more physically slight since he'd lost a few pounds to wrestle at a lower weight for competition. Dad had no idea whether his son was gay or not, but he did want Jeremy to know that he would love him regardless of his sexual orientation. While driving him home from a wrestling meet one night, Dad casually told him a story from his own adolescence.

"You know, my dad used to come to my wrestling meets, too. I wasn't as good as you, though. My dad was disappointed about that. He always needed me to be real macho. I don't want to be that way with you. I want you to know that the way you are, however you are, is okay with me."

Jeremy looked at his dad a bit quizzically, allowing the message to sink in. He wasn't exactly sure what his dad was getting at, but it felt good to know that he had his dad's acceptance.

These are delicate matters to broach. Even if we're fairly sure our teenager is gay, we shouldn't ask about it directly. We have to wait for them to be ready to tell us. However, we can give our teens the message that they are free to be whoever they are. Depending on what our own attitudes are, we may need to work on being able to accept our child's sexual orientation. We may have our own prejudices and disappointments to deal with. We can hope we will be ready to accept whatever we hear and our teenagers will be ready to be honest with themselves and with us.

Keeping Up with the Barbies (and Kens)

There is enormous pressure in our culture to look a certain way. Magazines, movies, and television all bombard us with images of physical perfection that are impossible for the vast majority of us to attain. Although this is a cultural pressure that females have dealt with for a long time, it's now becoming equally true for males. Not many teens, or adults for that matter, have bodies that are as slender, tall, sexy, or muscular as the images we see in the media around us. We now even have computer-generated virtual models that set a truly impossible-to-attain standard.

The discrepancy between such unrealistic ideals and the imperfect reality of our bodies can lead to a pattern of being excessively critical of and dissatisfied with ourselves. Teenagers are especially vulnerable to this kind of pressure for two reasons. First, they're already uncomfortable with their bodies due to the drastic changes in their hormones and their rapid growth. Second, their sense of self is not yet solid and secure enough to tolerate their own physical limitations. They haven't yet learned to accept themselves as they are.

"I don't have anything to wear," fourteen-year-old Rebecca complains to her mom.

We have to be careful how we hear this familiar cry of frustration from our teenagers. It doesn't necessarily mean that Rebecca is spoiled and just wants to go shopping.

"What's the problem?" Mom asks.

"Nothing looks right on me."

"Hmm, what do you mean by that?" Mom asks, trying to get Rebecca to clarify what's upsetting her.

"I don't like the way I look. Nothing looks right on me," Rebecca repeats, collapsing into a chair.

Rebecca doesn't need a new wardrobe—she needs understanding. Her body is changing so quickly that she doesn't feel comfortable with herself, no matter what clothing she puts on. She needs as much reassurance as her parents can give her. She certainly doesn't need to hear any criticism about her body from her parents. Even a single comment, intended to be humorous or helpful, such as "You look like you're putting on a little weight" or "You're all arms and legs these days," particularly coming from a father, can set off an intense storm of self-hatred.

Mom has a little more leeway in what she can say to her daughter, but she still needs to be both empathic and cautious in her remarks. And sometimes it seems that she just can't say anything right. Even a seemingly safe "I like the navy outfit the best" may not be acceptable if Rebecca is caught up in a cycle of self-criticism. "How can you say that, it looks just awful!" may very well be the response. Sometimes it can help just to be present while our teenager goes through the emotional crisis. We don't have to say anything—our calm, accepting presence can be soothing in itself.

We ourselves are not immune to the cultural pressures to be physically perfect, and many of us have our own body image concerns. We need to be careful about what we say about ourselves in front of our teens. Habitually commenting on our feeling fat, or not being well coordinated, can set up a negative model for them. Our teenagers have enough trouble learning to deal with their own inner critics—they don't need to listen to ours as well.

We want to give our kids a model of healthy self-acceptance when it comes to our physical appearance. This can be especially challenging for moms going through menopause. These moms have to deal with emotionally charged hormonal and body image changes at the same time their daughters are dealing with the equally upsetting hormonal and body image changes of adolescence. There's no question that this juxtaposition of life stages requires extra awareness and sensitivity.

We also want to think about how we can balance the ubiquitous media images with comments that are healthy, realistic, and more accepting. We can call attention to female athletes who are fit and certainly not model-thin, as well as to actors and media personalities who are not picture-perfect. We can remind our teenagers that different body builds are optimal for different sports or activities. It also helps to compliment our teens often on how they look and to be patient with their obsessions with their appearance. This preoccupation is actually an important part of adjusting to their changing bodies and developing a more stable self-image. The way our teenagers feel and think about their bodies is part of their developing sense of self. The more we treat our teens with kindness and acceptance during this time, the more likely they are to develop a positive self-image—and the better their self-image, the better they'll take care of themselves.

Setting a Good Example

For all of us, teens and parents alike, one of the most challenging health habits is to bring a steady balance into our daily lives, to consistently treat our bodies with kindness and care. We need to make time for recreational activity, socializing, and just plain fun, as well as time for revitalizing rest, quiet reflection, and creative pursuits.

Our teenagers need to develop their own formula for finding a balance between being overscheduled with activities and "vegging out," between being glued to the computer or TV and working out at the gym, between partying with friends and having dinner at home with their families.

Whatever habits our teenagers grow up with in their family will become their standard to either replicate or rebel against. What examples are we giving our teens? Do they see us working day and night and rushing around to do everything else? Do they see us reclining in front of the TV for hours on end? What do our lives look like to our teenagers? Do they see us taking good care of ourselves both physically and emotionally? How do we handle alcohol and drugs in our lives? Even though they're not around as much, they are still watching us, and they are learning from our example.

There is nothing we can say to our teens that will have a greater impact than our example. The strongest influence we can have on our teenagers' health habits is the way we live our own lives—including the wisdom and compassion we show when we treat our bodies with kindness.

If teenagers live with support, they learn to feel good about themselves

Supporting our teenagers is like creating the foundation for a building that we won't see for at least a decade—and won't be thanked for until long after that. Yet, as parents, we need to give our teens all the support we can through these years of big changes and difficult challenges. Whether we realized it at the time or not, this is part of the commitment we made to them when they were born. And whether they appreciate it now or not—and most of them will not—it's what they need from us.

Even though they're teenagers now and seem very independent, they still need our support. They need to know we care about them, that we will do our best to understand whatever it is they're going through, and that they can talk to us about anything. They need to feel implicitly, but with absolute certainty, that we're always there for them, ready to be on their side.

Adolescence can be a time of enormous, ground-shaking insecurity, and our teens rely on us to have faith in them, especially when they don't have faith in themselves. When times are rough, we can lend them some of our own stability and confidence. Our support helps them develop greater equilibrium and strengthens them during their frequent and intense moments of insecurity.

Jason and his dad had been studying aikido for years, attending classes together two nights a week. When Jason was fifteen, he was preparing to test for his brown belt, and he was quite nervous about it. The test involved fending off three other students who would be aggressively charging him. Jason would have to be able to throw them quickly, one right after the other.

As they were driving home together from class one night, sweaty and sore, Jason mentioned to his dad, "I hope I don't have to face Gerard. He's fast, and he's pretty rough, too."

"I know what you mean," Dad agreed. "I don't even like to practice with him." Then it dawned on Dad that his son was worried about his upcoming test. "But you know, your technique is better than Gerard's," he added. "You can outfinesse him if you plan ahead."

"How?" Jason asked.

"Let's watch him in the next couple of classes," Dad suggested. "I think you'll be able to figure out a strategy to handle him."

So Dad and Jason watched Gerard carefully, and they noticed that he generally approached from the left. This observation gave Jason the edge, as he could now predict Gerard's moves and be prepared for him. Jason's test did entail fighting Gerard, and because he was psychologically well prepared, he passed his test, and received his brown belt.

When they went out to lunch to celebrate afterward, Dad said, "You know, Gerard *is* bigger and faster than you."

"Tell me about it," Jason mumbled with a mouth full of hamburger.

"But you really threw him."

"Yeah, I did!" Jason reflected, pleased with himself.

"Remember, there's always a way you can handle guys like Gerard. You just have to use your brain to figure out a strategy."

"Yeah, you're right," Jason agreed, adding even more ketchup to his burger.

Dad is supporting and coaching Jason, not only for aikido but for life. He is showing Jason that he has confidence in him, even when Jason doubts himself. He doesn't ignore or discount Jason's fears, but acknowledges them, while helping him to build on his strengths. Jason happens to succeed in this example, but even if he hadn't, his dad would have been right beside him, helping him to learn from his experience and prepare for the next round of testing.

Adolescence is full of dramatic ups and downs. We want to be there for our teens, especially during their moments of self-doubt and insecurity, so we can help bolster their confidence in themselves. Often our support and faith in them provides the extra measure of courage and confidence that helps them rise to whatever challenges they're facing.

Gradually our teens' sense of self will strengthen, and they will be able to sustain their confidence in themselves on their own. They will learn to feel good about themselves for who they are and how they behave. This kind of learning continues over a lifetime. We need to help them understand that maturation is a slow and gradual process of development, and that it involves continuously learning from one's experiences. This is how they develop the personal foundation for their adult identities, as well as their capacity for healthy intimate relationships and meaningful work—the two elements that make for a full life.

Our Time Is the Most Important Gift

In order to give our teens this kind of support we need to know the specific challenges they're facing in their daily lives. A simple "How're things going?" while we're driving them to school or doing errands together gives us only the barest amount of superficial information. We need hanging-out time with our kids if we want to know what's really going on.

We can't schedule such time or put it on a to-do list, but that doesn't mean it's not important. We have to look for opportunities to join our teenagers and just be together. We may have to set aside something we were doing in order to do this, but that's what it means to make our kids our priority.

Mom was hanging out in fourteen-year-old Marie's room, watching her sort through her closet and try on different outfits. Every once in a while Mom would make a comment, or help Marie hang up an outfit, or they would find something to laugh at together. This rather aimless activity went on for over an hour. No major decisions were made, and the closet was not any cleaner or better organized at the end of the hour than it had been at the beginning. Marie was simply playing around with different "looks" the way many teenage girls can do for long periods of time.

"I like the other sweater with that skirt," Mom said.

"I'm not sure," Marie answered. "How about this one?"

"You're right," Mom agreed. "That's better."

The conversation was pretty ordinary, but Mom's presence sends an important message to Marie—I enjoy being with you, I'm interested in helping you figure out how you want to look, and being with you is more important to me than all the other things I have to do. Because this is the consistent message Marie gets from her mom, she knows that her mom will always be there for her when she really needs her. During this hour, Mom doesn't even think about the paperwork waiting on her desk—just being with her daughter is the priority.

Hanging out with Marie in this unstructured way gives Mom an important and informative glimpse into her daughter's life—the way she feels about herself and how she looks, little snippets of gossip about girlfriends, her thoughts about some of the boys, and her anticipation about upcoming events. Mom now knows, for instance, that she needs to keep a certain weekend clear for Marie, because that's when Marie's class picnic is. Mom is clearly connected and available, and Marie knows she's got her mom's support for what's important to her in her life.

Taking an Interest in Their Priorities

Our teenagers' priorities may be very different from our own. Many of the things they find important, we may consider trivial. We may find it hard to believe how much time our daughter can spend putting on makeup or e-mailing her friends, or how much time our son spends downloading music or browsing catalogues of wilderness sports equipment. We don't have to understand our teenagers' priorities, but we do need to pay attention to and respect them. Before our teens will respect what's important to us, they need to know that we will support them in whatever they consider important. Even though we may not think of something as being all that significant in the grand scheme of things, if our teenager does, then we need to be attentive and responsive to it. In other words, whatever interests our teens should interest us. This is how we support them and nurture our relationship with them.

Thirteen-year-old Neal is crazy about a new computer game. He plays it for hours on end, totally captivated. When he isn't playing, he tries to explain the intricacies of the game to his dad in mind-numbing detail. Dad is not a computer game buff, so most of the time he has no idea what his son is talking about; however, he is wise enough to hear his son's excitement and respond to it.

"So, all of your friends are playing the same game?" Dad asks, trying to get the whole picture.

"Yeah," Neal answers. "Sometimes we talk on the phone while we're playing."

"Do you share tips with each other?" Dad asks.

"Sometimes, but not all the time," Neal explains. "So you don't always know what someone else knows, and they can surprise you sometimes."

Dad doesn't ask, "What's the point of all this?" or "Wouldn't it be more fun to shoot some hoops?" Instead he enjoys Neal's excitement in the game and the opportunity to understand a little bit about Neal's private world. After all, Neal is spending a large percentage of his free time on the computer and if Dad doesn't express interest in it, he'll be cutting himself off from a significant portion of his son's life.

If Neal had been into bowling, Dad would have been a good sport and dusted off his old bowling shoes. In this case, he takes a deep breath, and says with convincing enthusiasm, "Can you show me how it works?" Supporting our teenagers in whatever their interests are requires a significant investment of time and energy. We need to be generous in the giving of ourselves to our teens.

Sometimes we just have to forget about how we could be completing our taxes, finishing a report for work, or just plain relaxing, and actively decide to spend quality time with our kids. If we catch ourselves becoming impatient as our daughter describes her day in excruciating detail or when our son wants us to help him reconfigure his skateboard ramps one more time, we need to remind ourselves that this is the way our kids connect with us, and they are trying to share their world with us. Even though we may not have any interest in the subject they're talking about, we are interested in *them.* This can be difficult to keep in mind, especially if we're feeling overwhelmed with our own demanding lives. But there is nothing more important we can do as parents.

Whatever They Say, They Still Need Us

If we were to ask our teenagers, especially the older ones, whether we really need to be at every game or every performance, they would most likely say, "No, don't be silly." Don't believe them. As teenagers mature, it becomes increasingly difficult over the years for them to admit they still want us around. We may even want to believe that our older teens don't need us very much anymore. After all, they're independent in many ways now—they're driving cars, earning money, involved with friends and have a life of their own quite distinct from that of the family. We may even think that when a problem comes up, we can just give them time and they'll figure it out on their own. Sometimes this might be okay, but at other times it can be a terrible mistake.

Older teens need our active support and involvement as much as younger teens do. They need us to be attuned to their needs and concerns in a day-to-day way, whether they're facing tough issues or fretting over insignificant ones. What matters is that we're there for them whenever they need us, for whatever reason. If we don't give them our support and guidance on the little issues, they won't turn to us on the big ones. And we don't want them to feel they have to face their problems alone. Without our caring attention, they can become overwhelmed and sink into discouragement or isolation.

Even if the problem seems small to us, we want to seek to understand it from our teenagers' point of view. Fourteen-year-old Lindsey was upset that some boys were teasing her at school. She casually mentioned this to her father, and, wanting to reassure her, he minimized the problem.

"Oh, that's just a guy thing," he explained. "It means they like you."

"Well, I don't like them," Lindsey replied.

"Then just ignore them," Dad said, dismissing the issue and putting an end to the conversation.

Lindsey really didn't know what to do about the problem. Although she tried to ignore them as her dad had suggested, they didn't stop teasing her. Lindsey became more anxious and withdrawn at school, and her grades began to slip. Admittedly, Lindsey hadn't told her dad how upset she really was. But she had tried, and she had been dissuaded from revealing the full extent of her feelings by his dismissive attitude. We need to pay close attention to what our teens say. Often they don't tell us the whole story all at once, but in tentative bits and pieces. If Dad had responded to Lindsey's remark about being teased by asking, "What are they saying to you?" or "What are they doing that bothers you?" she would have been encouraged to give him more information about what was going on, and he could have helped her look for a solution that might work for her.

Our teenagers often float conversational "trial balloons" to see if we're really listening and taking them seriously. In this case, Dad failed the test, and Lindsey is unlikely to raise this subject with him again. And that doesn't help her solve her problem. If we consistently miss our teenagers' cues or subtle requests for help, they'll stop turning to us for help.

Dealing with the challenges they face is a prime learning opportunity for our teens, and we want to be the ones who influence what they learn. We don't want them to get most of their advice from their friends. Too often kids turn to each other for advice about difficult issues, and, frankly, none of them has enough experience to know what's best to do. Also, their friends may become overwhelmed when they're asked for help and the problem is too serious.

When we know our teens are dealing with a difficult problem, we want to be the first to reach out and offer support. Our kids can always reject our offer, but it's our job to be available. It's always better to err on the side of giving too much than giving too little. And if they're not willing to turn to us, we want them to know they can seek out other adults—teachers, coaches, clergy, relatives, or even the parents of other teens. This is one of the reasons why an extended network of family and friends is so critically important when raising teenagers. We want to have a good number of adults available to our teens for support and guidance.

A Time of Emotional Storms

Teenagers are moody. There's an intensity during adolescence, perhaps in part due to wildly fluctuating hormones, that lends a dramatic emphasis to even the smallest upset. We're all familiar with the spectacle of a teenager turning the whole house upside down as he desperately searches for a favorite pen before an exam, or feeling that her social life is over because a facial blemish has appeared just before an important date. During the intensity of these psychic storms, teenagers need our support and faith in them to help them regain their equilibrium.

We have to let them know that this is not the end of their world, that this time will pass and that things will get better. And we have to do this in a way that doesn't diminish or dismiss the intensity they feel in the moment. On the other hand, if we get caught up in their emotional maelstrom ourselves, we can easily lose our bearings, too, and become as panicked as they are. When that happens, we're no help at all. So we have to strike a balance—being strong and calm for them at the same time we are being understanding and sympathetic.

Sixteen-year-old Rebecca had just had a big fight with Sherry, her closest girlfriend, and she was moping around the house.

"I don't have any friends," she moaned.

Mom answered calmly, "I know you're upset about your argument with Sherry, but you do have other friends."

"She's never going to talk to me again."

"Who apologized first the last time you two had a fight?" Mom asked.

Rebecca thought a minute. "She did," she admitted.

Mom gave her daughter a knowing look, but didn't say a word.

"Okay, okay, maybe I'll call her!" Rebecca said, and flounced out of the room.

Mom was supportive and sympathetic, but she did not allow Rebecca to drown in her feelings. She gave her a subtle hint about how she might reconcile the situation, yet didn't push her to do so. Mom allowed her daughter to come to her own decision in her own time. Later that evening, Rebecca called Sherry to apologize, and everything was back to normal before bedtime.

It would not have been helpful if Mom had asked in a gossipy way for the details of what had happened between the two girls, and then gotten caught up in Rebecca's feelings of being hurt and angry with Sherry. When parents overidentify with their kids or micromanage the details of their lives, they often lose the advantage of their adult perspective. That's not really being supportive. Sometimes parents even make things worse by taking sides.

We have to remember that we're the grown-ups in the situation. We've got the experience and maturity to know that our teenagers can survive the highs and lows in life, even the loss of a precious friend or love interest, if it comes to that. Still, it's very sad when that happens, and this may be our kids' first experience of a broken friendship. We have to find a middle ground where we can talk things through with our teenagers but not get caught up in the details and in taking sides. After all, in Rebecca's case, the two girls could be best friends again tomorrow, and then she'd be mad at her mom for whatever negative things she said about her friend the night before.

We have to take our teenagers seriously enough to respect their feelings, yet maintain our adult perspective so we don't get swept away by their dramatic intensity. This is quite a challenge for us as parents. Sometimes it's hard not to react emotionally, since watching our kids go through the storms of adolescence tends to rekindle old feelings of our own from high school. The combination of old wounds that may still be tender and our fierce desire as parents to protect our kids from pain can be a volatile one. Needless to say, we're not going to find that perfect middle ground every time. We can, however, be supportive of our teens by keeping all this in mind and making sure that we accept the intensity of their emotions while at the same time encouraging constructive action.

Encouraging Their Best Inner Qualities

In order to support our teens' unfolding sense of self, we need to be able to recognize their unique inner qualities. We can search for just the right words to describe these finer aspects of our teenagers, the ones we want them to develop. In practical and simple ways we can call attention to these inner qualities, so that our teens become more aware of themselves and who they are becoming.

Fifteen-year-old Ron was describing to his dad some of the infighting that had been going on within the basketball team.

"Everyone's fighting for the ball," Ron complained to his dad. "No one's passing."

"That happens," Dad said. "Even in the NBA that happens."

"Well, we're never gonna win that way," Ron said.

"You're playing for the team, and they're playing for themselves," Dad said.

"That's the problem," Ron agreed.

"Keep on being a team player, no matter what the other guys are doing," Dad advised. "It'll pay off, if not now, then later. Besides, that's what comes naturally to you."

Dad is not just supporting Ron's interest in basketball, he's supporting who Ron is as a person and helping him to understand who he is. With this kind of acknowledgment and support, Ron is able to strengthen his self-image as a good team player and trust in his decisions, even when they go against what his teammates are doing. Dad gives him the chance to see himself in a positive way and to feel good about who he is.

Ron is more than just a member of the basketball team who's willing to pass the ball, and he's more than just a guy who wants his team to win. He's someone who can put aside his own egotistical desires in the interest of a larger goal, and he is able to maintain that perspective. These are inner qualities that will serve him well in the future, in whatever career he chooses as well as in his intimate relationships.

Notice that the parental words of support in the above anecdotes are directed toward specific inner qualities; not to anything external that the kids may achieve, but to who they are inside. We want to support the *inner being* of our teenagers, not just their outer results. This is the best way to encourage our teens to develop their best qualities.

Complimenting Them on the Right Things

We also want to support our teens when they behave in ways we hope to encourage. Many parents think they're giving their teens support and increasing their self-esteem by giving them a steady stream of compliments: "You're wonderful!" "You're the best!" "You're so handsome/pretty." These vague pronouncements are likely to be ignored by our teens—worse yet, they may use them to become even more self-centered than most teens already are. Even though we may be well intentioned when we praise our kids in this way, our words can quickly become meaningless or have an undesired effect. It's better to give our teens specific compliments targeted to them personally—comments that show we've noticed the way they behave and admired them for it.

When we applaud our teens' accomplishments, we can also mention their inner attributes that enabled them to achieve. Our kids gain confidence in themselves as they realize they have what it takes inside them to succeed. The accumulation of many small successes as well as some big ones also helps our teens feel more competent and powerful. Little by little our teenagers learn to feel good about themselves and their growing independence.

One Sunday morning, Dad asked fourteen-year-old Brooke how her baby-sitting job had gone the night before.

"Okay," she said.

"I'm sure you're great with the kids."

"Yeah," Brooke yawned, still half-asleep.

This kind of vague support slides right off our teens and it doesn't really mean anything to them. We need to be more specific in our comments.

"How did the baby-sitting job go last night?" Dad asked Brooke.

"Okay."

"What was the hardest thing about it?"

Brooke thought a minute. "I guess getting them to go to sleep."

"How'd you do it?" Dad asked.

"I read to them for a long time," Brooke answered. "But I kept dimming the lights until I could barely see the book. That's when I noticed their breathing had changed, and they were asleep."

"How clever." Dad responded, impressed with his daughter's ingenuity. "That was a great idea."

"I thought so," Brooke agreed, and felt pleased with herself all over again for her ability to come up with a good strategy.

Which Values Do We Support?

It's quite natural for us to support some things our teens do and ignore others. Through the way we interact with our teens, we choose to encourage certain things, discourage others, and let some go. For example, we support playing the violin and try not to nag them about whiling away the hours in front of the TV. We hope we're making conscious choices about what we encourage based on our values and our teens' interests. We want to be sure that our support is encouraging good character development in our teens through both their values and their actions.

Fifteen-year-old Kelila was doing volunteer work at a nursing home to fulfill the community service requirement at her high school.

"I'll be finished with my twenty hours this weekend," Kelila told her mom, "but I think I'm going to keep going in to help out."

Mom could say a variety of things in response. She might say, "That'll look great on your college application," or she could say, "That's very sweet of you," or "I'm sure they'll appreciate your help." Each of these comments reflect different value systems. Instead she asked, "What are you learning there?"

Kelila had to think a minute. "I guess I'm learning the most from

Mrs. Carbonari. I like to sit with her and listen to her stories about Italy and her family. She had eleven brothers and sisters!"

Mom smiled. "I guess a lot of the people there have good stories to tell. It's wonderful you can learn from their lives. Tell me more about Mrs. Carbonari."

Mom is encouraging a certain depth in her daughter—the ability to understand other people's lives and to learn from their experiences. This isn't only about providing a required number of hours of community service, it's about how Kelila will grow and learn from her interaction with the residents at the nursing home. Mom is encouraging Kelila to be reflective about life—Mrs. Carbonari's life as well as her own. She is also showing her how service to others enriches our lives as well as the lives of those we serve.

Hanging In There When It's Hard to Do

One of the times it's hard to emotionally support our teenagers is when they're arguing with us. It's natural to become frustrated in that situation and want to fight to win. But we may lose something more important if we get caught up in winning. When we are in the middle of an argument, we need to step back and ask ourselves, "What's this conflict really about?" It's usually about something other than the seeming point of conflict.

Many times teens are fiercely fighting for their independence— what they perceive as *their* territory or *their* freedom. We want to recognize this and support their efforts to grow up as much as we can. We can do this by giving our teens as much opportunity as possible to be self-determining. We can have flexibility within our structure, respecting our teenagers' drive toward independence and our need to hold them accountable. If we can maintain this perspective during a disagreement with our teens, then our attitude will be different. We won't feel that we have to "win" every argument by exerting control over our kids, or squashing their spirit in a way we don't mean to. We'll be more able to find a compromise that will protect their sense of autonomy while meeting our standards.

"You know, your curfew is midnight," Dad says to sixteen-year-old Brett. "Yet you continue to come in at twelve-fifteen, twelve-twenty, every Friday and Saturday night. Why are you doing that?"

"I figure that's close enough," Brett answers.

This is an invitation to a big disagreement, but if Dad rose to the bait it would just become another painful and inconclusive parent-teen power struggle. Trying to overcontrol our teens can lead to destructive arguments that make everyone feel bad about themselves and each other. Dad doesn't particularly care about winning a debate on the issue of curfews, and he definitely doesn't want to undermine his relationship with Brett.

"I know you want to decide on your own when to come home, but your curfew is midnight," he says, acknowledging his son's striving for independence while maintaining his right to set limits.

"Whatever," Brett answers sarcastically, and leaves the room. Dad lets this remark go. This is another example of flexibility on Dad's part. Some parents would react to the sarcasm and get angry, demand an apology, or punish Brett. This is precisely the kind of fight to avoid—the familiar warning of "Pick your battles" is appropriate here.

Brett continues to arrive home fifteen to twenty minutes late every weekend, and Dad continues to restate the midnight curfew. If

Dad were to move the curfew to 12:15, Brett would come home between 12:35 and 12:40. So the curfew is actually working in a way—
there is a subtle sort of compromise that allows Brett to declare his
independence, while giving Dad the assurance that his son will
come home at a predictable, and safe, time.

This is a good way to deal with an argument of this nature. Neither party wins, but neither party loses, either—the struggle continues, with Dad setting limits and Brett resisting them. Actually, both
Brett and Dad are winning. Brett feels as if he is coming home on his
own terms by coming home late. Dad knows that his curfew is working because Brett always does come home within a reasonable prox-
imity of his curfew time. When Brett moves into young adulthood,
he and his dad will be able to laugh together at this contest of wills.
At that point, Dad will know he was wise not to quibble over the
principle of a few minutes, and Brett will appreciate the fact that he
didn't.

Encouraging Gender Freedom

Our culture reinforces certain gender stereotypes, and no matter
what our own values and attitudes are, our teens can be
strongly influenced by these societal biases. We don't want our teens
to be limited by cultural stereotyping of any kind. We want our sons
to be able to feel and express a wide range of emotions—and not just
on the athletic field. We want our daughters to feel free to use all
their strengths and abilities in whatever endeavors they choose
to pursue in life. Ultimately we want all our teens to be free to
choose how they want to live their lives, whether our sons want
to become stay-at-home dads or our daughters neurosurgeons. We
need to make an extra effort to support our teenagers' development

in ways that go beyond the limitations that society tends to place on them.

Seventeen-year-old Jenny thought her math teacher was favoring the boys in the class. He called on them more frequently, and seemed to help them think through the problems if they didn't know the answer right away. One day Jenny was at the blackboard, struggling with a particularly tough problem, and the teacher told her to give up and sit down.

"He completely humiliated me," she cried to her mother. "I could've gotten that problem, too."

"I'll make an appointment to talk to him," Mom said.

"No, don't bother with that, he'll just deny it," Jenny answered. "Call the parents of other girls. See what they say!"

Mom was taken aback by this idea. She wasn't the type to make trouble, but for her daughter, she'd do anything. Mom started calling a few parents and found that every single girl in the class agreed with Jenny and a number of the boys did also. Jenny's mom set up a meeting with the teacher and the head of the math department. The teacher expressed surprise at the allegations and promised to be more aware of his behavior. Jenny felt great that her mom was willing to stand up for her. Also, she was determined to show her teacher what she could do, and, in a surge of righteous anger, she aced her math final.

Gender stereotyping affects teenage boys as profoundly as it does girls, but in a different way. Dad was enjoying a glimpse of thirteen-year-old Russell playing Rollerblade hockey with some of the neighborhood kids one day. As he watched, he realized the kids were being particularly rough on one boy and then taunting him. Dad asked Russell about it later.

"That was a pretty rough game this afternoon," Dad said.

"Naw," Russell responded, "just the usual."

"It looked rough to me, especially on Robert," Dad said.

"Oh, Robert, he's no good, anyway," Russell said.

Dad got right to the point. "Look, I know how rough and cruel guys can be. I don't want you participating in that kind of behavior."

"Aw geez, Dad, it wasn't that bad."

"I watched. I know how these things go. I wouldn't want you to be the one that was being treated that way."

Russell looked at his father. "Okay," he mumbled.

Russell got the point. His father didn't want him participating in the kind of bullying that goes on regularly among groups of boys. Dad didn't tell him what to do or not do. He simply made a clear statement about his values—bullying behavior is wrong, no matter how commonly it occurs or who the victim is.

As parents we need to be willing to take a stand regarding gender socialization issues. We want to encourage our kids to develop a broader range of feelings, behavior, and future possibilities than the cultural norm has defined for them. They need our support to venture beyond the traditional gender roles and to develop the strength to sustain themselves when they differ from stereotypical expectations. Our teenagers need to understand that our strongest desire is that they be free to decide for themselves what kind of person—man or woman—they want to become.

In Times of Crisis

The way parents treat their children during times of stress or crisis makes an enormous difference in the child's ability to adjust to the trauma they're experiencing. Divorce is probably one of the most common family crises in a teenager's life, a time when kids of all ages clearly need extra support. It's not enough to tell our kids, "It's not your fault." Teenagers may intellectually understand that, but still feel that they are somehow responsible. Often they imagine that they should have been able to do something that would have kept their parents together.

We need to give our teens extra support during this time, even though we may doubt that we have it in us to give. But we really *must* pull ourselves together so we can be sure we're meeting their needs and giving them the extra support and reassurance they need through this family crisis. We might even consider babying them a little—tucking them into bed, for example, even if we haven't done that for years. At bedtime, teenagers, like small children, may be more open and willing to talk. This can provide us with an opportunity to listen to them and give them some of the extra support they need during a very difficult time.

Divorce can be such a rough time for parents that we may even be tempted to turn to our kids for support. But no matter how tempting it is, or how much *we* need a shoulder to cry on, we should resist this impulse. It's better for us to turn to friends or family or counselors for the support we need. Like younger kids, teens are likely to regress emotionally during a divorce, so this is not the time to expect them to take on more adult responsibilities. We cannot expect them to understand our stress or to relieve our emotional burdens. They have their own deep pain in the midst of a divorce. We need to be sure that we let them continue with their normal adolescence as much as possible. We have to reassure them that we'll be fine on our own, that it's not their job to take care of us, and that they have every right to continue with their lives uninterrupted, as much as possible.

Seventeen-year-old Stacey's family was going through a tough divorce. Over a long holiday weekend, Mom noticed that Stacey was hanging around the house more than usual.

"You're not staying home to keep me company are you, Stacey?" Mom asked.

"Who, me?" Stacey replied guiltily, as if she'd been caught. "No, of course not."

"Well, I'm fine at home alone," Mom assured her, "and I have friends to call if I want to go to a movie or something."

"I know that," Stacey said.

Still, she needed permission from her mom to live her own life. A few hours later, she asked to borrow the car, and caught up with her friends at the mall.

When we're going through a tough time with a divorce or some other crisis, we need to give our teens permission and support to continue living and enjoying their own lives. No matter how stressed we are, we need to remember that it's *our* job to take care of our teens, even if we have to muster all our strength to do so, and not their job to take care of us.

Giving and Receiving Support

The ability to both give and receive support is part of the essence of family relationships. An interdependence exists in intimate relationships, where we know we need each other and we want to be needed in return. We want our teens to learn how to give of themselves generously and how to accept from others graciously, too.

Fourteen-year-old Justin was raising money for breast cancer research by participating in a fifty-mile bike-a-thon. His mom was a breast cancer survivor, so this cause was very important to him. Justin asked family friends, kids at school, and local merchants for their support—a financial contribution for every mile he completed.

This kind of marathon is always more difficult in reality than in our kids' imaginations. Justin struggled for the last ten miles, and he needed all the support team had to keep going. They kept him hydrated, fed him orange slices, bandaged his blisters, and kept his spirits up. After he crossed the finish line, amid the cheers and the water spritzing, Mom hugged him and said, "Thank you, Justin. I'm so proud!"

Justin felt good about being able to support his mom and to contribute to breast cancer research, but he also knew that he hadn't done it alone. Without the support team, he might have given up during those last ten miles, and without the incentive provided by the financial commitments of all his contributors, he wouldn't have signed up for the bike-a-thon in the first place.

Justin originally set out to support his mom, but in the end he realized that he had received more than he gave. The experience of being helped through an intense challenge had a strong emotional impact on him. It opened him up to a greater understanding that we don't go through life alone—that we all need each other.

If teenagers live with creativity, they learn to share who they are

Adolescence is a time of inner reflection. Teenagers need to find out who they are, distinct from their parents, and eventually distinct from their peer group as well. During these years, they are grappling with the great philosophical questions of life: Who am I? Why am I here? What am I going to do with my life? And what does it all mean?

Our teens have to wrestle with these questions within their own hearts and souls. We cannot "give" them the answers. We can only encourage and respect them as they find their individual paths to self-discovery. This is a creative process, during which they learn to express who they are in the present and at the same time begin to define who they will become in the future.

Generally speaking, we adults are not in the midst of life changes as dramatic as the ones our teenagers are engaged in. However, the creative process of expressing who we are continues throughout our entire lifetime. We may not always think of what we do every day as being creative—decorating the house, preparing a gourmet dinner, designing a website, finding better business solutions. But any activity we're passionate about or deeply involved with can be an outlet for our creativity.

A creative approach to life—in which we are constantly developing, growing, and sharing who we are with others—doesn't require specialized artistic talent. Rather, what's required is being open to honestly and deeply experiencing one's inner world and being willing to express the insights gained in that process in the outer world.

Most teenagers have the opportunity to explore many different avenues of creative expression. They have leisure time and often the right kinds of classes, teachers, and even homework assignments that encourage them to stretch their imaginations and try new ways of seeing themselves and the world. Through this process of self-expression our teens can discover who they really are, participate in their own creation of themselves, and share who they are with others.

Seventeen-year-old Isaiah decided to take a series of photographs of his friends in their bedrooms. He was insistent that his subjects neither dress up nor clean their rooms for the portraits, which made everyone but the parents happy. Isaiah simply showed up at a prearranged time, set up his equipment, and shot some film.

The photos he came up with were revealing. One girl was sitting in bed reading, surrounded by her stuffed animals; a boy was lounging on the floor with his dog; another kid stood next to an overflowing closet; and still another was playing "air guitar" in his portrait. The kids' rooms were remarkably different. Most had wild accumulations of stuff layered around the room in interesting juxtapositions, but a few were neatly organized. It became clear from the photos that the teens' bedrooms, as well as their images, were creative expressions of the unique individuals they were.

Isaiah's imprint was on the photos, too. No one smiled. The teenagers looked straight into the camera, in total seriousness. Aside from the setting, this was Isaiah's only request and, of course, it set the mood for the entire series of portraits.

In addition to expressing his own vision, Isaiah's photos revealed an intimate vision of each teenager as he stared out at the camera, each from a room of his own creation. The portraits were a glimpse into another art form in progress—the development of a unique human being. Each teen was captured, at that moment in time, just being himself in his own world, and though the parents were somewhat embarrassed about the disastrous state of the bedrooms that had been documented, everyone loved the photos.

Discovering Themselves Through the Arts

Creative expression helps our teens discover who they are and connect with themselves in a deeper, more expansive way than they may be used to doing in daily life. It offers them the opportunity to experience universal feelings and moments of inspiration. It's a way they can identify with the whole of humanity, exploring the archetypes of birth and death, love and fear, community and isolation.

If we are open to our own process of self-discovery through the arts, our teens are more likely to be comfortable with this process as well. We can engage in the creative process through our work or our hobbies, whether we are professional musicians or avid knitters. We can also participate in the arts as members of an audience, attending a variety of performances, from opera to country-and-western concerts. Or we can make more creative choices in our own homes, tuning in to the arts on public television or radio. Creative expression comes in a variety of responses to everyday life—it doesn't just mean picking up a set of paints or participating in community theater.

The greatest impact we can have on our teens is through our example. Our authentic pleasure and love of all kinds of artistic expression is what will inspire our kids to explore these venues for themselves—the more open to the arts we are, the more open our teens will be.

Through us, our teens can learn how to behave in museums, to feel comfortable in concert halls, to dare to lift a paintbrush, or to take risks on stage. The arts enrich our lives and throw light on what it really means to be a human being in the never-ending process of evolving, growing, and becoming more whole. This is a way we can share who we really are with our teens, beyond the sometimes confining roles of parent and child, and beyond the predictable and inevitable skirmishes with our adolescents. Through art, we can just be people together, enjoying the creative experience.

Neither Dad nor thirteen-year-old Caesar was in a good mood; in fact, they were almost on the verge of an outburst. They were going to an art museum to complete one of Caesar's homework assignments, and by the time they got there, they were both miserable.

"Let's not rush through the whole museum," Dad suggested. "Let's just find something that you like a lot, and you can write your essay sitting in front of it."

"Okay," Caesar agreed.

They wandered through the galleries together, not saying much until Caesar plunked himself down on a bench by a large sculpture. "This is it," he said.

"Okay," Dad agreed. Caesar began writing in his notebook. Eventually Dad got bored, so he asked his son for a piece of paper and he began scribbling some words down, too.

After they left the museum and were having lunch, Caesar shyly asked his dad, "What were you writing?"

Dad smiled. "Oh, I was just jotting down some thoughts about the statue."

"Really?" Caesar asked, taking out his notebook. "What did you think?"

They read to each other what they had written in the presence of the sculpture. And they listened to each other as equals, a father and a young teenage boy, each encountering a classical work of art and trying to express what it meant to him.

On their way home, Caesar remarked, "That was fun."

"What was your favorite part?" Dad asked.

"Lunch," Caesar answered promptly, smiling, and looking directly at his dad.

Cultivating a Unique Voice

Creative expression does not necessarily require a specialized talent. Rather, it's the art of finding one's unique voice or singular perspective. It requires tuning in to one's deepest and most sincere inner self, connecting to that essential center, and then sharing that essence with others.

To do this, teens need to be able to "march to their own drummer," and be willing to risk being seen as different or weird. To find their own voices, all teenagers have to be able to express their own unique vision. Following their artistic impulses can help kids discover who they are, separate and distinct from their friends.

Everyone in the eighth grade had to take art, and at the end of the year there was a major project due. The projects were then to be used to decorate the auditorium for the middle school graduation ceremony. There were many talented kids in Anita's class, but she was not one of them. She didn't feel comfortable using any of the art forms they'd studied, so she asked her teacher if she could build something instead, and cover it with a collage. She knew she could at least hammer a nail and cut and paste.

With her art teacher's support, Anita built a freestanding archway made of corrugated cardboard. Then she covered it with an incredible array of intricately pieced-together magazine clippings. The whole project took much more time and energy than Anita thought it would, but she was so enthralled with the process that she didn't care. She spent long hours in the art studio, cutting and pasting, until she had covered the entire structure. Then she coated it with clear lacquer for protection. Without realizing or even planning it, Anita had created a sculpture. Both she and her art teacher were ecstatic.

Anita came into her own through her art project. She didn't start out thinking it would be quite so big. She just kept doing what seemed right to her and changing whatever struck her as "not right." She followed her intuition, and as she did, the sculpture seemed to grow organically. Through this process she learned to trust her inner self and feel more confident in other ways as well.

At graduation, Anita's sculpture dominated the auditorium. Everyone wanted to walk through and around it. It drew so much attention, in fact, that her parents were embarrassed and didn't know what to say about it.

"Do you like it?" Anita asked them.

"It's very interesting," Mom replied evasively.

"What's underneath it?" Dad asked. "What's it made of?"

"Do you like it?" Anita asked them again, insistent.

Finally Anita's parents responded that they loved it and were proud of her. But actually, they were shocked. They had never thought of Anita as someone capable of building and creating something so impressive. They felt as though they had to get to know their daughter again in a totally different way—and they were right.

Our teenagers can change so much during adolescence that they may become almost like strangers to us. This is one of the reasons we need to be closely connected to them on a daily basis. We want to know how they're evolving, what new directions they're exploring, who's influencing them, and what their current passion is.

In Anita's case, the change was a positive one. Under her art teacher's guidance, Anita had expanded her sense of herself as an artist and as a person, and had literally enlarged her vision of what she could create in the world. Anita's parents now have to catch up with their daughter, to get to know her again. They have to adjust to seeing their daughter as an individual in her own right, as someone who can express herself in the world in a unique and original way.

A Risky Business

Creative expression is an active process filled with risk—you invest yourself deeply in a process that often leads to an unknown destination, and along the way you reveal your most intimate thoughts and feelings, with no control over the way your creative efforts will be received. This type of endeavor is the exact opposite of being a "couch potato"—someone who wants to be entertained while sitting back passively. It's also qualitatively different from engaging in either athletic or academic competitions, because when it comes to artistic activity, there are no standardized rules or score cards. Creative expression is totally subjective—and it's a very personal process that is shared publicly. As such, it requires a good deal of personal courage and conviction in one's own beliefs.

The process of self-expression is fulfilling in and of itself. There's great pleasure to be found in following one's inner calling and allowing one's imagination to roam freely. The joy is in the act of creating, opening to the inner flow and expressing it in the outer world. However, sometimes in the midst of this wonderful creative process, our teens may hit a major snag—whatever they're creating doesn't look, read, or "work" the way they feel it should. Or no one understands them and what they're doing, and they feel isolated. Or other kids may laugh at them and think they're weird.

What can we say to them in these times? How can we give our teens the encouragement to continue to risk sharing themselves? We have to be very clear ourselves, and remember that the value lies in the creative *process,* and not with audience approval.

Seventeen-year-old Bruce read some of his poetry at an open-stage event at his high school. His poetry tended to be dark and obscure, and it was not well received by his fellow students. The kids were confused by or uninterested in his poetry, at best. Bruce came home in a funk.

"How'd it go?" Dad asked.

"Bad," Bruce mumbled.

"What happened?" Dad asked. He was not all that surprised.

Bruce explained what had happened in as few words as possible and then tried to retreat to his bedroom. But before he left, Dad asked Bruce one more key question.

"Do *you* like your poems?"

"Yeah, I like them. So what?" Bruce answered.

"Well, did you write them for yourself or for a high school audience?" Dad asked. That question stopped Bruce in his tracks. He realized that reading his poetry aloud had been an afterthought, and that writing the poems had been the best part of the experience. His dad's question also helped lead him toward the realization that his own opinion of his poetry was more important than the opinion of others.

"If you want to share your poems, there may be a better audience than a teenage crowd," Dad continued. "And the most important thing was writing them in the first place to suit yourself." Bruce didn't say much, but he did listen. Dad delivered his message strongly and clearly, in just a few words.

Dad could lecture his son about all the poets and composers who have died in obscure poverty and are now famous, but he doesn't. He could suggest that Bruce look into venues for publishing his poetry, but he saves that for later. Right now he focuses on helping Bruce get through the embarrassment and disappointment he is feeling in the moment, and on reinforcing his own positive feelings about his poetry. Dad is able to be there for his son because he knows what's going on—he knows about the poetry reading, and he knows about Bruce's writing. He isn't surprised by the reception Bruce got at the high school, and he's ready to lend an encouraging word at the right moment. This is the advantage of knowing what's going on in our teenagers' world on a day-to-day basis. When we're connected to our kids we can help guide them through their experiences with a minimal exchange of words.

But Is It Art?

It's relatively easy for us to appreciate art for its own sake when our teenagers are engaging themselves with the quieter forms such as drawing or watercolors. However, when their large metal sculptures are taking over the house, or they're enthusiastically pursuing a career as a rock star, complete with all the amplified electronic equipment, wild clothes, and endless rehearsals, it may be a bit more difficult for us to support our kids in their artistic pursuits.

When our kids write angry or depressing lyrics, scream out the words, and turn up the amplifiers to the point where we think we're going to lose our minds or get thrown out of the neighborhood, it may not seem like "creative expression" to us. However, this kind of expression may be the best way for our teens to feel as if they are truly sharing who they are, perhaps for the first time in their lives. It really doesn't matter whether or not they are any good. All that matters is that they feel fulfilled, through their own chosen form of creative expression.

"I'm going over to JJ's to practice," fifteen-year-old Luke told his mom. "I'll be home late."

Mom wishes Luke didn't waste so much time with his band. To her their music sounds awful, and she's not too thrilled with the lyrics, either. She's only grateful the rehearsals are no longer in her garage. But she answers her son calmly, saying, "Okay, just call when you're ready to come home."

We have to put our own preferences and judgments aside when it comes to our teens' creative expression. We have to admit that we don't always recognize what's valued by teenagers, and that our artistic opinions are not the ones that count in this matter.

Luke's band plays at a few of their old middle school's dances, where they are loud, keep a good rhythm—and the kids love them! Mom still thinks they are flat-out terrible, but she never voices her opinion. She treats Luke's rock group as seriously as Luke does throughout the life of the band.

When our teenagers find ways to express themselves, we need to be very careful not to react as if we've been personally offended. This is not about us. Our teens are exploring ways to share who they are and how they see things. We want to give our teens permission, support, and respect for whatever ways they find to express themselves creatively.

Keeping Up with the Stars

It may be difficult for teenagers who have exceptionally talented siblings to focus on their own creative expression, particularly in the same area of endeavor, and to be satisfied with themselves without comparing themselves to their siblings. As parents, we can affirm each child's uniqueness and encourage creative expression as a value in itself, but if there is an obvious star in the family, there's no way of getting around that fact. We can't pretend otherwise, or downplay the talented teen in a vain attempt to protect the other sibling from hurt feelings or feelings of insecurity.

Audrey's sister had an absolutely beautiful singing voice. She got all the solos in the school chorus and the lead in the school play. Audrey, who was two years younger, also had a nice voice, but it was nothing special. She loved her older sister, but she got pretty tired of all the attention she got for her singing. When Audrey began high school, she decided not to audition for the chorus.

"Why don't you go out for chorus?" Mom encouraged her. "I'm sure you'll get in."

"I'm not interested," Audrey declared emphatically, leaving no possibility of further discussion.

Mom realized that Audrey needed to find something completely her own, something her older sister wasn't involved in. But Mom couldn't really help her. This was something Audrey had to do for herself.

It can be painful for a parent to watch as a teenager struggles to find her own style of creative expression, a way of establishing who she is in her world. All we can do is be supportive as our teens seek to find their way through the maze. Mom encouraged Audrey in all the activities she explored and never pressured her to be "the best," but always expressed support, telling her just to have fun and "see if you like it."

After a few false starts—with the debate team, the student council, and on the yearbook—Audrey joined the newspaper staff. She began writing articles, but they didn't always get published, and when they did, they were so heavily edited that she hardly recognized them as hers. But Audrey loved working on the paper anyway, and her mom was glad she had found something she could call her own. One day the editor noticed her doodles on her notebooks and asked if she could draw a cartoon for the paper. That was the opportunity Audrey had been waiting for, without knowing it. The cartoons were the perfect outlet for her creative scribbling and her wry sense of humor. Audrey began to draw cartoons for the paper on a regular basis. She loved doing them, and they were very well received by her peers. Most important of all, she had found her niche and was no longer just the younger sister.

Mom was wise to understand that Audrey had to find her own opportunities for self-expression, quite apart from those of her older sister. She was careful not to pressure Audrey to excel, but to explore, relax, and have fun with her experimentation. With that kind of encouragement, Audrey was quite happy on the newspaper staff, even when her articles weren't published the way she had written them. She didn't care about that, because she had found a place where she could be herself and carve out her own domain, free from the shadow of her sister.

Developing her ability in cartooning was an extra bonus for Audrey. The key was that her mom understood her need to find her own avenue of self-expression and that she didn't pressure Audrey in any way. Sometimes when one teenager is highly successful in a certain area, the parents may assume that the other sibling needs to succeed at the same level in order to feel okay about themselves. Audrey didn't need to be a singing star. She just wanted to have fun and share who she was with others.

When Audrey was a senior, Mom found the perfect way to celebrate her daughter's contribution to the school newspaper with as much enthusiasm as she had her older daughter's vocal achievements. She collected all of Audrey's cartoons and put them into a scrapbook for her as a graduation gift. Audrey didn't say much when she opened the package, but she didn't have to—the look of pride and gratitude on her face said it all.

Following Your Passion

Creative expression can take many forms, and we don't want our teens to be limited by our own preconceptions of what they're doing. They may have a vision for themselves that's beyond our imagination. Sometimes their creative pursuits may appear obsessive or unusual to us, and we may even worry that our kids are not more well-rounded. We need to keep in mind that we may feel this way because of our own limited viewpoint. We've got to have faith in our kids to give them support and encouragement. We also need to keep in mind that the process is what's most important, not the outcome. Whether or not our teens succeed in what they are doing is secondary to the experience of pursuing their creative interests.

Seventeen-year-old Austin was spending all his free time on his computer, experimenting with writing different kinds of programs. For him, computer programming was an art form. Austin was passionate about what he was doing, but his parents were worried about all the time he was spending alone.

"What are you doing on your computer?" Dad asked him one day.

"I'm working. You wouldn't understand," Austin answered and Dad knew he was right. Dad was fairly computer-savvy, but he was no expert.

He tried again: "Well, are you working with the computer department at school?"

"No," Austin replied. "They're not doing anything interesting. They're too limited and restrictive."

Dad gave up this approach. He could see that Austin was entering a world that was beyond him, but he didn't give up on his son. He knew Austin was passionate about computer programming and that he was already too advanced for the classes that were offered at his high school. So he called a few of the nearby colleges to request computer programming course information. Austin was interested in one of the courses and took it, even though he didn't get credit for it. Pretty soon he was spending his free time at the college computer center. There he fit right in with a bunch of kids who were approaching programming as a creative challenge, in much the same way Austin was.

Dad supported Austin's creative passion even though he didn't understand it. He trusted his son's enthusiasm and excitement for the work he was doing and accepted it as an expression of Austin's creativity. He did everything he could to help Austin connect with the resources and opportunities he needed to pursue his interests at an advanced level. This is a good model for how we need to be connected to our kids and involved in their lives, as well as an example of how our teens need us to help guide them toward the appropriate resources.

Supporting Our Teens' Creative Process

There are many ways to encourage our teens to pursue their creative interests, and the most important one is that we take them seriously. This actually is the best way for them to take their own artistic efforts seriously. Our teens can become easily discouraged if we thoughtlessly make an offhand, disparaging remark or if we ignore their efforts and their creative explorations altogether.

We need to remember that our teenagers may not know how to ask for the support they need or even how to show appreciation for the support we give them. This doesn't mean that they don't want and need our help. They need us to help them find the right teacher or class, drive them to lessons, loan them the car, purchase materials or equipment, attend their concerts or shows, encourage them to practice, give them space at home for their workshop or studio— most of all, to be their biggest fans and encourage them to keep trying when they're discouraged.

Of course, we don't want to throw money away on a different hobby every month. However, we do want to encourage our teens to explore wherever their creative spirit leads them. Fifteen-year-old Taylor has taken lessons in piano, drums, computer programming, and drawing over the past couple of years—and now he's making his own animated film. This last interest is actually the culmination of all the previous ones. Taylor uses all the artistic skills he developed earlier as he creates and scores his own animated movies. But neither he nor his parents knew where all those lessons were leading as he moved from one seemingly disconnected interest to another.

Nobody knows whether Taylor will be any good at making animated films as an adult, or whether his interest in it will lead anywhere or even continue. As parents, we need to ignore these questions. There's no way to know the answers to them and they're the wrong questions to ask. Instead ask yourself, "Is she enjoying the lessons? Is he learning about himself and exploring his creativity? Is he having fun? Does she love what she's doing?"

"How's your project coming along?" Mom asked Taylor one afternoon.

"I don't know," Taylor answered. "I'm right in the middle of putting the scenes together."

"Well, do you want some lunch?" Mom asked.

"Lunch? What time is it?" Taylor asked, surprised as he looked up from his computer.

"It's 3:30." Mom laughed, realizing that her son was so absorbed in his project that he had actually forgotten about eating.

"Later," Taylor said.

If our teens are so caught up in their creative expression that they lose track of the time, if they are making their artistic projects a priority, and are choosing to spend time on it above other teenage activities, if it seems that they are irresistibly driven to do what they're doing, then we should invest as much as we reasonably can in terms of time, energy, and money to support our teens in their creative pursuits. If they are this dedicated to what they're doing, they deserve no less.

Respecting Their Privacy

Teens need private time to explore their creative pursuits, whether that means reading or writing poetry, listening to or playing music, or just plain daydreaming. We need to give our kids plenty of time and space and, most important, respect for their privacy. This means—unless there are serious signs of unacceptable behavior—no snooping in their papers, letters, journals, or diaries. When it comes to artistic freedom, we need to respect our teenager's creative process and privacy.

Teens often use journal writing to help them get through difficult times. Fourteen-year-old Katy was keeping a journal during her first year of high school. She copied into it quotations from books, poems, and her favorite pop songs. She also pasted in a random collection of mementos—a feather she had found, an ad from a magazine, ticket stubs, and some photos of movie stars. Mostly, though, she wrote in her journal about her feelings about going from a small middle school where she knew everyone to a large, anonymous high school.

"Mom," she said in a serious tone one evening, "did you move my journal?"

"I vacuumed your rug this afternoon. It was filthy, so I just sort of pushed everything off it," Mom answered. "Look under your bed. Some stuff got pushed under there."

Mom was grateful that she'd resisted the urge to peek at Katy's journal. This way she was able to answer her daughter's question in a straightforward, honest way. Mom knew that Katy was struggling to adjust to high school and that writing in her journal was helping her, and she didn't want to ruin this outlet for her daughter.

Writing about a difficult time for even just twenty minutes a day will help teenagers think through their problems more clearly. But for this to work, our teens need to feel that they can write down whatever is troubling them in full confidence that it will stay private. We want our teens to feel safe to express themselves in their own private world without having to worry whether we'll intrude upon them in any way. We need to respect our teenagers' privacy and freedom of self-expression. It's their decision how they choose to share themselves—with whom, when, and in whatever way they choose.

Even When It Hurts . . .

Sometimes teachers give creative assignments to teens that may involve revealing aspects of their family life. We need to respect our teens' privacy and give them creative license in these situations. Such homework assignments are between our teens and their teachers. It's not our job to edit or censor our teens' writing, even when it's about us.

Thirteen-year-old Casey told her mom that she had to write an autobiography for class and that she could use photos, drawings, or whatever she wanted to illustrate her personal story.

"I'm sure we can find some photos," Mom said. "I'd love to read your autobiography."

"Oh, yeah, right," Casey answered in a sarcastic tone.

"What do you mean by that?" Mom asked, leaping to the bait.

"Like I'm gonna let you see what I think of my life so far?" Casey said in total exasperation.

Mom was hurt and angry, though she wasn't surprised. Her daughter had clammed up recently and wasn't telling her anything anymore. Mom wasn't happy about this recent development. After all, Casey wouldn't have a life to write about if it weren't for her. And she didn't want Casey going into the gruesome details of her divorce, remarriage, and current separation. That was none of the teacher's business anyhow.

Mom needs to back off here and allow her daughter to claim her autobiography and her own life experience, separate from Mom. Casey has a right to tell her own story and Mom needs to respect that. We have to remind ourselves that our long-range goal for our teenagers is that they become independent. This means we have to lose a few of the disagreements along the way, allowing our kids to become increasingly self-determining. This is a good conflict to lose.

"Okay," Mom conceded. "I understand. It's your autobiography."

"Right," Casey affirmed, pleased with herself.

"I'll find the photos from when you were little if you want," Mom offered.

"Okay," Casey responded.

This is a great example of a thirteen-year-old's stage of development. Casey wants separation and privacy, yet she's also glad to have her mom's help finding the photos. It's difficult to become more independent while still needing help and support, yet this is the dilemma for teenagers and, consequently, for their parents as well.

We need to give our teens as much privacy, independence, and respect as we can, as graciously as we can whenever we can, without neglecting them or endangering them—while still staying connected and involved. Even though Casey's mom is at first personally offended by her daughter's remarks, she recovers quickly and regains her perspective. Mom strikes just the right balance between letting go and still being there to help her daughter with the photos.

Revealing creative projects require extra sensitivity from parents. They are not to be regarded as regular homework assignments. They are invitations from the teacher for our teens to share who they are, express themselves fully, and perhaps, in the process, discover what kind of person they'd like to become. This is their private exchange with their teacher, separate from us, even though they may reveal information about us as part of their story. We have to remember that this is *their* story to tell, not ours.

Expressing Loss

Many teenagers lose a grandparent during their adolescent years, and for many of them this will be the first death they experience up close. At this point, they are old enough to visit in the hospital, understand when an illness is terminal, and say good-bye. Teens feel their grief with their usual intensity, and are very sensitive to their family's mourning. However, it's not always easy for them to talk about these new experiences. Creative expression can help our teenagers deal with such a significant loss in their lives.

"I want to read something at Grandpa's funeral," fourteen-year-old Amy announced to her mom the day after Mom's dad died.

"That'd be nice, honey," Mom answered. She was too distracted with her own grieving and with making funeral arrangements to pay much attention to Amy. She figured her daughter would read a quotation or something from a book and that that would be okay.

At the funeral service, Amy pulled out two typed pages of her own writing. Mom had no idea what she would say. Amy read about the time her grandfather took her fishing. It had rained, and they had caught only one fish, but it was a great trip for both of them. Amy's story was heartfelt, funny, and totally appropriate. It was what people talked about at the reception after, often adding their own personal memories of the times they had shared with Mom's father.

In some ways our teens can be more able than we are to express what they're feeling. They can tune in to their emotions and share themselves in ways that are both bold and fresh. Their creative expression can be therapeutic for them and for us as well.

When everything was over that night, Mom sat down with Amy on the sofa. They were both exhausted.

"Your reading was wonderful, Amy," Mom said.

"I know," Amy answered honestly. "It was for Grandpa."

They sat quietly together for a moment.

"Did I ever tell you about the time Grandpa first took me fishing?" Mom asked her daughter. Then she went on to share one of her own favorite memories of her father. It was a wonderful moment for the two of them together, and a way to continue to feel the presence of their loved one after he was gone.

Creativity Is Natural for Teens

Our teenagers are constantly expressing who they are through quirky fashion combinations, wild body decorations, unusual hairstyles, their choice of music, the way they keep their rooms, the drawings on their school notebooks, their poetry, the notes they write to friends, the movies they choose, their favorite—and sometimes not very elegant—expressions, their dance styles, and even the way they walk. It seems that teenagers can't help but express themselves creatively—it's part of being a teenager. During adolescence, our kids are in the process of creating themselves, experimenting with various approaches to life, new and original ways to look; exploring the full range of their emotional lives; and trying out a variety of roles, personalities, and identities. These years will probably be the most creative, fluid, and experimental in their entire lives.

Our teenagers don't emerge out of this decade fully formed, but by the end of adolescence, they do achieve a relatively coherent identity. They know enough about who they are so that as young adults they can begin to move in a specific direction in terms of both career decisions and love relationships.

We don't want to restrict our teenagers' process of creating themselves by being critical, judgmental, or punitive. We want to see our teens as works of art in progress, creations that we may have started years ago, but that are now evolving along their own unique pathways. Our job is to guide and influence them, primarily through supporting and encouraging the qualities and behaviors we value most.

If teenagers live with caring attention, they learn how to love

L earning how to love is one of our teenagers' most important preparations for adulthood. We want our teens to grow up being able to love generously and freely. Knowing how to give love to and receive it from a life partner, children, extended family, and friends is what strengthens and nurtures relationships. We hope that our teenagers' significant relationships will be fulfilling and that as they mature, they will feel accepted, valued, and appreciated by their loved ones. In the final analysis, it's our closest relationships that are most important to us and give us the greatest satisfaction and happiness in life.

In order to be able to love generously as adults, our teenagers need caring attention. Every day. This means we must make an effort to connect with our teens on a daily basis so we're in touch with what's happening in their lives and are available for support or guidance. Our teenagers won't necessarily turn to us this often or even open up to share every day. The point is that we are there, available to them. They learn to trust that we will be there for them so that when they do need help, they know that they can count on us. It's our caring attention that fills them with the security of being loved. We want our teenagers to grow up feeling so well loved that they will have an abundance of love to share with those they care about.

Our teenagers learn about love from how we express love in the family. The day-to-day sharing of love is far more than saying, "I love you," or even just experiencing loving feelings. It's behaving in a loving way. This includes how parents treat each other. Our teens notice how we treat our spouses or significant others and absorb this as a blueprint for intimate relationships. This is a very sobering realization—the model of our marriage stays with our children throughout their lives.

Our teens also notice how we treat each child in the family, as well as extended family, friends, and neighbors. Our ability to be caring and loving in these relationships is the example our teenagers grow accustomed to and accept as the standard for family behavior.

Of course, our teens are primarily concerned with the way we treat them. Do we treat them fairly and with respect? Accept them for who they are? Give them our attention and support? And care about what's important to them? Caring about what our teens care about is the key to being able to connect with them on a daily basis. Respecting what they value opens the door to communication and sharing.

Our teenagers are sensitive to the moment our eyes glaze over when they're talking to us. We can't just pretend to listen while we're planning what we're going to say to them next. We need to give them our caring attention whether they're describing the current teen horror movie, complaining about a boring teacher, or asking us to listen to their favorite CD. We need to sit on the sofa with them and watch their teen television shows and favorite videos (no doubt repeatedly) so we know what our kids are talking about when they refer to them.

In truth, the current teen craze in clothes, movies, or music may not be very important to us, but if this is our children's main concern in life, then we also need to pay attention to these fashion trends. We don't have to like everything they like, but ignoring, making fun of, or denigrating what they care about is not loving behavior.

Giving such attention to our teenagers even when we don't feel like it is a living example of the decision to behave in a loving way. In long-term family relationships, love is as much a commitment as it is a feeling. When our teens see us get up in the middle of the night to talk with them about something that's bothering them, they understand that loving behavior is a decision.

Fourteen-year-old Mallory needed to find a white dress for middle school graduation. She had looked in all the stores at the local mall and didn't find exactly what she wanted, so she asked her mom to take her shopping at a larger mall about forty-five minutes away. Mom was busy with her own schedule and didn't want to spend a whole afternoon in search of the perfect white dress.

"Can't you just get that dress you tried on yesterday and said you liked?" Mom asked.

"I did like it," Mallory admitted. "But it's not what I envisioned for graduation."

"You're only going to wear the dress once and for just a few hours," Mom persisted.

"That's not the point," Mallory snapped back.

Mom didn't understand how Mallory could get so worked up over a simple white dress. It was only a middle school graduation, too, not even high school.

Mom has a point here about the dress but she misses the real opportunity to care about what's important to her daughter. As parents, we can be logically correct, yet not do the best thing for our relationship with our teenager. Mom needs to understand that middle school graduation is the most important graduation her daughter has ever experienced, and that it's very important to Mallory how she looks on that occasion. One of the ways Mom can express her love for Mallory is to take her concerns seriously.

A few hours later, after Mom had thought the situation through, she approached Mallory who was reading in her room. "I'm sorry," Mom said. "The truth is I'm just overwhelmed with things I need to do. I know graduation is important to you."

Mallory got up and gave her mom a hug. "Thanks."

Mallory was asking her mom for more than just a ride to the larger shopping mall. She really wanted her mom's attention and involvement in her preparation for graduation. Once Mom made the decision that Mallory was more important than her to-do list, she let go of feeling pressured and focused her attention on Mallory. Together they had a fun afternoon and they did find an "almost perfect" white dress.

It's Not a One-Way Street

In a loving family, the caring flows in all directions—between spouses, between parents and children, and between siblings. Teenagers are not exempt from this flow. Sometimes teenagers need to be coaxed out of their tendency to be self-absorbed and encouraged to behave altruistically and lovingly to others.

Mom asked sixteen-year-old Nathan to go to his little brother's soccer game. She couldn't make it, but she wanted a family member there to cheer.

"Aw, Mom, Kelly and I were going to hang out together after school. We don't want to go over to the elementary school."

"I know it's not an exciting proposition for you and your girlfriend, but this is what we do in this family. I went to all your games."

"Yeah, but . . ."

"Your brother needs someone in the stands."

So Nathan and his girlfriend went to see the little kids run around the field. Kelly thought it was cute, but Nathan didn't perk up until he got involved in the game. It was a close score and his little brother went for a goal. Nathan was cheering him on, but his brother missed the goal. Nathan continued shouting encouragement across the field. His little brother looked over at him on the sidelines and that was enough for Nathan to understand why he was there. Nathan didn't know watching his little brother's soccer game could feel so good. Plus Kelly was impressed with his being "such a great older brother."

Nathan learned some important lessons at that soccer game. First of all, he had to admit his mother was right—she had gone to all his soccer games and he now realized that this may have involved some self-sacrifice on her part. At the time, he had taken her presence for granted. It had never occurred to him that she might not have loved soccer.

Now it was Nathan's turn to give back. Nathan realized how

good it felt to give some caring attention to his little brother. He felt proud of himself that he could give to his little brother in the same way his mother had given to him. Scoring points with Kelly was an added, and unexpected, bonus. It was enough just to be there for his brother, loving him and cheering him on.

How Parents Treat Each Other

Whether we're married, dating, or in a significant relationship, our teenagers pay attention to how we treat and are treated by our most intimate loved ones. Through our relationships we give our teens a model of what it means to love and care for someone. Even if we tell our kids, "Don't make the same mistakes I made," the real message is conveyed through our behavior, not our words.

Our teenagers learn from our example how to treat their loved ones. They may want to follow in our footsteps or they may consciously decide not to repeat our patterns. Either way, they still have to deal with the imprint of our model in one way or another.

One of the most important legacies we give our teenagers is the experience of growing up in a loving, caring family. With this background, our kids will naturally gravitate toward friends and mates who know how to love generously.

Thirteen-year-old Carly's mom had been diagnosed with breast cancer, gone through surgery, and then had to undergo six months of chemotherapy treatments. She was weak and sick for much of this time and Carly's dad dedicated himself to taking care of her. He made special soup for her when she had no appetite and was losing too much weight. He surprised her with new hats each month as her hair fell out. He kept her company by playing cards, watching TV, or reading aloud to her.

Carly would often walk into their bedroom and find her parents holding hands or just sitting quietly together. Sometimes she would join them, lying on the bed next to her mom. Carly loved these times with her parents even though she was worried about her mother.

After Mom was declared free of cancer and was well recovered from the chemotherapy, she talked with her daughter about her experience. "You know what made the biggest different for me during the worst of it?" Mom asked her daughter.

"What?" Carly asked, just grateful it was in the past.

"Feeling so loved and cared for," Mom said. "By Daddy and by you."

Carly snuggled up to her mom, relieved and glad that the worst was over.

"I hope you find someone someday who will care for you as lovingly as Daddy cared for me during this time," Mom added.

"Me, too," Carly agreed wholeheartedly.

There's no question Carly will always remember the year her mother was sick, but she'll also have wonderful, warm memories of how her father lovingly cared for her mother during this time. Carly is likely to grow up expecting that she will be treated as lovingly as her father treated her mother.

Even if we don't have such a caring, loving relationship in our lives, we can still talk with our teens about what comprises a good relationship. There are other models we can point to among extended family, friends, or even parents of our teenagers' friends.

We hope that our teenagers will grow up to choose friends and spouses who will be kind and caring. We want our adult children to have successful marriages in which there is an easy sharing of attention and appreciation.

Resolving Differences

Disagreements are inevitable in every relationship. Hopefully we have found ways to deal with disharmony in our marriages and significant relationships without alienating affection. Just as our teenagers learn how to treat loved ones from us, they also learn from us how to resolve differences in intimate relationships. This essential skill is necessary for long-term relationships. Our kids know immediately when there's tension in the house even when we're making our best effort to put on a harmonious front. Teenagers easily recognize our patterns of dealing with conflict—our unique version of ignoring, arguing, discussing, compromising, fighting, problem solving, or all of the above.

Fourteen-year-old Maritza's parents fought often and with enthusiasm. A conflict would flare up and no matter who was around they let each other know their feelings, loud and clear. But in a few minutes it was over and Maritza's parents would return to laughing and having fun. Maritza was used to their pattern and would simply wait for the storm to blow over. But witnessing such fights made her girlfriend Lourdes upset.

"Do your parents always fight like this?" Lourdes asked Maritza one afternoon.

"Sure," Maritza replied, undisturbed. "They had a good one at back-to-school night in front of a teacher. It was really funny."

Lourdes was horrified. "Do you think they'll get a divorce?"

"No, why?"

To Lourdes, fighting meant there was a serious problem in the marriage. But Maritza knew this was just how her parents were. She even suspected that they enjoyed the fights. Still, she asked her mom about it later.

Maritza's mom laughed. "Divorce? Heavens no. I love your daddy. Why would you ask?"

Maritza explained Lourdes's questions.

"I get it now," Mom said. "Lourdes will get used to us if she hangs around more. She may even learn something."

"It's more fun here," Martiza agreed. "Her house is much too quiet."

It's not that any one style of dealing with conflict is better than another. What's important is that the style is mutual and works for the couple. Our teenagers need to see lots of mutuality, reciprocity, and flexibility in our relationships. A good sense of humor helps, too. They need to see us finding ways to resolve conflict, rather than getting stuck. What we don't want our kids to live with is a household filled with conflict and no resolution and lots of bad feelings. Living with that kind of frustration and tension is difficult for parents as well as their kids. How we deal with conflict affects our teenagers even if we think they don't hear us or we only argue when they're not around. Kids have a way of picking up on the atmosphere and if it's uncomfortable, they'll find ways to avoid coming home.

Forgiving and Letting Go

As adults, we know that no matter how much two people love each other, it's inevitable that feelings will get hurt or pride wounded somewhere along the way. We understand how important apologies and forgiveness are in relationships. Our teenagers need to see that we, as their parents and their first teachers, are able to apologize and forgive each other, to reconnect and get on with our lives. Harboring grudges in the family is a sad and terrible lesson to pass on to the next generation.

Fifteen-year-old Teri's dad was coming home from work each night grumpier than the night before. Things were not going well in the office and he had to lay off some employees. At home, Dad had no patience with anyone and would retreat to his computer as soon as he could. Mom was very understanding about his stress until the evening of her birthday, which he completely forgot.

Teri knew her dad was in big trouble then. She heard Mom say that being busy and stressed didn't matter, that there was no excuse for forgetting her birthday.

The next night Dad arrived home with flowers and a present. Mom was happy but Dad still disappeared into his study.

"How can you stand it, Mom?" Teri asked in exasperation. "What's the point of being married?"

Mom knew this was one of those big questions from her daughter, about more than just the current situation. "This is a tough time for him, but it's temporary. Things will get better and he felt really badly about missing my birthday," Mom explained. "I don't think he'll do that again."

Teri listened to her but didn't quite understand or agree. Then a few weeks later things got better at work and Dad came home in his usual pleasant mood. At that point, Mom reminded Teri of their talk. "See, this is what I meant when I said that stress was temporary. Marriage has its ups and downs, but it's still worth it."

Mom understood about Dad's going through a rough time at work *and* she let him know that she wanted him to remember her birthday. These are two separate messages that Mom was able to balance in her communication with Dad. She didn't give up her needs because of Dad's work stress, yet she was empathic about his situation. This is a wonderful model for Teri to see—Mom is both assertive and caring.

When Dad forgot Mom's birthday, he quickly realized his mistake and made amends with a belated gift. His responsiveness made it easier for Mom to forgive him and let go of her hurt feelings. Love includes getting through the tough times together and forgiving each other. Teenagers need to see this in action so they will know how to let go of hurt and disappointment in their adult love relationships.

Changing Needs

L ove needs to be a vital part of everyday life, expressed through small acts of consideration and caring. Mom leaves a note of encouragement in her son's math book. Dad remembers to ask his daughter how hockey tryouts went. Mom stops on the way home from work to buy colored pencils her daughter needs for a school project. Dad includes cartoons with his daily e-mail messages to his son. There are an infinite number of ways we can connect with our teenagers on a daily basis if we make the effort. Some of the ways we express our love are universal—like telling our kids we love them, for example. But we also need to attend to the details of our teens' individual lives so we can express our love in ways that are most relevant to them, especially as they evolve and mature through adolescence.

The ways we express our love for our teens have to be flexible, responding to their growth spurts, moods, and changes. We may spend time finding our thirteen-year-old the perfect birthday gift but buy a gift certificate for an older teen. Our loving concern for a younger teen can become overbearing only twelve months later. Our teens are changing emotionally as quickly and dramatically as their shoe size used to change when they were toddlers.

Thirteen-year-old Roger was happy to have his parents take him to school each morning. That was in May. Just a few months later, the following September, Roger's attitude was totally different.

"You can drop me off here, Dad," Roger said one morning a few blocks before his school. "Then you can get right on the expressway."

Dad slowed the car. "I don't mind taking you all the way."

"Please," Roger said, somewhat panicked.

"Oh." Dad got the picture and pulled over. "Ashamed of your old man?" he asked jokingly.

"No, Dad," Roger stammered, "it's not that."

"It's okay, Roger." Dad smiled. "Have a good one."

"Thanks," Roger said as he slung his backpack over his shoulder and set off into his world.

Our teens are experimenting with their independence, wanting to feel "on their own," if even for only a few blocks. Roger wants the appearance of arriving at school on his own, although he actually still needs his father and that ten minutes of time alone with him every morning. Being flexible in how we express our love for our teens means accepting and being responsive to their growing and changing needs for independence. This means we don't take it personally if our teen cringes when caught in public with us or shrinks away as we give a last-minute hug, and that we understand our teen still needs us even if not in public. There is a delicate balance between letting go gradually as our teenager matures and giving the same loving, caring attention that we gave when our kid was younger. We may even have to remind ourselves of both sides:

"She's fifteen years old. I can let her stay out a bit later," as well as "Even though she's now four inches taller than I am, she still needs me to support and reassure her."

Passion Is Not the Same as Love

Passion is not the same as love, despite Hollywood's portrayal of romance, lust, and love. If we believed everything we saw on the big screen, we would think love is about excitement, risk, and perhaps luxurious set designs. We have to imagine what happens five years after the so-called happy ending. But teenagers don't have that long-range perspective, and for them excitement and passion of the moment can easily be mistaken for love.

This is a particularly challenging distinction for teens to make when hormones are turned on, their impulse control is undeveloped and their romantic notions rampant. We want our teenagers to know the difference between passion and love so they can make wise decisions about their emotional involvements. In just a few short years our teens will be young adults and many of them will be making major decisions about life partners. We want them to know the difference between chemistry and enduring love.

Mom was watching Denis closely. She knew her sixteen-year-old son was seeing Bethany, one of the more popular and experienced girls at school, and she didn't want him to get hurt. But there wasn't much she could do to stop it or even slow it down. The kids' attraction to each other was stronger than anything Mom could say.

When they broke up after just a month or so, Denis was inconsolable. The good news was that he hung around the house more and even did some errands with his mom. While they were driving, Mom tried to open up a conversation.

"It's nice to have you around these days," Mom said.

"Yeah," Denis replied without much enthusiasm.

"I know it's because you're not seeing Bethany anymore," Mom continued.

"Yeah." Denis sighed.

"It wasn't a very long relationship," Mom observed.

"I guess she's not really into that," Denis figured. "It's more the beginning excitement."

"Oh," Mom said, knowing full well that this was a valuable observation her son was making, albeit a painful one. She refrained from criticizing Bethany, even though she was tempted. Mom kept her statements short and observational. She didn't make any assumptions or interpretations, leaving plenty of opportunity for her son to share whatever he was willing to talk about. Furthermore, Mom didn't push Denis to open up more by asking lots of questions, but listened thoughtfully to what he did say.

After a long pause, Mom said, "I'm sorry."

"Thanks," Denis said. "I'm going to go slower next time."

"That's a good idea," Mom agreed. "Then you'll have a better sense of whether the girl wants the same things you want in a relationship."

"Yeah."

Denis doesn't say much—some teens don't—but this brief conversation covers important territory. Mom manages to get her point across by building on a statement her son makes ("That's a good idea."). This approach makes it more likely he'll be able to hear her.

Besides learning about love from whatever example we set, our teens will no doubt learn about love the way we all do—through experience. And that usually includes at least one heartbreak. As difficult as it may be, experiencing a romantic disappointment during adolescence while our teens are still in the protective shelter of their families can actually be a valuable experience. If nothing else, at least they learn that their hearts can mend and life goes on. If your teenagers do have their hearts broken, please take their feelings seriously even if it seems as if it was only puppy love or the relationship lasted all of three months.

Teenagers are vulnerable to seduction by passion as well as romance. The hope of finding a true love that they can both lose themselves in and find themselves through is irresistible, but love needs time to develop and deepen, and our teenagers need time to mature enough to recognize this in themselves and others. From every experience, they'll learn more about what qualities to look for in a partner. We want to give our teens our caring attention during this process along with a few well-chosen words of advice.

Young Love

Although most teen relationships last a few weeks, months, or sometimes years, there are teenagers who fall in love and remain together for a lifetime. The lesson here is never to underestimate the power of love even in our own teenagers who seem so young and inexperienced. It's true most won't last, but a few teenage relationships will span a lifetime, surviving beyond us. These teens somehow manage to grow up both individually and as a couple, surviving long distances, inevitable temptations, and personal transformations. As adults we probably all know of such a couple from our adolescent years.

Dierdre and Todd had been friends since elementary school, and when they turned sixteen, they developed a romantic interest in each other. Dierdre's parents had always liked Todd, but now they had a different perspective. As the relationship grew more serious and involved, Dad began to question his daughter.

"What's going to happen when you two go off to college?" Dad asked her out of the blue one Sunday afternoon.

Dierdre looked at him in surprise. "I don't know. That's almost two years away. I'm not worried about that now."

"Yes, but you have to think of these things," Dad pressed.

"No I don't," Dierdre responded quickly. "And besides, Todd and I will figure it out when we're ready."

Silenced, Dad retreated, but not happily. He was worried about his daughter; he didn't want her to get hurt or to limit herself too soon. He didn't see any way these two kids could know what they want in the long run. They could barely parallel park.

If Dad had casually mentioned, "You know I really like Todd and sometimes I worry about the two of you," he likely would have had a more satisfying conversation.

"How so?" Dierdre would probably have responded, surprised and curious.

Dad might say, "Well, I don't want either of you to get hurt . . ." and pause expectantly, waiting for Dierdre to fill in the space.

"We talk about stuff," Dierdre might assure her father. "You don't have to worry."

This may sound like an ambiguous, little-nothing conversation, but in actuality it accomplishes a few things. First of all, the exchange would connect Dad and Dierdre rather than alienating them as the previous attempt did. Also, it would enable Dad to express his fondness for Dierdre's boyfriend and his support of their relationship, and at the same time give voice to his concerns. This brief exchange might set the stage for Dad to say sometime later, "I hope you and Todd will consider colleges that are best for each of you, rather than just the ones that are geographically close enough to visit each other." Such a comment would show concern for both Dierdre and Todd and demonstrate that Dad is taking their relationship seriously and cares about both of them.

We need to tread lightly on teenage relationships. Unless we think there's some kind of problem with the relationship, we would be wise to accept the possibility that it may be serious. Dad may be celebrating holidays with Todd for the next forty years. It makes sense to respect our teenagers' relationships and take seriously their capacity to love and to grow together in their love. Caring about our own kids can naturally expand into caring about their chosen partners. This is how families grow into extended families.

Sex and Love

Loving relationships naturally include sexual intimacy. It may not be comfortable to think of our teenagers as having any kind of sex, but we can begin to prepare ourselves. Keep in mind that our teens are learning about relationships, and that the physical expression of affection—from holding hands to intercourse—is a part of relationships and, we hope, not an end in itself. We need to be clear about our values with our teens—sex is part of a loving, caring relationship and not to be entered into casually.

If we want our kids to know what we expect of them in terms of how they deal with their blossoming sexuality, we have to be able to talk with our kids frankly and honestly. For instance, it's not enough to say, "I want you to be a virgin through high school." Plenty of teens, male or female, have agreed to that and lived up to their promise while being sexually active with oral sex.

Also, as our teens mature, their circumstances will change. The way we talk with our teens about love and sex needs to reflect their stage of development and be relevant and practical to their current life experience. We might say to our thirteen-year-old daughter, "I don't want you to go off alone with any boys at the party." But to a sixteen-year-old daughter in a six-month relationship, we would need a different statement depending on our family values. Some parents might say, "I know it's tempting, but I don't want you to become sexually involved at this age," or "I'm not sure what you're planning to do, but let's talk about sexually transmitted diseases and birth control."

Judy's mother gave her a specific message that seemed to be applicable all through adolescence: "Don't do anything you're not ready to do and will feel good about the next day." This worked for Judy when she was thirteen and kids were pairing up to make out through their braces. And it worked for her at fifteen when her boyfriend pressured her for sex. It also helped her at seventeen when it seemed as if she were the only one in her high school not "doing it." With her mother's support and advice to respect herself and trust her own decisions, Judy decided when and with whom she wanted to become sexually involved.

If we aren't able to talk with our teens openly, we may be faced with some version of a surprise—from finding condoms or birth control pills in our kid's room to an unexpected pregnancy. Hopefully we have been talking about sex as part of a loving relationship from the time our children first started asking where babies come from. There are two goals for talking with our teenagers about sex and love. First, we want to be open so our kids can say or ask anything they want. Second, we want to let them know what our values are and what we expect of them in terms of their behavior.

The central value here is that sex and love are intertwined, a natural part of each other. Casual sex, including oral sex and other substitutes for intercourse, are not acceptable behavior outside a loving relationship. Of course, teenagers will experiment with sex, but our stand can still be that sex is part of an intimate, caring relationship. We want to give this message to our teens in a way that suits their stage of development and is relevant to their experience. Then, as our teens grow and circumstances change, our conversations can evolve to be appropriate to their developing maturity.

Parent-Child Relationship

In the very beginning of adolescence, our roles are still clearly defined as parent and child. However, year by year, and sometimes month by month, our teens may challenge us. We love them just as much, but the relationship changes significantly. As they gain experience and independence, we may lose our position as the expert and ultimate authority. By the end of adolescence the relationship is totally different. As our teens become young adults, we begin to develop a more adult relationship and a new kind of appreciation for each other.

Our love for them needs to endure through all these sometimes painful transformations. Sometimes, it may seem that our teens don't even like us, much less love us. As they mature and gradually emerge from their adolescent need to push us away, however, they learn how to express their love for us in a totally new way.

Nineteen-year-old Dawn's mother was flying out to visit her at college. Dawn met her at the airport and they waited together to pick up the luggage. When Mom started to hoist it off the carousel, Dawn jumped in.

"I'll get it, Mom," she said. "It's a big one."

Mom backed off and let her daughter help her. "I couldn't decide what to bring so I just brought everything," she explained as Dawn took over managing the luggage. In that moment, Mom realized that their roles had switched, however momentarily. As Dawn started pulling the suitcase, Mom put her arm through her daughter's and said, "Thanks. It's really heavy."

Dawn just smiled. "No problem, Mom." And off they went to enjoy their weekend together at the college.

Way back when we originally decided to have children, we naturally hoped and expected that we would have a good relationship with our kids and enjoy them through the whole length of our lives. Dawn and her mother are just beginning the natural shift in their relationship that occurs as our teens approach young adulthood. At that point, we're getting older and our teens are becoming more mature. The roles of parent and child begin to be more flexible as our teens realize that they can rely on themselves more and become truly independent. The flowering of a parent-child relationship is when we can be adults together, able to both give and receive caring attention, love, and friendship.

Nothing Is More Important than Love

Expressing our love for our teenagers by consistently giving them caring attention is our most important parental responsibility throughout their entire childhood, including adolescence. Admittedly, our kids do not always make this easy, but we need to be clear that we love them, even though we may not like what they're doing. Teenagers who feel loved and cared for and connected to their parents make better decisions for themselves about the highest-risk issues in adolescence—drugs, alcohol, driving, and sex.

Growing up with the security of feeling loved allows our teens to become young adults who can begin to build their own lives with optimism and confidence. They will be more able to find their way in the world, discovering how they can both succeed and contribute. They will be more able to give of themselves in their love relationships and more likely to choose life partners who can love them generously in return. There is no question that feeling loved is the essence of our teenagers' psychological foundation for life.

☀

If teenagers live with positive expectations, they learn to help build a better world

Our expectations for our teenagers help determine their future. Whether we express our expectations openly or try to keep them to ourselves, what we expect of our teens somehow slips into their assumptions about themselves. Our hopes and dreams for them—along with our disappointments and frustrations—influence our teenagers' expectations for themselves, their lives, and their world.

The challenge for us, as parents, is to set our expectations so they're neither too high nor too low, realistic yet inspiring, appropriate for our teens and, at the same time, meaningful. If we expect too much, our kids may grow up feeling like failures, and if we expect too little they may not rise to their full potential. It's not easy to do, but we have to be able to see our teenagers as they really are, accepting their limitations and encouraging their strengths. For there's almost no way we cannot have some expectations of our teens. Even if we haven't put them into words, we have hopes and dreams about what kind of lives we want for our kids and what kind of world we want for their future.

Our expectations about life in general also set a tone for our teens. After all, they see the world through our eyes first. How we live life and what we believe, whether on the optimistic side or tinged with pessimism, are the model our teens grow up with and take for granted. Although our teenagers ultimately find their own stance in life, our attitudes toward the world and their future can limit or empower them during adolescence.

Fifteen-year-old Brooke and her closest friends wanted to raise money for a classmate who needed a bone marrow transplant. Brooke raised the idea of a bake sale with her mom.

"I don't know," Mom said. "Bake sales can only bring in a few hundred dollars. That's not going to make much of a difference."

"I guess you're right," Brooke responded, and dropped the idea.

Mom knew she was being realistic about the bake sale idea, but she didn't intend to discourage her daughter completely. The next day she reopened the conversation.

"Have you thought of any other ways to raise money?" Mom asked Brooke.

"Yeah, but I'm not sure it would bring in enough money."

Brooke's answer was a reflection of her mother's pessimism. This time, however, Mom realized she had to set aside her own cynicism in order to encourage her daughter's optimistic enthusiasm.

"What are you thinking?" Mom asked.

"Well, I still like the idea of a bake sale," Brooke said as Mom quietly and wisely just listened, "and I thought we could combine it with a car wash. People could have a snack while they're waiting for their cars. If they like what they eat, they'll buy more of it to take home."

"And you can charge a lot for the car wash because people will want to donate to a good cause," Mom added, ever the practical one.

Brooke took off after that brief conversation to call her friends and begin to organize. The car wash/bake sale ran over a three-day weekend and raised almost five thousand dollars. All of a sudden everyone was baking, getting their cars cleaned, and contributing to the medical fund.

To her credit, Mom realized that she needed a larger focus than the financial bottom line. Brooke's bake sale idea was an expression of her compassion and desire to contribute to her classmate's recovery. After thinking it over, Mom understood that what was most important was to support her daughter's concern for her classmate. As parents, we need to maintain a wide perspective regarding our teens' undertakings. We can ask ourselves such questions as: How will our teenager grow as a result of this situation? How will this experience contribute to her development as a person? What will she learn as a result of her efforts?

Our teenagers' altruistic impulses are youthful and idealistic. Some projects will succeed better than others, and some won't work at all. Whatever the outcome, our job as parents is to nurture our teens' good intentions. We don't want any of our accrued experience or knowledge of the world to limit their inspiration. We want to believe in our teenagers' visions and in their capacity to make a difference, for they are building a future for themselves and for the world.

Tailor Your Expectations to Your Child

Since it so often seems that their only goal is to defy us, we may need to remind ourselves that our teens really do want to live up to our expectations. They don't want to disappoint us and may fear or even dread that they will fail us. So we don't want to set our expectations unrealistically high. Nor do we want our teenagers to become obsessed and perfectionistic in trying to please us. Often if our goals for our teens are inappropriately high, it is our problem and not theirs. We must be very honest with ourselves, so that we don't expect our teens to fulfill our egotistical needs.

The other aspect of keeping our expectations realistic is that we may have to face some real disappointments. Our teens may not be able to be everything we had hoped they might be, and we may simply have to accept this fact. The more graciously we can accept our teens for both their strengths and their weaknesses, the easier it will be for us to let go of our unrealistic expectations.

Seventeen-year-old Darlene was a talented athlete, no doubt headed for the all-state basketball team as well as a full college scholarship. Her mother was proud of her and attended all her games, yet Mom carried a private disappointment.

Darlene was not an intellectual like her mother. She didn't read anything she didn't absolutely have to for school, didn't think conceptually or question others' philosophical assumptions. Mom was having trouble letting go of her need to have a daughter who would think like her and share her interests. She gave Darlene a carefully selected book at every birthday, even though Darlene never seemed to get around to reading them. Lately Mom had given up on books and was now clipping newspaper and magazine articles for her daughter.

"Did you read that article I left out for you from Sunday's sports section?" Mom asked her daughter. "It describes the mental preparation that Olympic athletes use. I thought you'd be interested in it."

"Not yet, but thanks, Mom," Darlene answered cheerfully on her way to practice.

Mom knew Darlene probably wouldn't read even the brief newspaper articles she gave her. Darlene just didn't seem to stop long enough to focus. Still, it was a continual source of frustration and disappointment for Mom.

Harboring inappropriate expectations for our teens just creates disappointment. In this example, Darlene is simply being who she is. Her mom would be wise to keep her expectations realistic and enjoy her daughter for who she is in her own right—a cheerful, optimistic kid who happens to be a star athlete.

Letting Expectations Go

The more we can tailor our expectations to our teenagers, the more we will be able to see and appreciate them for who they naturally and uniquely are. We may even be able to envision them in the future as young adults—and not just as our kids.

Imagining what our teenagers will be like as young adults allows us, first of all, to realize how little time we actually have left with them. When we understand this, we realize how much more we want to teach them before they go off on their own. Also, picturing them as twenty-somethings helps us recognize and develop their potential interests and talents now.

Fourteen-year-old Dimitrios was a born entrepreneur. By eighth grade he was buying sports-related memorabilia and then selling it on an Internet auction site at a profit. He started out with baseball cards and gradually expanded. His parents failed to realize either the business potential in what their son was doing or his passion for it. Instead, they had their hopes set on Dimitrios' going to medical school. They had always dreamed of having a doctor in the family and science came easily to Dimitrios. Unfortunately for them, he just wasn't interested.

"Why do you waste your time on the Internet?" Dad asked late one evening.

"What do you mean, 'waste my time'? I'm working," Dimitrios responded, full of adolescent self-importance.

"Working?" Dad asked half-mockingly.

"Yeah. I've made about fifteen hundred dollars so far this year," Dimitrios answered, knowing that this would shock his father into taking him seriously.

Dad did listen that night and got a real lesson on the new economy. Frankly, he could hardly believe what his son was doing and how much money he was making. Dad began to understand that Dimitrios was running an Internet *business,* and he began to see his son on his own terms rather than as an extension of himself and his dreams.

This was a first step for Dimitrios's parents, who will have to let go of their dreams and align their expectations with their son's talents and interests. This may not be easy to do, even though he's doing well in his ventures. His parents can still have goals and standards they want their son to meet, but they need to adjust them to be relevant and appropriate for Dimitrios.

As parents, many of us need to let go of our specific plans for our teenagers and respect their right to determine their own destiny. Nonetheless, we can maintain our more general hopes and expectations, such as wanting our teens to find meaningful careers, to develop loving friendships, to create families of their own, and to contribute in their own unique way to building a better world.

Expecting the Best

We want to be able to maintain our faith in our teenagers and to be able to sustain our positive visions of them no matter what they're doing. Admittedly, this isn't always easy, especially when we're upset about their behavior or attitude.

A neighbor came by one summer night around dusk to talk with thirteen-year-old Doug's parents. It seemed that Doug and his buddies had been playing baseball and trampled the neighbor's flower beds—more than once. Dad responded with a mixture of embarrassment and apology and waited for Doug to come home later that night.

When Doug got home, his dad met him at the door with a flashlight in hand. "Let's go for a little walk," he said.

Surprised and intrigued, Doug followed his dad out the door. "Where're we going?"

"I hear you've been having some pretty good ball games in the neighborhood this summer," Dad said.

Doug was just beginning to suspect that he was in some kind of trouble. When his dad shone the flashlight on the trampled flower bed, Doug realized what the problem was.

"We tried to be careful, Dad," Doug protested, "but I guess the ball did roll in there a few times."

At this point it would have been easy for Dad to yell at Doug, threaten punishment, and imagine his son is on his way to even bigger trouble. But Dad made a clear decision to see his son as a well-intentioned young teenager who just needed to learn about respecting his neighbor's property. With this positive perspective, Dad offered guidance and mentoring to his son and expected Doug to rise to meet his expectations.

"I think we need to plant some new flowers for our neighbor," Dad suggested. "Maybe you can get some friends to help."

"Right," Doug responded, staring at the flower beds.

"I don't think marigolds are that expensive," Dad said pointedly.

"I think I'll call the guys tonight," Doug said, already planning to spread the expense and workload around.

It's easier to guide our teens toward doing the right thing when we expect the best from them, rather than getting caught in imagining the worst. Our teens will tend to live up to our expectations whether they are positive or negative, so we would be wise to expect the best and do everything we can to make it easy for our teens to meet our positive expectations.

The next weekend Dad drove Doug and his friends to the nursery to pick up the new plants. As the boys worked in the garden, Dad chatted with the neighbor and kept an eye on their progress. Just as the kids were finishing up and watering the new plants, a delivery van arrived with the pizza Dad had ordered. By investing his own time and energy, Dad created a situation in which his son could behave responsibly as well as live up to his father's expectations. Dad turned a potential problem into a neighborhood picnic by maintaining his faith in his son and providing just the right amount of guidance, supervision, and support.

Our Expectations Become Theirs

In a few years, when we look back on our children's adolescence with the wisdom of hindsight, we will be more able to realize the impact we have had on them. Even as they separate from us and seem to contradict everything we say, they are still sensitive to our expectations. This sort of realization is difficult to perceive when we are in the midst of a turbulent adolescence. Some things can only be seen years later.

Lucy dropped out of college to travel hippie-style throughout the world. Her parents were devastated. They would have gladly paid for an extended travel tour as a graduation present, but Lucy was un-deterred. Her parents thought she'd get this out of her system in a semester or two and return to college. A few years later, when Lucy was still traveling, they seriously wondered what they had done wrong.

Eventually Lucy returned to the States and finished college when she was in her mid-twenties. By then, she and her parents were able to talk about things with a different perspective.

"You know, we had given up on your returning to college," Dad said while they were out to dinner celebrating her graduation.

Lucy was surprised. "I always knew I'd finish school."

"We didn't," Mom added.

"I couldn't imagine not getting my degree," Lucy said.

It was only then that Lucy's mom and dad realized the full effect of their expectations. They had always assumed that their daughter would finish her education, and Lucy couldn't imagine *not* doing so. Long before her parents had given up, their expectations for her had already become a part of her. For Lucy, the decision to graduate from college was made long ago. She would just do it on her own terms.

The expectations we have for our teenagers help set their direction in life even after they've left home. Our teens incorporate our hopes for them, often accepting them as their own. In this way, our influence stays with our children into young adulthood and continues to inform their life decisions. We just have to wait until they're well out of their teens for them to acknowledge that they actually listened to us. By the time our adult children are about twenty-five years old and finding their own way in life, they can begin to admit to themselves and to us how important our influence has been to them.

Community Service

Our expectations for our teens include how we envision them as future citizens, relating to their larger community. It's quite a developmental leap for teens to expand their focus beyond their own lives and understand the needs of others. Teenagers are often consumed with themselves—how they look, who their friends are, whether they're cool enough, and how their love life is progressing. Such self-absorption is a normal part of their developing sense of self, and doesn't mean that they'll always be this way. In fact, concurrent with their self-absorption there's often a real concern for issues like human rights, animal welfare, and the environment.

One of the best ways to encourage our teens to participate actively in community service is to involve them while they're still in the early stages of adolescence in a project that we're working on. This way they'll learn for themselves how satisfying and fulfilling it can be to make a difference in their local community. We want our kids to grow up feeling confident that they can have a positive impact and change things for the better.

"I suggest you go to bed early tonight," Mom said to fourteen-year-old Tobin one Friday evening. "We have to be on our way when it's still dark so we can catch the sunrise."

"What's this for again?" Tobin asked, wanting to know why he was getting up so early on a Saturday morning.

"You promised to take photos of the land we want to save for conservation," Mom reminded him. "Your photos will inspire people in the community to sign the petition for open spaces."

"Oh, yeah." Tobin now remembered his promise to help with this project.

"You know my grandfather—your great-grandfather—helped create the park by the river," Mom said. "So we're following a family tradition."

"Right," Tobin said with a little more commitment. "I'll check my camera to make sure I have enough film."

"That's a great idea," Mom said calmly. She was prepared for a last-minute emergency about not having film and she had already picked up some extra rolls just in case. Her expectations were realistic for Tobin. She knew she might have to drag him out of bed the next morning, but that he'd become enthusiastic once he was out on the land.

By expecting our teens to participate with us in community projects, we show them how they can have an impact on the world. Tobin's photos became an important part of the campaign for land conservation. He saw them on posters everywhere he went in town and in the local newspapers.

Tobin's mom succeeded on many levels in this example. She transmitted family values that extended across many generations so Tobin felt connected to the family tradition of community service. She leveraged his limited involvement into maximum exposure. And, the campaign worked. The open space is protected and Mom can begin to focus on her next environmental project. Tobin has learned that giving his time and energy to a good cause can be fun as well as satisfying. Perhaps more important, he also learned that he can make a difference in the world and that community service, especially land conservation, is an ongoing process.

Taking a Stance

During adolescence teenagers discover their own ways of relating to the world. They become more aware of global issues and societal problems and search for things they can do to help. As their awareness expands, they may begin to question many of the assumptions they grew up with. As part of this process, their ideas, beliefs, and approach to life can begin to diverge from that of their family. Parents can sometimes overreact to their teenagers' questions and explorations, almost as if their teen is personally betraying them and all that they hold dear.

If we expect our teens to adopt new ways of thinking, to test previously held assumptions, then we'll applaud their exploration as a developmental milestone, rather than seeing it as rebellious or rejecting. Our teenagers have to discover for themselves what they believe in and how they want to live. The best approach we can take is to be open and interested in our teenagers' thinking, to ask questions, and listen respectfully. We can even engage in some debate, but not with the intention of proving our kids wrong. We can have a lively discussion and still accept their right to come to their own conclusions.

While shopping for a pair of shoes, Mom noticed that Helena, her fifteen-year-old daughter, was more concerned about what the shoes were made of than the style.

"I don't want anything that's leather," Helena stated. "No animal products."

Mom was surprised both by Helena's announcement and by her seriousness. "Why not?"

"I don't want to kill animals for my shoes," Helena answered.

"You're not exactly killing them," Mom pointed out.

"I don't want to contribute to their death by buying the shoes," Helena explained.

"Oh." Mom thought about this new decree. "What about the new pocketbook?"

"That was before I made this decision," Helena said. "I've thought about that and there's nothing I can do about it, but from here on in . . ."

"And hamburgers?" Mom asked, knowing that they were a staple of her daughter's diet.

"No more burgers," Helena answered without hesitation. "I'm a vegetarian now."

Mom looked at her daughter as if she couldn't believe her ears. "Okay . . . Well"—she hesitated—"we'll have to figure out what we'll need in the house for meals."

Helena has taken a philosophical stand on animal rights and is willing to make personal sacrifices as part of her commitment. Although caught by surprise, Mom is open to and accepting of her daughter's announcement. This is Helena's way of making a difference in the world. It's something she can do, that she has control over and believes in. Mom doesn't agree with Helena, but she's proud of her daughter's integrity and determination to live by her values.

The challenge for us, as parents, is to view our teenagers' philosophical explorations as their approach to building a better world. Whether they're protesting the death penalty or abortion, are liberal or conservative, agree with our outlook or oppose it, we need to see that they're trying to make the world a better place.

The Spirit of Generosity

Among fourteen-year-old Janelle's holiday presents was a simple envelope that had come in the mail and been tucked away as a surprise. Mom looked on as Janelle, full of curiosity, reached for it. She read the card stating that a donation had been made in her name to help support a weaving business in Central America. The card showed a group of village women dressed in handwoven clothing, all beaming at her from another world.

Janelle looked at her mother, not quite understanding. Mom explained, "The donation I gave will help women buy looms for their weaving. Their business will grow and they'll be able to hire other women and help them make money."

"And this donation was made in my name?" Janelle asked, still staring at the smiling faces on the card.

"Yes," Mom answered simply.

As soon as she understood what the gift meant, Janelle was thrilled. "What a great idea!"

The spirit of generosity needs to be gently transmitted. We can't *make* our teenagers become generous by forcing them to donate their own money, but we can guide them toward an appreciation of the experience of generosity and a glimpse into what it means to others. Janelle's mother gives a donation that brings her daughter into the experience of contributing to others. It expands Janelle's vision about what's possible and connects her to village women in Central America. This kind of gift is a wonderful way to introduce our teenagers to the experience of generosity.

If we want our teens to develop an openhearted generosity, then we need to be generous with them—not necessarily with money or material things, but with ourselves. They need to feel filled up emotionally so they grow up with a sense of personal abundance. We need to give them our time, attention, and energy, and to respond to their changing needs as a way of guiding them through adolescence. Giving of ourselves is perhaps the best model we can give our teens. Through our example they can learn how to respond generously when they perceive a need, giving both their time and their resources.

Opportunities to Make a Difference

It's very important that our teenagers grow up with the expectation that they can make a difference in the world. Making a difference doesn't always mean getting involved in a large, long-term project. Even small things done on a daily basis can have a constructive impact. For instance, being friendly to an elderly neighbor or kinder to a younger sibling or recycling trash and conserving water are just some of the everyday things teens can do.

As parents, we can encourage our teenagers to value their individual contributions by noticing and acknowledging the little things they do, especially when they don't give themselves credit. Teens often underestimate what they can contribute, especially within the context of all that's needed to improve the state of the world.

Dad and thirteen-year-old Connor were out fishing one day by the bank of a local stream. Every once in a while they would move downstream to what they hoped was a better spot. Each time Connor would pick up any trash that was lying about. By the end of the day he had a garbage bag full of candy wrappers, water bottles, and beer cans.

As they began to hike back to the car, Dad turned to Connor and said, "Here, let me carry that for you."

"I've got it," Connor replied.

"You did enough for one day, picking all the stuff up," Dad persisted. "At least let me help carry it out."

"Oh, okay." Connor hadn't thought of it that way. He was just cleaning up so it would be nicer where they were fishing. He didn't think of it as cleaning up the stream. Dad's comments helped him to see the big picture and his role in it.

When our teens are doing something positive, we want to acknowledge it, and help them see their actions in a larger context. When they realize that they're already doing something that makes a difference, they feel empowered to do more. In this way, teens learn to develop the confidence they need to believe that they can build a better world.

The Global Community

Our teens are growing up in an accelerated world with changes coming at an ever-increasing rate. We can hardly imagine what the world will be like when our teens are our age. However, we *can* be sure that the world will still need them to be contributing to the greater good. Some things don't change, and the greater good in the future is likely to be defined as the global community.

The world will need new generations who have grown up with a humanitarian worldview, who realize that the poorest among us must be fed and cared for in order for all of us to live in peace. We would be wise to value and nurture this global viewpoint when we see it developing in our kids.

Children of all ages naturally identify with other children all over the world. National boundaries and cultural differences don't stop them from feeling another child's hunger, pain, or loneliness. Young teenagers don't see why we can't send food and medicine to wherever they're needed. They see innocently simple solutions: we have more than we need, so we can share. Older teens begin to think about going to other countries to work locally and make a difference. They know it's not enough to send supplies; we also have to teach and build from village to village.

If we seriously listen to our teenagers, we will likely discover that they have probing philosophical questions about justice and equality. They are struggling to understand the dynamics of the dichotomies that challenge all of us—fate and self-determination, development and protection of resources, wealth and poverty. We need to encourage their questioning of the status quo as a way to nurture their longing to build a better world.

We must be sensitive to each stage of our children's visions for the future. These are their dreams for the time when they will be in charge, a time we can hardly even imagine. We must be sure that our viewpoints, fears, or negative expectations don't limit our teenagers' dreams of building a better world.

Sixteen-year-old Dean wanted to join a summer program of volunteer work in Peru. The group of teens was planning to raise money during the school year to pay for the trip in the summer. His parents were worried about a long list of things, from tropical diseases to kidnapping.

"This group's been working in the village for years," Dean explained. "There've never been any problems."

"But you'll be so far away," Mom said.

"Not so far, Mom," Dean answered. "I'll have access to e-mail."

"That only means I'll find out sooner that you're sick," Mom responded.

Dean laughed. "To me it means that I won't be so far away after all."

This is a generational difference in their perception of the world. Dean's mother sees the world in terms of geographical miles, and to her the distance is great. Dean sees the world electronically, and to him there is no distance.

We need to acknowledge and respect this shift in perception. Our teenagers will grow up to see their community as a global village, far beyond our limited identification. They will see themselves as part of all humanity and, in this way, they are truly our hope for the future.

The Next Generation

As we watch our children grow up through adolescence and into young adulthood we come to the recognition that the world will soon be in their hands. Theirs will be the next generation to take care of the planet, to try to bring peace, and to create abundance for everyone. This may be difficult to imagine when our teens are still struggling with Algebra 2, but in the blink of a decade they will begin their tenure.

Perhaps our children are our greatest contribution to building a better world. Who our teenagers are as people—their values, their integrity, and their compassion—will help create a new vision for the future. Every teen has a unique perspective, something original to contribute. We want to give our teenagers everything they need to grow into their full potential, live meaningful lives, and perhaps become the kind of people who really can build a better world.

We need to have faith in our teens and in their generation, and hope in the possibility of a better world. We need to graciously accept our limitations and failures and hope that following generations will develop a greater capacity for love and compassion.

Our positive expectations are conveyed in our hopes and dreams for our teens and for the world they can create. This is one of the gifts we give to the next generation—our expectations will become a part of who they are and help them to build a better world.